Integrative Psychotherapy In Action

Integrative Psychotherapy In Action

by

Richard G. Erskine

and

Janet P. Moursund

SAGE PUBLICATIONS
The Publishers of Professional Social Science
Newbury Park Beverly Hills London New Delhi

For information address:

SAGE Publications, Inc.
2111 West Hillcrest Drive
Newbury Park, California 91320

SAGE Publications Inc.
275 South Beverly Drive
Beverly Hills
California 90212

SAGE Publications Ltd.
28 Banner Street
London EC1Y 8QE
England

SAGE PUBLICATIONS India Pvt. Ltd.
M-32 Market
Greater Kailash I
New Delhi 110 048 India

Printed in the United States of America

Library of Congress Cataloging-in-Publication Data

Erskine, Richard.
Integrative psychotherapy in action.

Bibliography: p.
1. Eclectic psychotherapy. I. Moursund, Janet.
II. Title.
RC489.E24E77 1988 616.89'14 87-27511
ISBN 0-8039-3108-5

FIRST PRINTING 1988

Contents

To my mother, my wife, and
my daughters

—Richard

To Sue, Lance, and Roberta,
with my respect and my love

—Jan

Preface

In order to talk about what a psychotherapist does, there must be a context, a background. Our work as therapists is rooted in our assumptions about what people are like, how they get that way, why they change or stay the same. And, unlike the quantitative sciences, physics or chemistry or mathematics, these assumptions in psychotherapy cannot be easily specified. They don't hold still; they are not always the same for each of us. Each therapist borrows from theory and past experiences in a different and subjective way. Over the years, we each construct our own unique, personal ideas of human behavior; we base our understanding of our clients, as well as of ourselves, on these ideas. What we, the authors of this book, believe or disbelieve about personality, about human development, about the way change occurs, shapes our beliefs and practices in psychotherapy, and will certainly affect the way we talk about it. What you believe—and what you believe we believe—will shape the way in which you understand us. So explanations and foundation-laying are important. But where to begin?

It really is an endless progression, this business of describing how we have come to understand our human condition. As long as people have been self-aware—have been able to think about themselves—they have been building assumptions about how those selves operate: why we do what we do, how we learned to do it, whether and why and how we might do it differently. These kinds of interests form the basis for most, if not all, literature. The ancient storytellers, Biblical prophets, and Greek playwrights were really the first to describe human functioning. Psychologists came later—

much later—and psychotherapists, as we understand the term, were later still.

Integrative Psychotherapy is one of the most recent of psychotherapeutic schools. The term *integrative* refers both to the full synthesis of affective, behavioral, cognitive, and physiological theory and methods of psychotherapy and also to the outcome of psychotherapy—the integration or assimilation within the client of the fragmented or fixated aspects of the personality. In developing this approach, we have built extensively on the work of three of our predecessors, two men and a woman who were psychotherapists and theoreticians and, in their own ways, poets as well. This preface seems a fitting place to acknowledge our gratitude and respect for them.

Eric Berne was originally trained as a psychoanalyst. Berne was interested in how people structured their identities (egos), in the transactions between people, and in how people organized their life courses. His published work in what became known as Transactional Analysis began in 1957 with the appearance of a paper, "Ego States in Psychotherapy," in the *American Journal of Psychotherapy*. The term *transactional analysis* (TA) appeared in print a year later.

During that same year, 1958, Berne also began what was to become a laboratory for developing and applying transactional analysis theory: the San Francisco Social Psychiatry Seminar. This seminar grew, split, grew again: Debate, consultation, and training in theory and treatment were then and are now a primary concern of TA therapists. Berne was the quintessential teacher, delighting in the arguments, the case presentations, the vehement discussions that often lasted until the small hours of the morning. His enthusiasm and excitement were contagious, and though he died in 1970 he remains the euhemerist leader of the International Transactional Analysis Association.

Frederick Perls, another therapist/theorist who has shaped our work, was born and educated in Germany. He summarizes his career as a progress: "From an obscure middle class Jewish boy to a mediocre psychoanalyst to the possible creator of a 'new' method of treatment and the exponent of a viable philosophy which could do something for mankind." Fleeing Germany at the outset of Nazi oppression, he went to South Africa to train psychoanalysts and then emigrated to the United States in 1948.

Perls became intrigued by the idea that Sigmund Freud, in developing his theories, had neglected the importance of early oral aggression: the teething stage, during which children first begin to resist, to aggress against actively, and to say "no" to that which they dislike. He maintained that this is a crucial developmental period in the formation of ego. For Perls, this ability to resist is an essential aspect of mental health. His interest in the relationship of ego to healthy aggression and resistance led him to consider resisting and pushing against as a form of contact, and this, in turn, led to exploration of the whole notion of contact and withdrawal in human relationships. The capacity for contact, he concluded, is health; the absence of that capacity is nonhealth. Analyzing and correcting the ways in which a client distorts and denies contact is a major—perhaps the major—goal of Gestalt therapy, the school of psychotherapy developed by Frederick and Laura Perls and their trainees.

While Frederick Perls was the major author of the early Gestalt therapy literature, his wife Laura, a Gestalt psychologist and practicing psychoanalyst, also made important contributions. The publications that bear her name are limited; therefore, the full extent of her influence is not often appreciated, but it is clear that the theory was significantly shaped by her training in existential philosophy and in Gestalt psychology, and her interest in child development. Laura was quiet, calm; Fritz (as he came to be known) was dramatic. Fritz became the guru of Gestalt therapy and the humanistic psychology movement, and Laura moved into the background, intent on training competent psychotherapists in New York City. The reader is invited to recall the unsung, but nevertheless important, influence that Laura has had on the developing theory of Gestalt therapy. In these pages we shall refer to both Perlses' contributions.

Although we have highlighted these three psychotherapists and theorists whose work has stimulated much of the theoretical exploration in this book, I (Richard Erskine) would like to express my gratitude to several other psychologists who have had an important influence in my training and supervision—an influence that has truly been an integrating of approaches. In 1967, while I was teaching psychology at Chicago City College, two very different psychotherapists left their indelible mark: Fritz Perls stimulated my excitement with his unique approach to psychotherapy, and Robert

Neville, through his consistent consultation, made client-centered and child psychotherapy come alive. My appreciation extends to David Kupfer for his teaching of transactional analysis theory and to Hedges Capers for his uplifting sense of how to reach people gently; to Hobart Mowrer and Sid Beajeau for their interpretation of behaviorism; to Georgia Pitcher (Baker), who expertly taught applied child development; to Laura Perls and Isidore From for their personal interest and exploration of Gestalt therapy theory and practice; to Herman Eisen for stressing the importance of deep affective psychotherapy; and, most of all to my mother, Lucille Koniecki, who set a healthy model of respect for the Child in all of us. There are countless numbers of authors whose ideas have been borrowed and augmented and scores of students and clients with whom integrative psychotherapy emerged and continues to be refined. Thanks to the members of the Professional Development Seminar at the Institute for Integrative Psychotherapy for their input on theoretical ideas and to Kate Barton for her thorough reading of the manuscript, and to Alan Jacobs for his thought-provoking position.

I (Janet Moursund) also owe a debt of gratitude and affection to those who have shaped and stimulated my thinking as a psychotherapist. First among these is Roy Heath, who opened my eyes to the very existence of psychology as a discipline. Carl R. Rogers, with whom I worked as a graduate student, and Eugene Gendlin, coworker and friend during those student years at the University of Wisconsin, gave me much more than I knew at the time. Later—much later, after years of working in the field of educational psychology and learning theory—I was introduced to the ideas of TA and Gestalt therapy through a program known as the Quest Fellowship, developed by Dale Jamtgaard of the Lutheran Family Service agency in Portland, Oregon. Dale developed the Quest Fellowship as a way of making the concepts of Gestalt therapy and TA available to healthy folks, folks who were functioning adequately in their relationships; Quest was, for me and for many others, a truly life-changing experience.

Since those first, heady days of discovering a whole new way of looking at myself and others, and of developing a new professional identity as a psychotherapist, I have had many mentors: Claudette Hastie, Carol Ormiston, Mari Panzer, Norma Ragsdale, to name a few. My colleagues at the University of Oregon have supported my efforts, making it possible for me to read and learn and integrate the new and the old; my students have helped me to remain a student myself as I share their excitement, their confusion, and their growing competence.

Both of us, Richard and Jan, owe a special debt to Rebecca Trautman, cotherapist in much of the work to be presented in this book. Personally and professionally, she has literally made our collaboration possible; she has provided a kind of quiet energy that pervades the work we have done together. Her continual discussions of theory and treatment planning and, most important, her relentlessly seeing the OK-ness in people, has shaped integrative psychotherapy as it is today.

Finally, we have both grown in many ways from our association with each other in creating this book. The long hours of discussion, argument, agreement, and challenge have helped both of us to clarify our ideas, to defend our theories, and to organize what we do in a form that can be understood and communicated to each other—and, by extension, to you the reader. As the writing process draws to a close, we want to acknowledge publicly the warmth and respect that we have come to have for each other.

—Richard G. Erskine
—Janet P. Moursund

1

INTRODUCTION

Most psychotherapists date their beginnings from the work of Sigmund Freud. It was Freud who first attempted a detailed explanation of the way in which unconscious processes affect behavior and of the way in which early patterns of feeling and believing continue to shape how we think and feel as adults. Freud's "psychodynamic" approach became a touchstone of modern psychology. Except for the strictest of behaviorists, no psychotherapy is unaffected by Freud's work, though some schools of thought borrow from and build upon it more directly than others.

During the early decades of the twentieth century, Freud's version of psychotherapy dominated clinical practice in both Europe and America. To be sure, there were occasional exceptions—physically oriented treatments like complete bed rest, regimens of strenuous exercise, education and exhortative programs, or the use of hypnosis in treating mental disturbance—but these were small islands in a sea of treatment by "psychoanalysis."

By the 1930s, a new generation of therapists was emerging: among them Carl Jung, Alfred Adler, Wilhelm Reich, Otto Rank, Karen Horney, and Harry Stack Sullivan. As their voices and influence grew stronger, they not only expanded the vision of psychotherapy beyond Freud's vision (Geiwitz & Moursund, 1979) but also contributed many of the essential concepts of integrative psychotherapy.

The first obvious break in the monolithic structure of psychoanalytic and neo-psychoanalytic dominance occurred in the 1940s. Perhaps we should say "breaks," for there were suddenly not one but two major alternatives to psychoanalytic thinking: humanistic psychology, articulated by Abraham Maslow (1954, 1962) and Carl Rogers (1942, 1951), and the behavioral approach to therapy that grew out of the experimental work of Ivan Pavlov (1927) and B. F. Skinner (1938, 1953) and the learning theory of O. Hobart Mowrer (1950).

Behaviorism has traditionally involved itself in demonstrating that universal laws govern the behavior of all organisms, from microbe to man. Understanding these laws would allow the creation of a technology of behavior, by means of which all undesirable behaviors could be eliminated. The early behaviorists were explicitly and vehemently uninterested in "thoughts" or "motives" or "emotions" as such. If it couldn't be measured, or somehow observed by someone else, then it was nonexistent—or at least of no real importance. "Don't talk about being depressed," said the behaviorist, "tell me what you do when you're depressed and I'll help you to find a way to stop doing that and start doing something else instead." When the behavior changes, went the theory, the internal experience (whatever that is) will also change. The behavioral approach to therapy (Bandura, 1969; Dollard & Miller, 1950) considered many of the concepts developed by Freud—instincts, defense mechanisms, the unconscious, focusing on the historical "why"—to be irrelevant. What mattered were the contingencies that maintained a "problem" behavior and what the new behavior would be. The model was clear and logical. Moreover, it was research-based: Behaviorists could prove that their methods worked. Study after study claimed dramatic changes in client's behavior in a variety of problems ranging from agoraphobia to voyeurism.

In contrast to the relatively mechanical approach of the behaviorists, the humanistic psychology movement focused on the uniquely human attributes of the individual. Human beings are more than machines, are qualitatively different from rats or pigeons. Yet humans are not, as Freud would have us believe, driven relentlessly by sexual and aggressive urges, helpless to do more than make the best of a whirling chaos of animal instincts. Abraham Maslow saw men and women as self-actualizing creatures, motivated by the need to become the best that we can be. The basic premise of humanistic psychology is that people must be understood in the context of their unique humanness. Health, growth, and fulfillment, rather than the temporary surcease of drives or the achievement of reward, are the human goals; the quest for one's own potentiality is the human birthright. People are born healthy and, given good growth conditions, will stay that way. Things go awry and dis-ease occurs when those growth conditions are not met. Carl Rogers (1951) applied these humanistic concepts in his formulation of client-centered therapy, in which cure is a matter of restoring the conditions of growth—understanding, unconditional acceptance, genuineness of relationship. Given these necessary conditions, people will naturally and automatically begin to respond in healthy ways.

Maslow's and Rogers's ideas were exciting to a new generation of psychologists, tired of the limitations of psychoanalysis and behaviorism. Their position was simple, direct, optimistic. It offered hope. Moreover, Rogers offered a clear and understandable set of directions for actually working with clients. Carl Rogers's nondirective approach—client-centered therapy—changed the face of psychotherapy forever. Nearly every psychiatrist, psychologist, counselor, and social worker now practicing, of whatever orientation, began his or her training by learning basic active-listening techniques that grew directly out of Rogers's work.

Thus the stage was set for the Great Psychological Debate of the 1950s (Rogers & Skinner, 1956), a debate that still rages among psychologists (albeit somewhat more quietly now). It was called humanism versus behaviorism, and it pitted the people-are-unique-and-unquantifiable group against the behavior-can-be-measured-and-predicted-and-controlled group. The softheads against the hard-noses. The poets against the pragmatists. The development of the nondirective and behaviorist schools had another effect as well: It was the breach in the dam through which eventually poured an ocean of alternative theories and therapeutic approaches. The admixture of ideas from Freud and his colleagues, from Skinner and the behaviorists, and from the client-centered school begun by Rogers provided a fertile ground for the growth of therapeutic practice. And it is at this point that our story, until now somewhat academic and removed, becomes directly and immediately related to the ideas to be presented in this book. For three of the newer theorists—each emerging from and trained in the discipline of psychoanalysis, yet all inevitably affected by the climate of the Great Psychological Debate—contributed two specific psychotherapeutic models upon which integrative psychotherapy rests. These theorists were Frederick and Laura Perls and Eric Berne.

PERLS AND GESTALT THERAPY

Frederick and Laura Perls's contribution is known as Gestalt therapy, taking its name and underlying ideas from the Gestalt psychology of Wertheimer, Kohler, and Koffka (Perls, 1947; Perls, Hefferline, & Goodman, 1951). Gestalt psychology is concerned with the experiencing organism's tendency to perceive and remember wholes rather than collections of parts. The tendency extends to the "closing" of perceptions or experiences in memory, even though the actual stimuli may not form a completed whole. Four unjoined lines, arranged in a roughly square pattern, will be perceived as a square or a box. A story will be recalled with missing elements neatly filled in. So it is, said Perls, with our emotional experiences. The normal and natural human pattern is to complete an experience and with completion comes a sense of wholeness and of being finished. We are then free to move on to the next thing that claims our attention.

Primary and Secondary Gestalts

A need is felt, it is met; the whole is completed and we are done with it. We do not tolerate incompletion, and if the environment fails to provide us with the means for completing our experiences (our gestalts), we will fill them in artificially—for example, with substitute satisfactions, feelings, and fantasies. Such artificial closure results in a "secondary gestalt" in which the self-generated closure brings short-term relief from tension, but the individual must inevitably repeat the pattern because the closure is not one that allows him or her to move on to deal with the next natural and organically occurring experience (L. Perls, 1978a). Over time, these secondary gestalts tend to rigidify and become fixed patterns of perceiving, of thinking, of feeling, and of behaving. In part, the "fixed" perspective serves to keep old desires, unmet needs, and uncomfortable experiences out of present awareness. The fixed gestalt does not allow for full contact here and now between the current needs of the person and the people or objects in the environment.

As an example, consider Gordon, an obese 36-year-old man. In childhood, Gordon tended to be slow and clumsy and had trouble making friends. He often came home from school in tears because of the way his classmates alternately ignored or tormented him. His mother's response was always the same: "Don't feel so bad; it will be all right. Let's sit down and have a little snack together." Gradually, Gordon learned to stifle his natural craving for peer contact, his need to grow into healthy interdependence with others, by stuffing down food and leaning on Mother for comfort. Today, whenever Gordon finds himself feeling "frustrated" (the only word he can find to identify that archaic, formless need for social contact), he turns to food and/or the maternal comfort that his wife obediently provides. Indeed, he truly experiences and identifies his contact need at such times as a feeling of physical hunger. For the moment, food and the soothing presence of his wife help; the "hunger" is satisfied. But the discomfort always returns, as mysterious and as confusing as ever.

Like the thirsty man who puts a pebble in his mouth because he has no water, the temporary relief that Gordon gets from eating must eventually give way to an even greater sensation of need. The pebble serves as a secondary, artificial relief of the sensation of thirst, but the primary need for water remains, even though the man is less consciously aware of it. In a similar way, Gordon has set up an artificial means of dealing with his unmet psychological and social needs, finding temporary relief or distraction while continuing to repeat what is unfinished from the past.

The Structure of Personality

In addition to the concepts of primary and secondary gestalts, Gestalt therapy continues to draw upon a number of psychoanalytic ideas, particularly the concepts of "ego" and "id" (Freud, 1923/1961) and the notion of defense mechanisms and how they are manifested in contact interruptions (Perls, Hefferline, & Goodman, 1951). The ego is defined as the identifying and alienating aspect of self. It is the sense of "me" or "not me." It internalizes and discriminates and is the organizing factor whereby people interact with the external world. As needs, appetites, and desires of the organism—the collection of urges that psychoanalysts refer to as "id"—come into awareness, it is the identification with or alienation from these sensations that in part constitutes the ego. When a person knows that he or she is hungry, or wants to sit down, this awareness of bodily sensations in part defines who he or she is at that moment—ego. The constant shuttling back and forth between awareness of internal experience and awareness of the environment, along with accepting or rejecting what the environment offers, is the essence of ego. Healthy ego, then, is a process, a verb rather than a noun. It is ongoing movement. It is a shifting, a changing, an existing in the endless moment of "now." It evaluates what the current environment presents and assesses internal sensations, bringing the internal and the external together in a never-ending series of experiences.

Although the notions of ego and id are basic to Gestalt therapy, the other structural division of psychoanalysis—the superego—is not. Nor is Freud's notion of *the* unconscious, a reservoir of memories barred from conscious awareness, useful to Gestalt therapists. Instead, Gestalt therapy (Perls, 1947) emphasizes how introjection and repression—basic defense mechanisms—serve as interruptions to contact. In an attempt to cope with needs not being met, and with a lack of needed contact with people, we suppress our awareness of both internal and external events. The result is that we are then unable to be in full contact with ourselves or with what is going on around us. This loss of awareness of needs, feelings, experiences, and memories is *repression*—a defensive, active "forgetting" or shutting down of some part of our thinking and feeling. Repression always involves a corresponding muscular inhibition within the body as an active means of maintaining distraction from full awareness.

As a consequence of active repression, the possibility exists for *introjection,* an unaware defensive internalization of elements of the personality of other people. With introjection, we metaphorically "swallow whole" that which is presented to us by others; we are unable to integrate it so that it becomes a part of the responsive, changeable, ongoing self. It sits within the ego like an indigestible lump, neither contacting nor contactable.

Introjection is only one of a set of contact-interrupting defenses that maintain repression. A second is *projection,* wherein a part of the self—thoughts, motivations, feelings—is perceived as being in another person. The projecting person is not conscious that the sensations are within himself; he responds, not to the real other, but to his own projected images. *Retroflection* is the holding back of action that could be expressed outwardly, as when we carry on an internal dialogue with ourselves rather than interacting with the outside world; or we tighten muscles instead of screaming or hitting. *Deflection,* the lessening of the significance of internal sensations or feelings and screening out or fending off attempts at contact that others may make, is also a way in which we interrupt contact. And finally, *confluence*—losing our boundaries, experiencing self and other as one unit—destroys contact because self and other are now fused and there is no longer any "other" and/or a distinct self with whom to be in touch. Contact interruptions or defense mechanisms maintain repression: The person using them represses his or her awareness of the real (or potential) interaction between him- or herself and the external world, and maintains the belief that his or her particular way of not making contact is, in fact, the only way to interact in that situation. Dealing with contact interruptions, often through the medium of the therapist's own openness to contact, and restoring awareness of both the internal and the external world, are hallmarks of integrative psychotherapy.

BERNE AND TRANSACTIONAL ANALYSIS

In developing the theory of Transactional Analysis, Eric Berne—like the Gestalt therapists—used the definition of ego as a basic element. Berne, however, viewed the ego in a different way than did the Perlses and their students: while the Gestaltists considered the ego as an indivisible and continually emerging process, Berne described it as consisting of various clusters or states, each with complete and coherent patterns of thoughts, feelings, and behaviors. Berne expanded on the ideas of psychoanalyst Paul Federn (1953), who reported that his clients seemed to have distinctly different egos at various times during their therapy. At times, for example, clients would have full awareness of what was occurring both inside and outside their organism in a way appropriate to their developmental age. This contact function of the ego accounts for and integrates what is occurring moment by moment, internally and externally. It also integrates past experiences and their resulting effects, along with the psychological influence of other significant people. Berne colloquially referred to the neopsychic state of the ego as the "Adult." The Adult ego state consists of one's current age-appropriate motor behavior; one's emotional, cognitive, and moral development; one's ability to be creative; and one's full contactful capacity for engagement in meaningful relationships.

The here and now psychological state of the ego (neopsyche or Adult) can be contrasted with an archaic ego state, consisting of encapsulations of the thoughts, feelings, and behaviors of earlier developmental stages. These archaic ego states are analogous to a collection of fixed gestalts (in Perls's terminology) in that these childlike states of the ego are "fixated" or stuck in the past. This aspect of ego perceives the external world, as well as internal needs and sensations, as the person did in an earlier developmental stage. Although the person may appear to be relating to current reality, he or she is actually experiencing what is happening with the cognitive, emotional, or behavioral capacities of a child. He or she has regressed, internally, to the point in development at which an unresolved trauma or confusion originally occurred. Berne colloquially referred to this aspect of the ego as the "Child" ego state.

It should be noted that using the term ego *state* in the singular is somewhat misleading. A child develops through a number of phases and stages—as Jean Piaget (Phillips, 1969), Erik Erikson (1950), Margaret Mahler (1968, 1975), and others have described—and at any of these phases and stages there may be repression and fixation. Under the influence of one set of stressors, we may think and feel and act much as we did when we were six years old; under another, we may regress to an unresolved adolescent problem or even back to early infancy.

In later psychotherapeutic work, Berne explored Federn's observations that the constant psychic presence of parental figures influenced the behavior of many of his clients. This internalized parental influence is that of real people, who years before interacted with and had responsibility for the client when he or she was a child. The parental presence is more tangible than the Freudian concept of "superego"—it contains traces of what was actually said or done with the individual as a child, by whom, and when. Through introjection, the child made the parental person a part of his or her psychological self, that is, ego. Although this aspect of ego can be acquired through internalization of people other than one's actual parents (any of the "big people" in a child's life can be introjected and made a part of the ego), Berne used the designation "Parent" to differentiate this state of ego from the Adult and Child states.

The Fantasy Parent

Neopsyche (Adult), *archaeopsyche* (Child), and *exteropsyche* (Parent) are the three major states of the ego described by Berne. Both archaeopsychic and exteropsychic ego states are fixations of early reactions and experiences or unaware internalizations (introjects) of significant others. In addition, integrative psychotherapy posits another process by which ego state fixations can be acquired.

As a normal developmental process in early childhood, children will often create an *imago*, a fantasy figure, as a way to provide controls, structure, nurturing, or whatever that young person experienced as missing or inadequate. Some children create their own personal "boogeyman," a frightening creature who threatens them with dire consequences for minor misdeeds. Investing the fantasy parent with all the bad and scary aspects of being parented allows them to keep Mom and Dad as perfectly good and loving.

Throughout his elementary and junior high school years, Richard was haunted by the boogeyman. As he developed into a teenager, the boogeyman ceased to be a concern; however, there was always the possibility of a stern teacher or policeman who could punish him if he got out of line. In his late twenties, Richard's grandmother died and he helped the family clean out her house. As he cleaned under her bed and in her closet, he felt extremely anxious. He anticipated some terrible punishment and, although he told himself that his thoughts were not rational, he kept expecting to find the remains of the boogeyman. Working with his therapist, Richard began to remember that as a young child he thought the boogeyman "lived" in grandmother's bedroom, and that he also had the capacity to follow Richard to school or at play. If Richard misbehaved, the boogeyman was sure to punish him. In the process of therapy, Richard began to remember a spanking at age 4, which was administered by his mother, in grandmother's bedroom during a family party. Shortly after the spanking, Richard developed his belief in the boogeyman and could then turn to his mother for comfort, protection, and reassurance. The fantasy of the boogeyman helped the four-year-old Richard remain adapted to external parental controls and at the same time experience his mother as all loving and fully tolerant of his behavior.

Others may create a fairy godmother sort of fantasy parent who loves and nurtures them even when their real parents are cold or absent or abusive. This created image serves as a buffer between the actual parental figures and the desires, needs, and feelings of the young child. The inevitable discomforts of growing up in an imperfect world are more tolerable because the fantasy figure provides what was missing in the real parents.

Anne-Marie, for example, had periods of depression in which she would eat a large amount of food. During this time, she would long for her dead grandmother, whom she described to her therapist as affectionate, understanding, consoling, and who she said used to bring her wonderful food to eat. The therapist, out of curiosity, asked how old Anne-Marie had been when her grandmother died and she replied, "14 months." A 14-month-old infant was not likely to have the experiences with a grandmother that Anne-Marie reported. As the therapist began to explore the discrepancy between Anne-Marie's longing for her grandmother and the fact that the grandmother had been dead since infancy, the client began to remember experiences from childhood that had been lost from memory for many years. Anne-Marie had repeatedly been abused by both mother and father and had often been locked in the wine cellar for days at a time without food. Anne-Marie related how the grandmother would "appear" to her after the beatings or in the dark wine cellar to comfort her, to encourage her, and to promise her wonderful meals. By creating these images of grandmother, Anne-Marie was able to satisfy in fantasy some of the needs for appropriate nurturing that were drastically lacking in her parents' behavior toward her.

As they mature to later developmental phases, children often let go of their self-generated images. But when the child represses his or her awareness of needs, feelings, and memories in order to survive in the family, the self-created image is fixated and does not become integrated with later developmental learning. Whatever the characteristics of the fixated self-created Parent, over the years it comes to operate similarly to the Parent ego state described by Berne. It functions like an introjected personality; however, it is often more demanding and illogical and unreasonable than the actual parent was (after all, it had its origin in a small child's fantasy). The self-created parent made from fantasized images provides an encapsulated, nonintegrated package of thoughts and feelings and behaviors to which the person responds as if they were truly internalizations from the big people of early childhood.

Ego State Function

Berne used the term "ego state" to describe a state of mind with a coherent system of internal feelings and thoughts and a corresponding system of postures, facial expressions, and other external behaviors. The pattern of behaviors and the state of mind that a person experiences and exhibits at any given moment forms the active ego state. It is from these *active ego states* that people communicate. Sometimes people talk to others from their Parent ego state, with all the feelings, attitudes, and expressions that their mother or father used years before; at other times, they may react as a little child, perceiving the situation as they did when they were only five or six years old. They may then switch to the Adult ego state and react to their environment (and the people in that environment) with the emotions, ideas, and behaviors that are situationally and developmentally appropriate and unencumbered with internalizations from parents or fixations from childhood.

Knowledge of ego defense mechanisms is integral to understanding ego state functioning and how ego states are activated. *It is because of the fixation of defense mechanisms that the archaic (Child) or introjected (Parent) aspects of ego remain separate states and do not become integrated into neopsychic (Adult) awareness.* Adult ego state awareness of needs, desires, memories, and external influences remain blocked through the maintaining of infant defenses of avoidance, freezing, and fighting (Fraiberg, 1983); the late oral defenses of splitting (Fairbairn, 1954) and transformation of affect (Fraiberg, 1983); and the early childhood defenses described by Anna Freud (1937). Additionally, full Adult ego state functioning is inhibited by the complex defense mechanisms of introjection, projection, retroflection, deflection, and confluence (as defined in Gestalt therapy). Thus ego state function is the dynamic interaction of these intrapsychic processes and the observable behaviors.

Because of the fixation of defense mechanisms, ego state function can either be *active* or remain an intrapsychic *influence*. We can observe the manifestation of the exteropsychic (Parent) ego state when a person actively feels, perceives the environment, or acts as the parents did years before. The active Parent ego state is most typically seen in the person who talks to her own children just the way she was spoken to as a child. Suzanne, for instance, yelled at and ridiculed her children when she felt pressured or under stress. Throughout Suzanne's own childhood, her mother screamed insults and denigrated Suzanne's way of doing things. Even though Suzanne once vowed to herself that she would never treat any child that way, she reported that "the yelling just slips out" of her. At such moments, her introjected Parent ego state was active.

When the Parent ego state is influencing someone intrapsychically, that person is most likely to exhibit childlike behaviors. These behaviors will reflect the age at which the child experienced conflict with his or her actual parents or when there was a significant absence of contact. The person actively feels or behaves like the child he or she actually was years before, with the same childhood defense mechanisms. The childlike reasoning, perceiving, feeling, and behaving is a reaction to the *internal influence* of the Parent ego state. Suzanne reported that, after she yelled at her children, she would say to herself, "You're no good for anything!" and "You're the dumbest person in the world!" Then she would feel "upset" and ashamed of herself and would apologize repeatedly to her children. She would often bring them presents "to make up for the bad way" she behaved.

Tim described how every time he was about to start a new legal case for the law firm where he was working he would become sad, would feel sick at his stomach, and would procrastinate in response to a continuous thought: "Who are you fooling?" In the course of therapy, Tim remembered that these were his father's actual words just before Tim had a music recital at age 11 and again at high school graduation. The internal dialogue stopped when Tim felt his anger and expressively imagined telling his father to stop that kind of put-down and that he was a competent attorney now.

As a defense against the intrapsychic influence of the introjected parents or significant others, an individual may project the introjected personality onto another person, such as a spouse, teacher, or therapist, and then perceive and react to that person as he or she did at the time of fixation. This projecting of the introjection and reacting regressively is *transference* and often provides a relief from the internal stress of the intrapsychic conflict. Through transference the conflicts of childhood are once again experienced as originating with people in the environment. Through close observations of these transference transactions, the therapist can understand the intrapsychic influence of the Parent ego state and the child's actual or wished-for response to the discomfort of the conflict. Barbara, late for an appointment with her dentist, trembles as she imagines his anger at her. In actuality, it is neither her concern with promptness nor the dentist's possible reaction that scares her. Rather, it is the memory, of which she is unaware, of a mother who became furious when she was even a few minutes late from school.

The primary ways, then, in which people react to the intrapsychic conflict between ego states are (a) regression to Child ego state in response to the internal influence of the Parent ego states (Tim's sadness and sick stomach); (b) active manifestation of the contents of Parent ego states, directed at someone else as an attempt to avoid the internal pressure (Suzanne's yelling and ridiculing her children); and (c) transference, where the introjected and/or fantasized parent is projected onto another person with a corresponding reaction to the projection as the child actually reacted, or wished she could have reacted, years before (Barbara's trembling).

Psychological problems emerge when introjected and/or archaic ideas, images, and emotions contaminate the here and now perceptions of the Adult ego state. When Adult ego state contamination exists, the subjective experience of the person is that he or she is processing current stimuli, accounting for current sensations and feelings, and behaving appropriately to the situation; when, in fact, this is not so. But because the person is unaware that introjected ideas and emotions and/or childhood decisions and feelings are infringing on present perceptions, he or she has no reason to challenge or update the inappropriate reactions.

Just as parents and children inevitably experience conflict, so conflict between the introjected Parent and Child ego states is virtually inevitable. The healthy ego is one in which the Adult, with full neopsychic functioning, is in charge and has integrated (assimilated) content and experiences both borrowed from others and fixated in earlier development. When the Adult ego state is contaminated by Parent and/or Child, or when the boundaries between ego states are too loosely defined, the Adult ego state cannot be fully in charge of thoughts, feelings, and behaviors. The resulting war between what was introjected into Parent ego state and what is a fixated reaction of the Child ego state is one of the most common dysfunctions: The exteropsychic state of the ego is overly demanding or overprotective of self and others; the archaeopsychic ego state attempts to protect itself by means of outmoded and largely ineffective defensive maneuvers; and the neopsychic ego state becomes deenergized. Energy is drawn into the internal conflict (or avoidance of it) and less attention is available for ongoing contact between the environment and the present needs of the organism.

Ego State Identification

The analysis of ego state *cathexis*—the source of psychic energy at any point in time—is dependent upon the correlation of four determinants: phenomenological (subjective), historical, behavioral (developmental), and social (transferential). The first is the phenomenological or subjective experience of the client, including the sensations, feelings, and beliefs that shape his or her perspective. In identifying the subjective experience, the therapist inquires as to *how* the client feels or *what* it is like to live in his or her skin or how the client reacts internally to his or her own behavior. Joyce responded to such questions with, "I was feeling scared and reacting to my university professor just as though I was still in third grade." Bob reported that, although at times he was ashamed of his behavior toward his son, he often felt compelled to use the same voice tone and the same words that his father used 33 years earlier when he criticized Bob. Over a several-week period, John was angry with the people at work because they did not share his enthusiasm. The therapist suggested that he just stop feeling angry and enjoy his own contribution to the project. John responded with, "I have to feel angry." The sense that he had no other choice was a clue to the therapist that his anger might have been introjected, but the therapist could not yet rule out that the anger might have been based on fixated decisions in childhood. Both Bob's and John's responses indicated the need for further inquiry into their subjective experiences and a clear picture of their life histories.

The historical experience of the client is assessed by creating a supportive environment in which the client is free to talk about his or her memories. Inquiry into the dynamics between the child and others or the relationship between mother and father provides essential information regarding early conflicts. The therapist can assist this process by asking *who* and *when* questions, such as "Who in your family also felt or acted that way?" "When you were in the third grade what was happening between you and the teacher so that you were scared?"

The answers to these questions may lead to more specific inquiry as to the client's family or school history or to going back to the phenomenological experience. For example, "How did you feel and what did you do inside when your father criticized you?" or "How did you cope when you were in conflict with the third-grade teacher?" invite the client to reexperience past events. In the interweaving of phenomenological and historical information, the therapist collects significant data as to which ego state is active or internally influential.

The behavioral or developmental focus is the third indicator for the therapist to evaluate. Here the therapist assesses the client's current observable behavior by drawing on observational information and research from the field of human development. What psychologists have learned over the years about early mother-child interaction; motor and language development; emotional, cognitive, and social development; defense mechanisms; moral development; and adult life transitions all serve to provide a background of information to assist in determining the stage of development at which emotions, behaviors, or interactions have become fixated.

When Fred was about to try something new, he would begin walking flat-footed with a choppy movement and with his stomach protruding. His body and posture looked like that of a toddler. Using this as a clue, the therapist inquired about this stage of his life and learned that his mother had been hospitalized for an extensive period of time when he was about two years old, and he had felt frightened and insecure—a feeling that continued into adulthood whenever he found himself faced with a new challenge. The feeling was manifested in his toddlerlike walk.

Behavior that is not congruent with the current context may have been normal and appropriate for a child at a specific developmental stage or may be an indication of how the client defended him- or herself in a traumatic situation. When Mary noticed tension developing between two people, she would begin making irrelevant comments and trying to change the subject. As the therapist explored this behavior, Mary remembered as a child trying to distract either one of her parents when she felt an argument coming on because it usually ended in violence. Mary's irrelevant comments in tense situations today are a regression to her childhood defense of deflection in the face of conflict.

When an introjected parent frequently functioned from his or her Child ego state, the client may also behave in a childlike way. Here again the therapist will have to interweave the developmental assessment with the historical or phenomenological to determine if a specific defensive reaction, behavioral pattern, or emotion is the manifestation of an exteropsychic state of the ego or of an archaeopsychic fixation. Steven reported getting depressed often, particularly when things were going well in his life. An exploration of the current situation and thinking patterns did not reveal anything significant, and neither did an investigation of childhood experiences. Finally the therapist explored what Steven's mother was like and learned that she had suffered a series of major losses in her life. Her emotional response as an adult to happy experiences was to shut down emotionally and not let herself anticipate anything positive out of fear that something "terrible" could happen. Even though she did not seem overtly to say anything to Steven about not feeling happy or excited, Steven, without awareness, internalized her response and made it his own.

The fourth determinant of an ego state is the social or transferential. The analysis of transactions provides further data to indicate which ego state is active, the nature of the intrapsychic influence, and what stimulus from the therapist served to trigger the cathexis. Transactions between client and therapist, or, in group therapy, between client and client, may reflect a current transference, an attempt by the client to put into action that which he or she has difficulty remembering or putting into words. The desires, expectations, and reactions of the client as well as the projections and/or refusal of a transferential relationship all serve to describe the client's family system, the developmental age fixation, or aspects of personality of significant people who may have been introjected.

The therapist will sometimes clarify or restate to a client what he heard the client say in words or behavior. Jenny would generally respond with anger to these clarifying statements. She frequently denied what she had just said or accused the therapist of criticizing her. As the therapist explored this pattern, he learned that Jenny's father used to turn things Jenny said around in such a way that he either criticized or made fun of her. When the therapist addressed Jenny's Adult ego state with clarifying statements, she would move to her Child ego state, reacting to the therapist as if he were her father. The analysis of this transferential transaction helped the therapist to understand Jenny's developmental fixation, the internal conflict between her Parent and Child ego states, and to identify the interventions appropriate for a child who was constantly criticized and ridiculed.

When the analysis of transactions is correlated with the phenomenological, historical, and behavioral (developmental) assessments, the therapist has a usable hypothesis as to which ego states are influential or active. Making use of this hypothesis helps the therapist to select effective interventions.

SCRIPTS

As infants and small children (and perhaps even before birth), we begin to develop the reactions and expectations that define for us the kind of world we live in and the kind of people we are. At first encoded physically, in body tissue and biochemical events, then emotionally, and later cognitively, in the form of beliefs, attitudes, and values, these responses form a kind of blueprint that guides the way we live our lives. Alfred Adler referred to this blueprint as "life style" (Ansbacher & Ansbacher, 1956); Sigmund Freud used the term "repetition compulsion" to describe similar phenomena (1920/1961); Eric Berne termed this blueprint a "script" (1972); and Fritz Perls called it "life script" (1973).

Formation of Script Beliefs

The story of life scripts is the story of contact and contact distortion between an individual and the outside world of people and things. To the degree that the ego is involved in a healthy contact process internally and externally, needs will arise, be experienced, and be acted upon in relation to the environment in an organically healthy fashion. A felt need arises, is met, and is let go; the person moves on to the next experience. When contact is distorted or denied, however, needs are not met. The experience is not closed naturally, but must find an artificial closure. These artificial closures are the substance of childhood reactions and decisions that become fixated and may also create a situation where introjection of another person's personality is likely to occur.

The life script is a self-protective plan that emerges from the introjections, survival reactions, and decisions of childhood; it is a fixated series of defenses that prevent the feelings and unmet needs of childhood from coming into awareness. It is the guideline—the plot and subplots—around which our actual experiences revolve. The *script limits spontaneity and flexibility in problem solving and in relating to people* because the story of one's life, including the ending and all the major events, is already written, usually in early childhood. In essence, the script answers the question, "What does a person like me do in a world like this with people like you?" Life script is a repetition of the unresolved dramas of childhood.

Introjection. The script can be established in two ways—through the defense mechanism of introjection and/or through the child's self-protective reactions and decisions. First, a child may internalize the image of parental figures—introjection—which includes their emotions, thoughts, beliefs, behaviors, and style of perceiving the world. Introjection is most likely to occur in the absence of contact and/or the presence of conflict. Children internalize the threatening or damaging qualities of parents or other significant people in order to control those characteristics ("If it's in me then at least I'm in charge of it") and to keep awareness of unmet needs and related feelings repressed (L. Perls, 1978b). When parental nurturing is inadequate or inappropriate, there is a lack of contact; children may also internalize the ostensibly good and loving aspects of parents in order to experience themselves as good and loving and acceptable—like Mom and Dad.

Parental injunctions and definitions of the child are introjected by that child and later in life function as an intrapsychic influence, shaping his or her beliefs, emotions, and behavior. Parents and significant authority figures frequently provide two types of messages: those that tell the child what he or she must do or feel and those that tell the child who he or she is.

Script-forming messages may be either direct or indirect, and are often given in both ways simultaneously. For example, a mother often ignored her son's requests and told the boy, "You don't need anything." The child might have internalized this definition of himself literally, reacting with a life plan of denying wants and needs. Or the message can be inferred as a directive: The ignored child may understand that he is not supposed to be who he is, or even to exist at all. The message, "Don't exist," would then become a part of his life script, to be compliantly played out later in self-effacement, failure, or suicide.

Script decisions. The second way in which a script is formed is through the child's reactions and decisions about life, based on his or her perceptions of which options are open to him or her.

Irene, a harried executive, grew up with an alcoholic mother who was often incapable of preparing the family dinner or relating to Irene's needs for nurturing. At about age five, Irene decided that the best way to deal with life would be to become competent and efficient. Today she is highly organized, controlling, and overworked. Her sense of "responsibility" gets her into difficulties with other people at work and at home.

Tom, in contrast, is now 31 years old and is on his fifth menial job. He puts no energy into accomplishments and has turned down training that could advance his current job. In elementary school, he had some dyslexia and when he compared himself with his father, a distinguished university professor, and his mother, an avid reader, he decided that he was "dumb" and that there was "no use to try." Today he maintains the beliefs "I'm dumb" and "What's the use of trying? I'll fail anyway" as a way to make his life predictable and justifiable.

Childhood reactions and decisions begin as a means of coping with discomfort and, with internal and external reinforcement, shape a person's overall belief system. Such script beliefs begin to develop when a child is under pressure from parental behavior or from environmental trauma, particularly in circumstances where expressing feelings does not result in needs being met. Through the process of cognitive mediation (an intellectual defense against uncomfortable emotions), the child attempts to understand and explain his experiences and his unmet needs by making decisions about himself, others, and the quality of his life. The decisions "I'm dumb" and "What's the use of trying" were Tom's coping mechanisms 20 to 24 years ago; those decisions are maintained today as script beliefs. Script beliefs are usually experienced in similarly concrete terms—the way young children think—and serve as a cognitive defense against awareness of selected childhood emotions and unmet needs.

As another example of how the introjection of parental definitions and injunctions is used in conjunction with childhood decisions in forming a life script, consider Mary, a young woman who was extremely quiet and uncommunicative about her wants and needs. In therapy, she reexperienced having to suppress her joy and enthusiasm for life while living in a home with a bedridden grandmother who spent several years in pain. Mary's normal playful sounds often wakened the grandmother, and then Mary would be defined as "bad" and scolded or punished. She was repeatedly told, "Don't make noise." Her way of making sense of and dealing with this situation was to decide that her wants were likely to hurt other people. She continued to live out this decision years later with her husband, children, and friends. She experienced her own urges and desires as "bad" and quietly kept them to herself. She often resented others, however, because they failed to respond to what she had hidden with such skill and determination.

For simplicity's sake, the early survival reactions and decisions or the formation of script beliefs are often described as though they occurred at one particular time in a child's life. It is important, however, to keep in mind that a script decision may be acquired over a long period of time. It may arise out of the child's interaction with fantasy parents as well as with real people, or out of imaginations and dreams as well as from actual occurrences. To the child, the decisions that are made seem to be the best possible choice, under the circumstances, as a means of solving the immediate problem. Once adopted, script beliefs influence what stimuli (internal and external) are attended to, how they are interpreted, and whether or not they are acted upon. They become a self-fulfilling prophecy through which the child's expectations are inevitably proven to be true. Life script, then, is a repetition throughout life of the events and reactions of childhood.

Script maintenance. As a person grows older, the life script is maintained in order (a) to avoid reexperiencing unmet needs and the corresponding feelings suppressed at the time the child introjected the parental injunctions and definitions and/or made the script decisions, and (b) to provide a predictive model of life and interpersonal relationships. Prediction is important, particularly when there is a crisis or trauma; most of us feel uncomfortable when we don't know what is coming, don't understand what is happening, or don't know how our behavior will be received by others. Although the script is often personally destructive, it does provide psychological balance or homeostasis: It gives us at least the illusion of predictability. Any disruption in this predictive model produces anxiety; to avoid such discomfort, we organize our perceptions and experiences so as to maintain our script beliefs.

Eric Berne used the term "script" to refer to a longitudinal life plan formed from introjects and decisions. When we look at script as an intrapsychic and interpersonal system, we can observe how the script is lived out day by day, how the script plot is reinforced, and how others are manipulated into the roles the script requires. The life script becomes a self-reinforcing, distorted system of feelings, thoughts, and actions. In addition to script beliefs (Tom's "I'm dumb" and "What's the use of trying; I'll fail anyway"), the script system has two other interrelated and interdependent components: the script display (Tom puts no energy into accomplishments) and the reinforcing experiences (Tom remembers losing four other jobs).[1]

Script Display

When current needs are not met in adult life, script beliefs and related feelings may be stimulated as they were at the time the script was written. The person is then likely to engage in behaviors that verify script beliefs. These behaviors are referred to as the *script display* and may include any observable behaviors (choice of words, sentence patterns, tone of voice, displays of emotion, gestures and body movements) that are direct manifestations of script beliefs and of repressed needs and feelings (the intrapsychic process). A person either acts in a way defined by script beliefs, for example, saying "I don't know" when believing "I'm dumb," or may act in a way that socially defends against the script beliefs, for example, excelling in school and acquiring numerous degrees as a way of keeping the "I'm dumb" belief from being discovered by others.

Children test a whole range of behaviors throughout childhood in order to discover which will elicit responses confirming what they believe. Confirming responses, which reduce anxiety, tend to shape the behavioral repertoire, while nonconfirming ones are

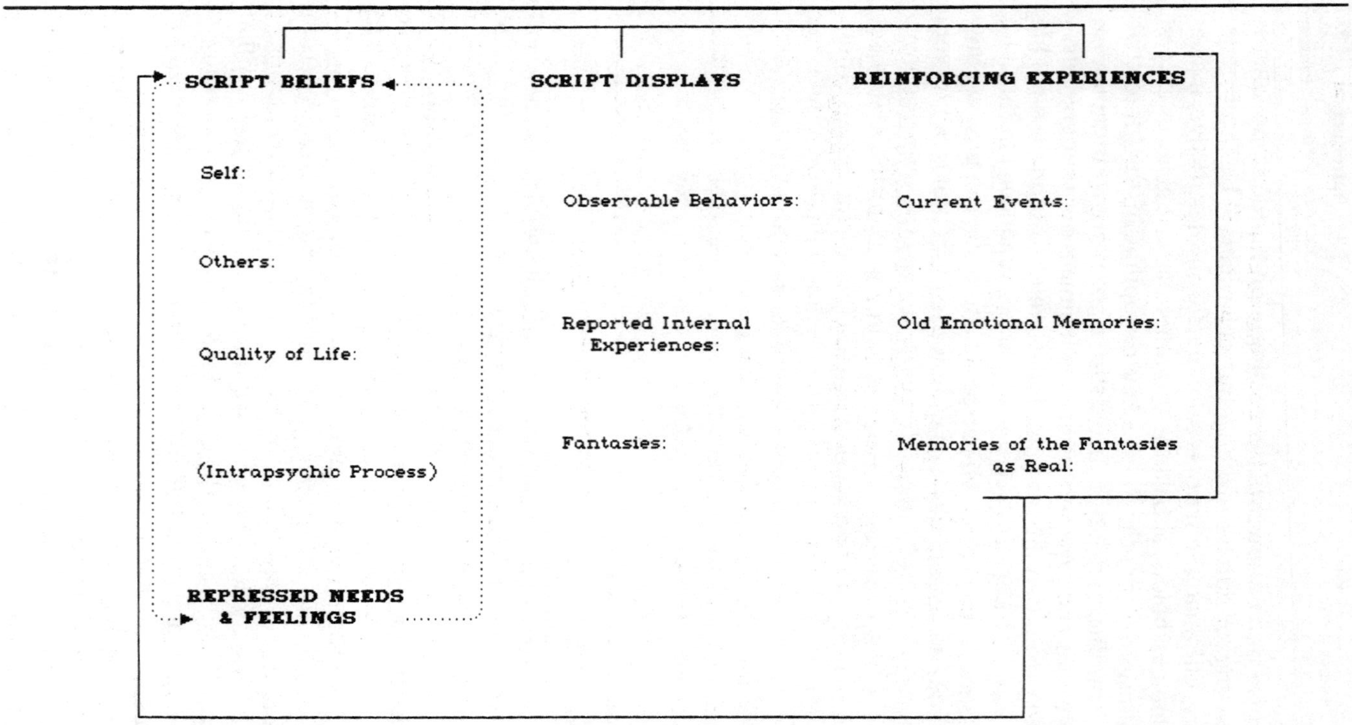

SCRIPT BELIEFS

Self:

Others:

Quality of Life:

(Intrapsychic Process)

REPRESSED NEEDS & FEELINGS

SCRIPT DISPLAYS

Observable Behaviors:

Reported Internal Experiences:

Fantasies:

REINFORCING EXPERIENCES

Current Events:

Old Emotional Memories:

Memories of the Fantasies as Real:

Figure 1.1 The Script System

more likely to be discarded. Eventually the child settles on a specific group of behaviors, including displays of emotion, and uses them repeatedly, especially in situations where the script beliefs are most active. These behaviors extend into adult life and continually tell the story of the original school environment or family system.

As a child, Jean decided that she wouldn't get what she wanted and learned to laugh rather than feel the resulting discomfort. In adult life, Jean seldom asks for what she wants and, whenever she does ask, covers it with a laugh. The laugh helps her to remind herself not to be disappointed when her prediction ("I won't get what I want") comes true. It also tells others that she really doesn't expect them to take her request seriously; thus the prediction is set up to be fulfilled.

As part of the script display, individuals often have physiological reactions in addition to or in place of the overt behaviors. These internal experiences are not readily observable; nevertheless, the person can give a self-report: fluttering in the stomach, muscle tensions, headaches, colitis—myriad somatic responses to the script beliefs and repression of needs and feelings. Body tensions help to maintain needs, memories, feelings, and reactions, while at the same time keeping them from awareness. Persons who have many somatic complaints or illnesses frequently believe that "something is wrong with me," and use physical symptoms to reinforce the belief—a cognitive defense that, again, serves to keep the script system intact.

Script display also includes fantasies in which the individual imagines behaviors, either his or her own or someone else's, that lend support to script beliefs. Jean, whose script belief is that she won't get what she wants, imagines that people won't respond to her. As she becomes aware that she would like her husband to remember her birthday, she fantasizes his coming home empty-handed, or his deciding to work late at the office that evening. These fantasied behaviors function as effectively as overt behaviors in reinforcing script beliefs/feelings—in some instances, even more effectively. They act on the system exactly as though they were events that had actually occurred.

Reinforcing Experiences

Any script display can result in a reinforcing experience—a subsequent happening that "proves" that the script belief is valid and thus justifies the behavior of the script display. Reinforcing experiences are a collection of emotionally laden memories, real or imagined, of other people's or one's own behavior; a recall of internal bodily experiences; or the retained remnants of fantasies, dreams, or hallucinations. Reinforcing experiences serve as a feedback mechanism to reinforce the script beliefs; only those memories that support the script belief are readily accepted and retained. Memories that negate script beliefs tend to be rejected or forgotten because they would challenge the belief and the whole defensive process.

Another example of the script system illustrates the interaction among script beliefs/feelings, script displays, and reinforcing experiences. Beginning with the birth of her first sibling, Louise made a decision, based on the care her sick sibling received and her own being "pushed off," that she (Louise) was not important. At the time her mother was under great emotional pressure and was psychologically unavailable, her father was frequently away. The early decision, "I'm not important," was reinforced with the birth of each successive sibling and in a series of traumatic home situations where, because she was the oldest, Louise's needs were ignored. Louise reported in therapy that she often experienced her parents' nonverbal attitude as an injunction: "Don't be important." At an early age, she discovered that one solution to the problem of not being important was to take care of others—siblings and parents. This would make it possible to get some of her needs met, even though she herself didn't really matter.

In adult life, Louise's decision was observable in her choice of a career in the helping professions. Her general demeanor was quiet and withdrawn, deferring to others. The social response from others was that she was ignored and often did not get what she wanted. This reinforced her belief that she was not as important as others. Her affective behavior was one of sadness mingled with periods of depression and/or severe headaches. Louise's fantasy life often centered on the belief that if she were good enough to someone else they would love her and take care of her. As a contrasting theme, she also occasionally fantasized ending up alone, poor, and unloved.

Interlocking scripts. Louise's family of origin provided the matrix within which her script system developed. Predictably, when she found a partner with whom to build a family of her own, it was someone who fit neatly into her system. Both Louise's family of

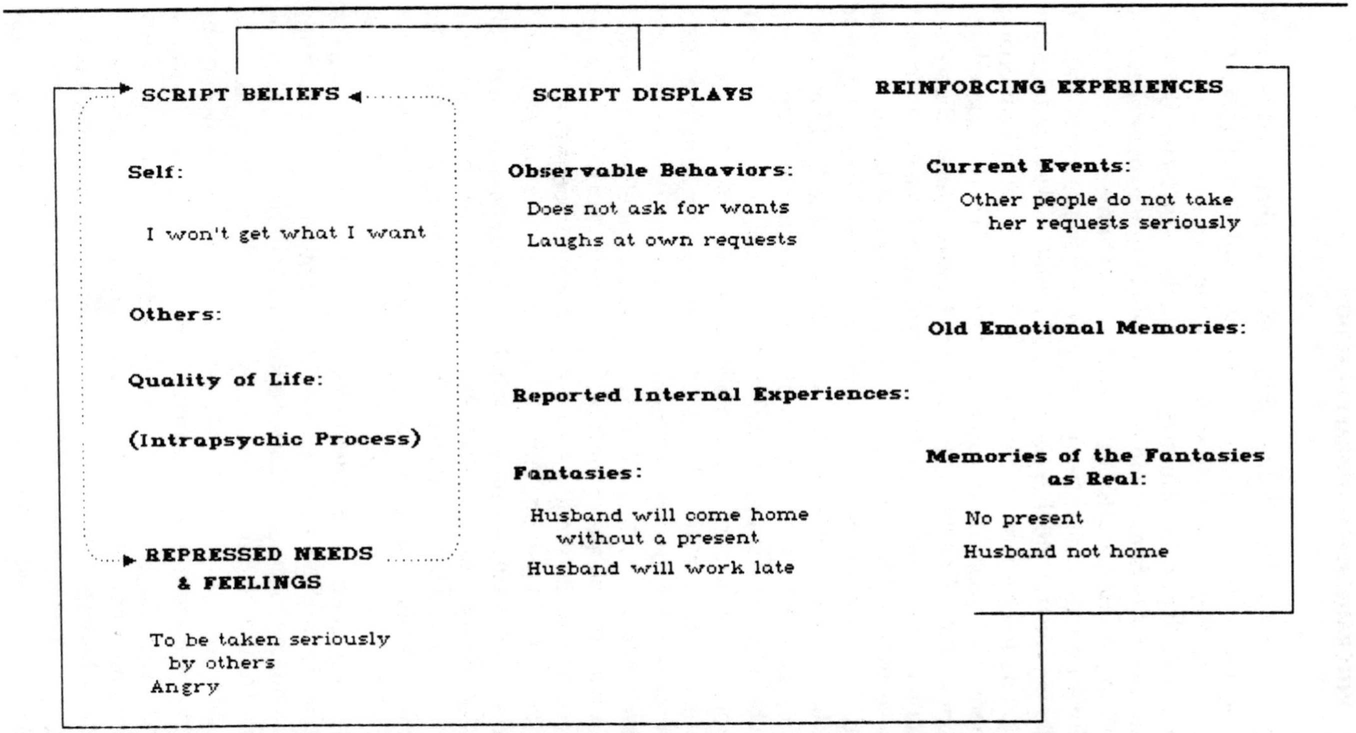

Figure 1.2 Jean's Script System

origin and her current relationship with her husband and children can be seen as interlocking script systems in which family members attempt to live out their respective scripts. In such interlocking systems, each person influences and is influenced by the behavior of others in the family who provide reinforcing experiences that confirm the script beliefs. Louise's behavior at home often consisted of long periods of silence, spending time alone reading, and not initiating contact with her husband, Bill. When Bill wanted contact with Louise, he would use Louise's behavior as a reinforcing experience to confirm his own script belief, "There is something wrong with me." During the periods of Louise's silence, Bill would fantasize a variety of things that he might have done wrong to lead Louise to avoid him. In each fantasy, he would collect further evidence to support his script belief. He then would defend against the belief by angrily telling his wife and son what they had done wrong. Louise used the memory of Bill's angry criticism to reinforce her belief, "I'm not important" and withdrew, providing further support for Bill's script belief. While Louise was at work, she would repeatedly remember Bill's criticism from the night before, each memory serving to stimulate her childhood sadness and anger and old script decisions. In order to repress the old feelings, she would work harder to please Bill, anticipating all the things she could do to please him, while simultaneously expecting none of her efforts to be successful in the long run.

The interlocking script system helps us to understand how each family member supports and helps others to carry out day to day their own script beliefs. It describes both the interpersonal and the intrapersonal dynamics of dysfunctional families or groups. Each person's script beliefs provide a distorted framework for viewing self, others, and the quality of life. In order to engage in a script display, individuals must discount other options; they frequently will maintain that their behavior is the "natural" or "only" way they can respond. When used socially, script displays are likely to produce interpersonal experiences that, in turn, are governed by and contribute to the reinforcement of script beliefs. Thus each person's script system is distorted and self-reinforcing through the operation of its three interrelated and interdependent subsystems: script beliefs/feelings, script displays, and reinforcing experiences. *The script system serves as a defense against awareness of childhood experiences, needs, and related emotions while simultaneously being a repetition of the past.*

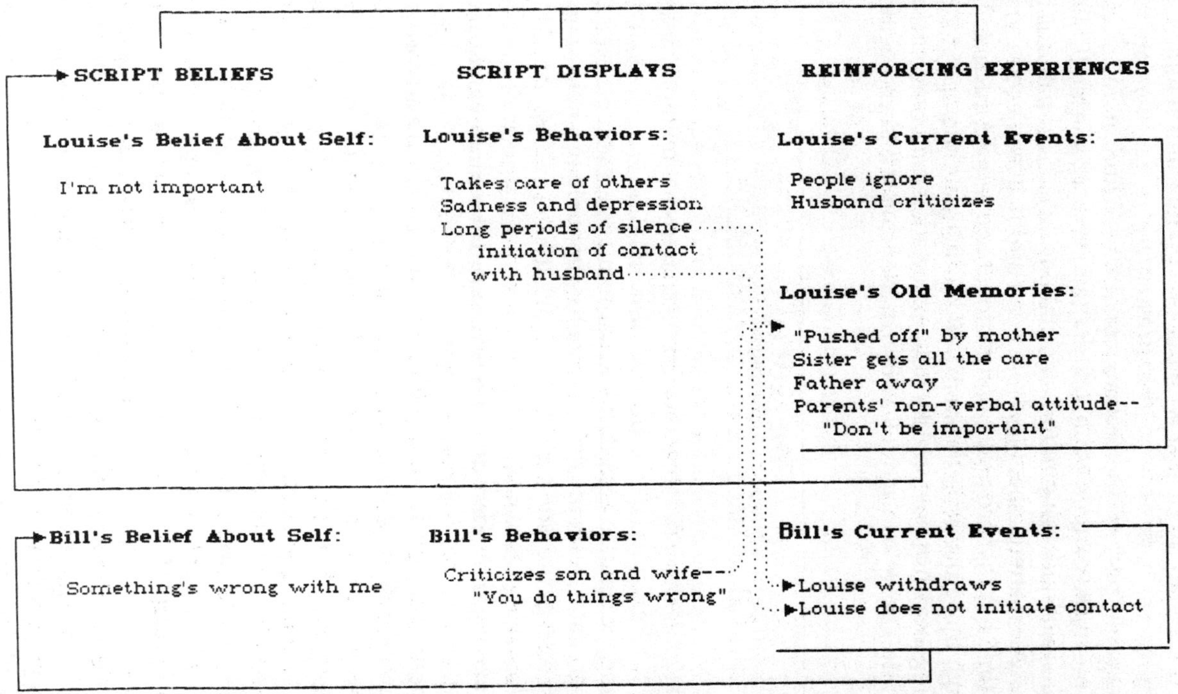

SCRIPT BELIEFS	SCRIPT DISPLAYS	REINFORCING EXPERIENCES
Louise's Belief About Self:	**Louise's Behaviors:**	**Louise's Current Events:**
I'm not important	Takes care of others Sadness and depression Long periods of silence initiation of contact with husband	People ignore Husband criticizes
		Louise's Old Memories:
		"Pushed off" by mother Sister gets all the care Father away Parents' non-verbal attitude--"Don't be important"
Bill's Belief About Self:	**Bill's Behaviors:**	**Bill's Current Events:**
Something's wrong with me	Criticizes son and wife--"You do things wrong"	Louise withdraws Louise does not initiate contact

Figure 1.3 Interlocking Script Systems

It is through script that we limit our options and reduce our ability to react flexibly to the stresses and crises that are an inescapable part of the human condition. When under stress, nonintegrated exteropsychic (Parent) and archaeopsychic (Child) ego state misperceptions and expectations dictate old patterns of response—patterns that may have been useful, even necessary, at one time but that are now nonfunctional and self-destructive. To change those patterns, the person must integrate the ego states, moving away from old, rigidly held expectations and perceptions and into a more contactful way of experiencing self-in-the-world.

THE PROCESS OF INTEGRATIVE PSYCHOTHERAPY

The *integrative* of Integrative Psychotherapy has multiple meanings. It refers, first, to the process of integrating the personality: helping the client to assimilate and harmonize the contents of his or her ego states, relax the defense mechanisms, relinquish the script, and reengage the world with full contact. It is the process of making whole: taking disowned, unaware, unresolved aspects of the ego and making them part of a cohesive self. Through integration, it becomes possible for people to have the courage to face each moment openly and freshly, without the protection of a preformed opinion, position, attitude, or expectation.

The *integrative* also refers to the integration of theory, the bringing together of affective, cognitive, behavioral, physiological, and systems approaches to psychotherapy. The concepts are utilized within a perspective of human development, in which each phase of life presents heightened developmental tasks, need sensitivities, crises, and opportunities for new learnings. Integrative psychotherapy takes into account many views of human functioning: psychodynamic, client centered, behaviorist, family therapy, Gestalt therapy, Reichian, and Transactional Analysis. Each provides a valid explanation of behavior, and each is enhanced when integrated with the others.

Freud, in asserting that the experiences of infancy and early childhood form a foundation upon which the adult personality is based, blazed a trail for later therapists to follow. The behaviorists laid out the laws of learning, of stimulus and response and reinforcement, which explain just how the early responses are acquired and how they are maintained and elaborated through the years. And Rogers, with his humanistic perspective, added another essential piece: People are uniquely different from animals, and do respond in innately healthy and growthful ways when provided with appropriate emotional and cognitive nourishment.

Freud, Rogers, and the behaviorists are the foundation stones of integrative psychotherapy. The actual "structure" of our work is found primarily in the ideas of Berne, Perls, and the developmental theorists. Frederick and Laura Perls provided the concept of closure and the idea that closing an experience prematurely or artificially creates a fixed gestalt, which continues to operate as an unmet need; they also emphasized the importance of contact and defined the ways in which psychological problems result from a distortion of contact. Berne's notions of the structure of the ego (that is, of ego states), and of the nature of script, form another major influence. Developmental theory provides the basic understandings of how humans develop into and through adulthood, allowing us to diagnose unresolved developmental issues and make specific interventions to address those needs.

We continually draw upon the theory and research-validated knowledge of normal developmental processes in the various stages of the human life cycle. We assess the client's behavior as it relates to physical, emotional, cognitive, and social development. We include understandings of child-parent interaction, language acquisition, the formation of morality, and the child's perceptual development as they emerge in each sequential stage. We apply our knowledge of human development to the therapeutic situation in designing interventions that either address adult developmental transitions or dissolve childhood defense mechanisms and allow for full contact with and integration of the fixated Child ego states into the Adult ego.

The basis of integrative psychotherapy is strongly theoretical and offers a unique organization of theoretical ideas; however, its vitality is found in a living, working process. Thus *Integrative Psychotherapy in Action* is a collection of verbatim transcripts of actual therapeutic sessions together with explanatory comments, which illustrate not only how we think about clients but also what we actually do in our work with them.

Students often say that they learn best about psychotherapy by doing it, either as client or as therapist, or by watching someone else do it and then asking questions about what happened. Therapists, too, comment that they teach their craft best with this sort of framework: presenting a case and using questions from students/ colleagues to "pull out" the ideas that might otherwise be taken for granted. There is an old Chinese saying that fish don't know that they are wet—given that water is the only element they know, "wetness" is a meaningless concept. So it often is with therapists: We swim in our own therapeutic waters so long that we fail to notice the quality of our own theoretical and practical perspectives. The transcripts in this book, then, give us a framework to ask and answer questions about what integrative psychotherapy is and how it works. They allow us to "pull out" of ourselves the explanations that will help others to understand our approach. And (by no means least important) they keep us from becoming pedantic, dry, from hiding behind theory so as to stay removed from the often not-so-clear world of actual clinical work.

In order to understand fully the transcripts to be presented, however, it will be helpful for the reader to have some prior knowledge, not only of the theory underlying the therapy (we've provided you with a brief introduction to that), but also of some of the techniques that we have found helpful and that will be used in the work. The final portion of this introductory chapter will, therefore, present a framework for understanding the actual therapeutic interventions that we utilize with our clients. Again, this presentation will be an overview, an introduction; the work itself, and the accompanying comments, is where the real "action" is.

Principles and Domains

Whatever the specific therapeutic intervention may be, two principles guide all integrative psychotherapy. The first has to do with our commitment to positive life change. Integrative psychotherapy is intended to do more than teach a client some new behaviors, a handful of coping skills designed to get him through today's major crises. It must somehow affect that client's life script. Without script change, therapy is in danger of affording only temporary relief: The surface may look different for awhile, but the underlying maladaptive structure remains intact. We frequently frame our work, therefore, in terms of script: What are the script beliefs and feelings underlying these symptoms? How do the symptoms fit into the overall script display? How can the client's narrative help us to understand the way he or she collects experiences into a store of script-reinforcing memories? Because life script-reinforcing implies a limit to flexibility and spontaneity in problem solving and relating to people, we wish to help each client integrate his or her fixed perspectives into a flexible and open acceptance of learning and growing from each experience.

The second guiding principle is that of respecting the integrity of the client. Through respect, kindness, and maintenance of contact, we establish a personal presence and allow for an interpersonal relationship that provides affirmation of the client's integrity. This respectfulness may be best described as a consistent invitation to interpersonal contact between client and therapist, with simultaneous support for the client to contact his or her internal experience and receive an external recognition of that experience. Withdrawing from contact will often be pointed out and discussed, but the client is never trapped or tricked into more openness than he or she is ready to handle.

It has long been known that clients bring to therapy both openness to work and resistance to change. They experience anxiety or pain and they want relief from those feelings. Yet the script system, uncomfortable though it may be, feels protective—perhaps even life saving. Clients want to be different, but they are apprehensive about what "different" will turn out to be. Both the desire for change and the resistance to change are useful in the therapeutic process. Resistance to being hurt, overwhelmed, confused, or defeated is the energizing force in script formation; that same resistance to dis-ease brings the client into therapy. Rather than fight against resistance, we encourage it and support the client's personal integrity: We want to help the client to learn to use his or her resistance in the service of his or her goals, as he or she would use any other resource.

There are four major domains in which therapeutic work can take place: the cognitive, the behavioral, the affective, and the physical. Cognitive work takes place primarily through the therapeutic alliance between the client's neopsyche—Adult ego state—and the therapist. It includes such things as contracting for change, planning behavioral strategies (here "cognitive" and "behavioral" often blend together, and many of our interventions are indistinguishable from the array of strategies used by behavior technicians), and the search for insight into old patterns. This latter can be very important following a piece of affective work, providing a cognitive frame within which the client can understand and "tag" his or her work for future accessing.

Behavioral work, the second therapeutic domain, concerns itself with engaging the client in new behaviors—behaviors that run counter to the old script system and that will evoke responses from others inconsistent with the collection of script-reinforcing memories. We assign "homework" of this sort, so that the therapeutic experience can be extended beyond formal therapy sessions. We invite the client, during sessions, to behave differently with us, with other group members, and (in fantasy) with those people who helped him or her build and maintain the life script through the years. In residential workshops, participants have a rich opportunity for this sort of behavioral work; "therapy" time blends imperceptibly into "nontherapy" time, and the entire 24-hour day becomes a laboratory for script cure.

Affective work, while it may involve current feelings, is more likely to involve archaic and/or introjected experiences. In order to deal with affective issues, we must help our clients to bypass their usual cognitive controls and defense mechanisms and move directly into the realm of feelings. More often than not, moving into this feeling world involves "going back," experiencing oneself in the age when the original introjects were taken on or life script decisions were made, or when those introjections or decisions were strongly reinforced. The client, in this regressed state, feels and thinks like a younger version of him- or herself. There develops within the regression a reconstruction of many attitudes and decisions that went into the creation of the person's life script. And in this supported regression there is an opportunity to express the feelings, needs, desires that have been repressed, and to relax the defenses to contact that have become habitual. The inhibiting decisions of years before are vividly recalled and can be reevaluated and redecided. We find ourselves using techniques borrowed from psychodrama, variations of Gestalt therapy "chair work," and various forms of quasi-hypnotic induction in order to accomplish these regressions.

The fourth major avenue into script is the physical: working directly with body structures. As Wilhelm Reich (1945) has pointed out, people live out their character structures in their physical bodies. Life script decisions inevitably involve some distortion of contact, and such distortions always require a degree of muscular tension—of holding in (retroflection)—in order to be maintained. Over time, the tension becomes habitual and is eventually reflected in actual body structure. Working directly with this structure, through deep muscle massage and manipulation, pacing and leading breathing patterns, and encouraging or inhibiting movement, we can help the client to access the old memories and patterns and experience the possibility of new options, options that may not have been available at the time of original script formation. In general, then, these are the four avenues or domains that we use to help clients fully access the work they need to do: cognitive, behavioral, affective, and physical. In the chapters to come, you will notice techniques and interventions involving all of these avenues, although we have not included sessions that are primarily physically oriented because these are largely nonverbal and don't lend themselves well to a transcript-based presentation. You will also notice that we seldom limit a piece of work to a single domain; most of the work eventually involves several facets. This is another aspect of the integrative nature of our work. When a person is not defended against his or her own inner experience, he or she is able to integrate psychological functioning in all domains, taking in, processing, and sending out messages through each avenue and translating information easily from one to another internally.

The Ego State Focus

Another way of looking at integrative psychotherapy is in terms of the primary ego state focus of the work. A given segment may deal primarily with Child, with Parent, with a Child-Parent dialogue, or with Adult ego states. We have chosen our examples so as to provide illustrations of the most common types of ego state foci.

Work with the Child ego state usually opens with some sort of invitation to the client either to remember or to relive an old experience from childhood: to let the child he or she once was take over or emerge. Actually, the invitation is directed toward both Child and Adult ego states, given that the Adult ego must relinquish control in order for the client to experience Child ego functioning fully. In the Child ego state, the client has direct access to old experiences and is able to relive those memories and dissolve the fixations. The invitation may be a simple and direct, "Go back to a time when you were seven years old," or it may be a more elaborate invocation of visual, auditory, and kinesthetic cues that assist the client in moving into old memories, memories unavailable to Adult ego state awareness. In some situations, physical movement or massage work will be used to stimulate cathexis of the archaeopsychic experiences. The therapist often paces and leads the client into childhood experiences through a series of verbal interchanges during which the Child ego state cathexis is gradually strengthened. Occasionally a structured relaxation exercise is used as a lead in, helping the client to let go of the script-related tensions that he or she habitually (outside of awareness) uses to block experiencing of those Child responses.

Once the client has chosen to accept the invitation into Child ego state and has been assisted in accessing those old experiences, regression work proper begins. Through talking with the Child (with the Adult ego state as a sideline observer of the process), the therapist begins to uncover the way in which the life script was formed and played out through the years. The client remembers or relives the early trauma, the early unmet needs, and reexperiences the process of reaction or decision through which he or she created a defensive artificial closure to deal with those needs. This re-creation of an old scene is both the same as the original experience (the feelings, wants, and needs are felt again, along with the constraints that led to that early resolution) and different from the original (in that the presence of the observing Adult ego state and the supportive therapist create new resources and options that were not available before). It is these new resources that make possible a different decision this time around. Because the self-in-the-world is literally experienced in a different way in the therapeutic regression, making a change in the archaic survival reaction or decision can break the old life script pattern. The client sees, hears, and feels him- or herself and the world in a new way and can, therefore, respond to self and others in new ways. This is the essence of the integration of the archaeopsychic ego state into the neopsychic ego.

When the script pattern is primarily linked to an internally influencing Parent ego state (introject), treatment often focuses on that Parent state of the ego. The client is invited to cathect Parent: to "be" Mom or Dad and to enter into a conversation with the therapist as Mom or Dad would have done. This work begins, as we shall see, in a rather conversational style. The therapist gets acquainted with the introjected Parent just as if a new and unknown person had actually come into the room. As the Parent ego state begins to experience and respond to the therapist's joining, the quality of the interaction gradually shifts into a more therapeutic mode and the Parent is encouraged to deal with his or her own issues. This is literally therapy with the exteropsychic state of the ego: working through the life script issues of the parenting person that the client has taken on for him- or herself. Many of the methods used with treatment of the Child ego state may be used here if the Parent needs to deal with repressed experiences; or we may intervene on behalf of the client's Child ego state—as a child advocate—providing protection if the introjected Parent is unyielding or continues to be destructive in some way. The historical accuracy of the portrayal is not particularly relevant; what is important is the parent-as-experienced by the client. A person introjects not so much what his or her parents "actually" thought and felt and did, as what he or she experienced them thinking and feeling and believing about him or her, about themselves, and about the world. And again, as the Parent begins to respond to challenges to his or her life script pattern, the introject loses its compulsive, binding, no-other-way-is-possible quality. The thinking process, attitudes, emotional responses, defense mechanisms, and behavioral patterns that were introjected from significant others no longer remain as an unassimilated or exteropsychic state of the ego but are decommissioned as a separate ego state and become integrated into an aware neopsychic ego.

Most enduring and problem-creating life script patterns are maintained by both Parent and Child ego states—that is, they contain elements of both Child ego state decisions and Parent introjects. Once the Parent ego state material has been brought to full awareness and the possibility of change at this level has been experienced, the client will still need to deal with Child ego state decisions and reactions made in response to the introjects. Thus, to facilitate full integration into Adult ego, a given piece of therapeutic work may involve both Parent and Child ego states, either in sequence (as the therapist deals first with the Parent, brings that segment to closure, and then helps the Child to explore and respond to the new information) or in the form of a dialogue between Parent and Child ego states.

Our work also incorporates direct interaction with the client's Adult ego state. Indeed, the ability to access neopsychic sensations, perceptions, and emotion, and to use adult levels of cognition, is virtually a prerequisite for effective work with the exteropsychic and archaeopsychic states of the ego. We often open a piece of work with straight contactful conversation and engage in a contracting process, through which the person clarifies (for both self and therapist) what it is he or she feels upset or confused or discouraged about. During the course of work with Parent or Child ego states, the Adult ego state is present as an observer and may be called upon to offer insights or support when needed—the availability of and protection and groundedness that he or she needs in order to work in previously forbidden territory. Finally, the therapy work ends with the recathecting of Adult ego and a discussion of what has happened—or, alternatively, an explicit agreement *not* to use old cognitions to interrupt the changes that the work with Parent and/or Child ego states has set in motion. Many clients use their defense mechanisms to block out the pain and frustration of childhood decisions and parental introjects, thus stopping the process of neopsychic integration. It may be useful to restrict this protective or defensive process contractually in order to experience the full impact of affective work.

For some clients, psychotherapy requires neither focus on fixated defense mechanisms or regression to childhood traumas that have been unresolved, nor a decommission of introjections, but rather attention to the concerns of the adult life cycle. We evaluate what the client presents in light of developmental transitions, crises, age-related tasks, and existential experiences. We may make use of the therapy session as an arena wherein clients can talk openly about their children, careers, and religious or spiritual quests. A frequent focus is on aging and death—either one's own or of parents and friends. Work with grieving is often here-and-now oriented with an emphasis on expressing the appreciations and/or resentments that need to be said before a "good-bye" is possible. When life cycle transitions and existential crises are respected as significant and the client has an opportunity to explore his or her emotions, thoughts, ideals, and borrowed opinions and to talk out possibilities, there emerges a sense of meaningfulness or purpose in life and its events.

Contact

Finally, pervading all of our work is an attention to contact. Contact is the full awareness of internal desires, needs, perceptions, emotions, or thoughts, with the concomitant ability to shift to full awareness of what and who is in the environment—a rapid oscillation between the internal and the external, between the self and the other person. When there is a lack of contact between the caretakers and a child, through under- or overnurturing or a failure to appreciate fully the child's uniqueness, that child's physical, emotional, and/or social needs, crucial to healthy development, are not fulfilled. Defense mechanisms are created as a protection against the discomfort of the unmet needs, and it is these fixated childhood defenses that limit contact—internal and external—in life today.

The contact between client and therapist is, of course, a major medium through which the client's contact with others, as well as internal contactfulness with him- or herself (i.e., awareness of his or her own processes and perceptions) can be explored. When the client "goes away" into withdrawal, or distorts the interaction with the therapist by means of retroflection, projection, deflection, introjection, or attempts at confluence, the therapist may confront the behavior directly or may respond in such a way as to restore healthy contact. Or the distortion may be allowed to continue, perhaps even be exaggerated, in order to understand its function in the client's overall maladaptive system. Sooner or later, however, disruptions in contact must be healed; psychological health requires the ability to make clear, clean, nondistorted contact both internally and externally.

Work with contact disruption and distortion is easy to overlook as we examine a piece of therapy. The attention to contact is subtle, and, because of the consistency of the therapist's modeling of contactful behavior, this aspect of the work may go unnoticed. Yet, like the substructure of a building, which cannot be seen but undergirds and supports all that is above the ground, contact healing is an essential foundation of both the theory and the practice of integrative psychotherapy.

Contact is possible when the therapist has a sense of being fully present: when he or she is attuned to his or her own inner processes and behaviors, continually aware of the boundary between self and client, and thoroughly observant of the client's psychodynamics. Contact is enhanced through a genuine interest in the clients' welfare and a respect for their unfolding experiences.

Each of these facets of integrative psychotherapy—work with the exteropsychic ego state (Parent), with the neopsychic ego state (Adult), with the archaeopsychic ego state (Child); accessing through thinking, feeling, behavior, and body responses; and the constant attention to contact and defense mechanisms—will be illustrated in the transcripts to follow. The discussion that accompanies the transcripts will further elaborate the concepts and the specific interventions.

The Setting

The workshops from which our transcriptions were made were 10-day residential experiences, sponsored by the Institute for Integrative Psychotherapy. A total of 18 to 20 participants attend these workshops to enhance their professional skills and to deal with personal issues. Indeed, the distinction between personal and professional growth is largely illusory, given that moving out of the restrictions and limitations of one's own life script is a prerequisite for working effectively with others. Two therapists, Richard Erskine, Ph.D., and Rebecca Trautman, R.N., M.S.W., conduct the sessions. All of the work presented in these transcripts is therapy-in-the-group, done with an individual participant who has requested therapeutic time, with the rest of the group observing. We have found that the presence of the group has a number of beneficial effects; the most noticeable is that the group provides support and encouragement for the individual client. In a residential workshop, the group provides an arena in which clients can experiment safely with the new responses and behaviors that emerge from a piece of work. A frightened, confused, or reluctant participant can model the therapeutic risk-taking of other group members, and can deal with his or her own issues vicariously through "piggybacking" on the work of others. Finally, the presence of an involved and caring group, with all of the complex emotional crosscurrents that develop over the course of the workshop, creates a kind of emotional hothouse, an ambiance that intensifies and encourages the expression of thoughts, memories, and feelings that are ordinarily kept out of awareness.

During the course of the workshop a third of the time is devoted to therapy-through-the-group-process, an approach in which each participant is active in the group dynamics, where therapy occurs in the transactions between each and every group member. In the "group process" time, participants contract to be open and honest with what they are perceiving, thinking, and feeling and to take responsibility for being active in the group. Because of space restrictions, we have chosen not to present this approach in this text. We have instead selected examples of intensive work with individual clients as the format that can best illustrate a large number of the principles of integrative psychotherapy.

The segments presented in the following chapters are largely unedited. The names of the participants have been changed. We have summarized sections that did not contribute new ideas or information to that which has already been presented, especially when the complete piece would have become long or tedious. Excluded segments are usually introductory cognitive work, or wrap-up work in which the emphasis shifts to theoretical discussion. The main body of each piece, however, is intact—complete with pauses, stutters, and colloquial grammar. In giving you these verbatim transcripts, we hope to share the pace and rhythm of the therapy, the pattern of slowing down and intensifying that typifies our work. We also hope to show the way in which the therapist's style changes to match the ego state that the client has cathected. And, finally, while the written transcript cannot hope to capture the emotional intensity of the actual work, we hope that clients' and therapists' actual words may help to convey some of the affective involvement that gives integrative psychotherapy impact.

NOTE

1. These ideas were originally published by Richard Erskine and Marilyn Zalcman in "The Racket System: A Model for Racket Analysis" (1979). Eric Berne applied the term "script analysis" to the deciphering of a lifelong plan designed in early childhood and predicting all the major events and relationships in life, including death. Marilyn Zalcman uses the term "racket analysis" to refer to the intrapsychic processes and behavioral manifestations of the script that are currently occurring. The term "life script" is used in this book to refer to both meanings: the current intrapsychic and manifested aspects of a longitudinal life plan.

REFERENCES

Ansbacher, H. L., & Ansbacher, R. R. (1956). *The individual psychology of Alfred Adler*. New York: Basic Books.

Bandura, A. (1969). *Principles of behavior modification*. New York: Holt, Rinehart & Winston.

Berne, E. (1957). Ego states in psychotherapy. *American Journal of Psychotherapy, 11*, 293-309.

Berne, E. (1958). Transactional analysis: A new and effective method of group therapy. *American Journal of Psychotherapy, 12*, 735-743.

Berne, E. (1961). *Transactional analysis in psychotherapy*. New York: Grove.

Berne, E. (1972). *What do you say after you say hello? The psychology of human destiny*. New York: Grove.

Dollard, J., & Miller, N. (1950). *Personality and psychotherapy*. New York: McGraw-Hill.

Erikson, E. (1950). *Childhood and society*. New York: Norton.

Erskine, R., & Zalcman, M. (1979). The racket system: A model for racket analysis. *Transactional Analysis Journal, 9*(1), 51-59.

Fairbairn, W.R.D. (1954). A revised psychopathology of the psychoses and psychoneuroses. In *Psychoanalytic studies of the personality (An Object- Relations Theory of the personality)*. New York: Basic Books.

Federn, P. (1953). *Ego psychology and the psychoses*. London: Imago.

Fraiberg, S. (1983, Fall). Pathological defenses in infancy. *Dialogue: A Journal of Psychoanalytic Perspectives*, pp. 65-75.

Freud, A. (1937). *The ego and the mechanisms of defense*. London: Hogarth Press and the Institute of Psychoanalytic Studies.

Freud, S. (1961). Beyond the pleasure principle. In J. Strachey (Ed. and Trans.), *The standard editions of the complete psychological works of Sigmund Freud* (Vol. 17). London: Hogarth Press. (Original work published in 1920)

Freud, S. (1961). The ego and the id. In J. Strachey (Ed. and Trans.), *The standard edition of the complete psychological works of Sigmund Freud* (Vol. 19, pp. 3-66). London: Hogarth Press. (Original work published in 1923)

Geiwitz, J., & Moursund, J. (1979). *Approaches to personality*. Monterey, CA: Brooks/Cole.

Mahler, M. (1968). *On human symbiosis and the vicissitudes of individuation*. New York: International Universities Press.

Mahler, M. (1975). *The psychological birth of the human infant*. New York: Basic Books.

Maslow, A. H. (1950). *Motivation and personality*. New York: Ronald.

Maslow, A. H. (1962). *Toward a psychology of being*. Princeton, NJ: D. Van Nostrand.

Mowrer, O. H. (1950). *Learning theory and personality dynamics*. New York: Ronald.

Pavlov, I. (1927). *Conditioned reflexes*. London: Oxford University Press.

Perls, F. S. (1947). *Ego, hunger and aggression*. London: George Allen & Unwin.

Perls, F. S. (1973). *The Gestalt approach and eye witness to therapy.* Palo Alto, CA: Science & Behavior Books.

Perls, F. S., Hefferline, R. F., & Goodman, P. (1951). *Gestalt therapy: Excitement and growth in the human personality.* New York: Julian Press.

Perls, L. (1978a). Conceptions and misconceptions of Gestalt therapy. *Voices: The Art and Science of Psychotherapy, 14,* 31-37.

Perls, L. (1978b, Winter). An oral history of Gestalt therapy, Part I: A conversation with Laura Perls [Edward Rosenfeld]. *Gestalt Journal,* pp. 8-31.

Phillips, J. (1969). *The origins of intellect: Piaget's theory.* San Francisco: Freeman.

Reich, W. (1945). *Character analysis.* New York: Farrar, Strauss and Giroux.

Rogers, C. R. (1942). *Counseling and psychotherapy.* Boston: Houghton Mifflin.

Rogers, C. R. (1951). *Client-centered therapy.* Boston: Houghton Mifflin.

Rogers, C. R., & Skinner, B. F. (1956). Some issues concerning the control of human behavior: A symposium. *Science, 124,* 1057-1066.

Skinner, B. F. (1938). *The behavior of organisms.* New York: Appleton-Century-Crofts.

Skinner, B. F. (1953). *Science and human behavior.* New York: Macmillan.

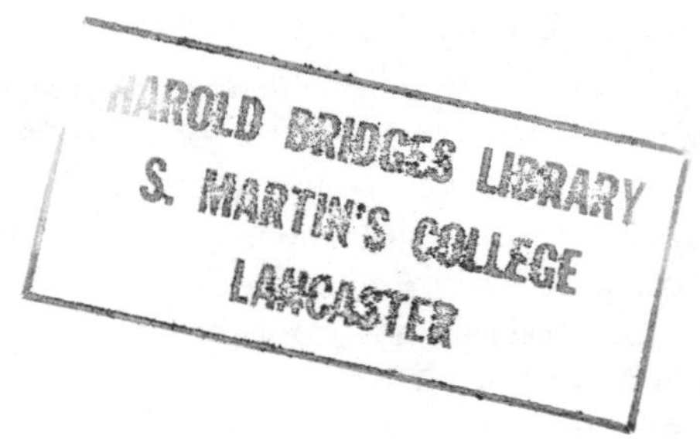

2

CONRAD
Regression and Redecision

The script is our personal blueprint for how we will live our lives: how we experience ourselves, others, the world around us; what we expect will happen if we behave in one way or another; how we feel and what we tell ourselves about those feelings. Begun in earliest infancy, the script comes together into a more or less coherent whole during childhood and is elaborated on and added to throughout our lives. Psychotherapy, if it is to effect lasting change, must affect script. It is script change that allows the client to experience him- or herself as truly different. As the script changes, new options for thinking, feeling, and behaving become salient. In Chapter 1, we described four domains of script-changing therapy: cognitive, behavioral, affective, and physical. Script may be changed through discovering new ways to think (and fantasize) about self and others; through trying out new behaviors in an "experimental" way; through making changes in biochemistry, musculature, or movement patterns; or through reworking the feelings present when the script was formed and as it becomes reactivated in later life. All four of these domains may become involved as the client is led to return, emotionally, to the point in time at which the early decisions and beliefs and perceptions were acquired, and to literally reprogram replacements for that which is no longer working.

Regression work, in which the client is allowed to go back in fantasy to a time of script formation, forms a major part of integrative psychotherapy. Regression encourages and empowers the client to redecide, to use the superior resources of the "now" to assist his or her confused or fearful or angry child "then." As is illustrated in the segment presented in this chapter, successful redecision involves not only cognition (through which the client comes to understand the old decision and how it is now getting in his or her way) and affect (which allows the client to access the deep, out-of-conscious-awareness parts of him- or herself that must participate in the change if it is to have any permanence), but also intent: a clear and conscious choice to go a different route than before. All three of these processes need not be operating in any single piece of work, but sooner or later each must contribute its part in order for a full redecision to take place. Conrad's work provides a good example of the integration of all three processes in a single episode of redecision work.

One reason why Conrad is able to work so efficiently with all three of the redecision components may be the nature of the group climate in which the work was done. The group had been together for some time—it was the eighth day of a ten-day workshop—and there was a high level of group cohesion and trust. A well-run group acts as a kind of sounding board for feelings, heightening and enhancing whatever is going on emotionally for each participant. At the same time, it provides a protective and supportive environment, in which it is safe to regress, to "be little," to act and feel in ways which would not be tolerated in the world outside. Conrad reflects this climate as he opens his work:

Conrad: I'm afraid if I don't work now, I'll fade away.... Last night, yesterday afternoon, not doing it good enough, just triggered a whole chain of things.

Richard: You mean when I made that comment . . .

Conrad: It's going on now. Feelings will rise up, they'll be there as they were just a few moments ago; and then it's like the plug is pulled in a sink. And, I do something with them, I don't know what. And I can do this very well; this was my scare, that if I didn't work this morning . . . and now the feelings are, I don't know how to let them . . .

Conrad is ordinarily a highly controlled and intellectualizing person, a successful academic who thinks, rather than feels, his way through life. In this introduction, he is describing a rather typical reaction to the emotional "hothouse" of an extended workshop: Feelings ordinarily denied and suppressed are breaking through the cognitive barrier, demanding his attention. He experiences a tug-of-war between his affect (feelings "rise up") and his cognitive defenses ("like the plug is pulled in a sink"). Physically, he reflects his internal state in the tension of his body, and the flush in his cheeks; and the very act of speaking up, asking for group time, is an important behavioral shift for him. The final ingredient, intent, is clearly present as he makes the conscious choice to deal with the feelings, to invite them into awareness rather than force them back.

A danger for Conrad, however, is that he may misuse the work he is about to do, by evaluating it so as to reinforce his old scripting. In an earlier piece of work, Conrad told of a grade-school incident in which he was cruelly humiliated by a teacher; his experience translated into a script belief that he was not as "good" (an adult might use words like competent or intelligent or socially acceptable, but for a little boy good refers to the totality of his being, his very essence) as the other children. Believing that he is basically not "good enough," that what he does can never quite measure up, he is likely to view his therapy through the same filter. Thus whatever he may accomplish, rather than moving him toward genuine script change, could be experienced as falling short of some vague and unreachable standard of performance and "prove" that the script belief is, in fact, accurate. To forestall this outcome, the therapists choose to set the stage for a challenge of the overall pattern, a challenge that can be strengthened later on if Conrad does revert to script in this way.

Richard: Let's just deal first of all with the "not good enough."

Conrad: It's, I'm not good enough to belong, to be a part of. I can't recall ever . . . (*pause*) I go in and out. I can't remember, I can't recall ever being invited to join a social organization. And as soon as I said that I remembered that last night George invited me, asked me to go with him to the waterfall today, during the break. And my first, immediate thought was that Patricia had said something to him. And I checked with Patricia, and she hadn't.

Here is an excellent example of the way in which reinforcing experiences are selected and augmented by fantasy. Conrad and Patricia are the only married couple in the workshop, apart from Richard and Rebecca. Patricia is somewhat overprotective of Conrad. When he is invited to join in socially, an event quite at variance with his script experience and expectations, he immediately fantasizes that Patricia has intervened on his behalf. "Yes, George did ask me to go, but not because I'm good enough—Patricia asked him to do it, because she too knows I'm not good enough to make it on my own; and George complied out of pity for this not-good-enough person." Some combination of the work that Conrad had done the day before, and the support and nourishment of the group climate, however, provided the impetus for Conrad to question his imagining, rather than simply accept it as reality. The discovery that Patricia had had nothing to do with the invitation further upset the script pattern and widened the breach in his old defenses.

Rebecca: You mean you thought Patricia set him up to ask you.

Conrad: Yeah. And my first . . . sense of belonging, of not being wanted, of not being welcome . . . (*his voice trails off; he is near tears*)

Richard: Yeah, and I think there's more involved than just leftovers from that day in school situation. What I was thinking of last night, when I was focusing on you, after I had gone to bed—

Notice the insertion, almost as an afterthought, of another script challenge: You are good enough for me to want to spend even extra, "off duty" time thinking about you.

Richard: (*continuing*) . . . was what made that school situation so devastating is that it was a reinforcement of what had occurred. To a child, a child who had good support at home, that child would not have been so wiped out by the teacher. What was going on, preschool, at home, Conrad?

The school incident, alone, did not seem to be traumatic enough to justify its importance in Conrad's mind. Remember that the "script decision" is often a long process, built up out of a whole series of experiences. What happened at school was probably a potent reinforcer in that decision-making process, and it may also serve to screen the earlier, ongoing, and even more influential scripting experiences.

Conrad: I don't know. I can remember when I was four my brother was born; I don't know what changes that made. Let me tell you some fragments of things. Used to love to climb trees. And I remember a neighbor had some trees, about 20, 30 feet high. I used to love to climb to the top of these, they were saplings, and then just let them bend over and go down to the ground. I'd climb on roofs. Have a memory of a peach tree in a friend's yard. I'm at the top of the tree, and my friend, Jimmy, was down below. I'm saying, "Shall I make it widdle, Jimmy?" My mother's voice, "You come down here, Conrad Stamfield, I'll make you widdle!"

Richard: "Widdle" meaning?

Conrad: Wiggle. Shall I sway it back and forth. Don't know why I said it that way; course I knew the difference. I knew the difference between widdle and wiggle.

Richard: What was the difference?

Conrad: In what?

Richard: What did that mean to you? That experience?

Conrad: I don't know what it meant.

Richard: What did you feel?

Conrad: I have no recollection. Although when you ask that, there's anger. The word that comes is "anger."

As was pointed out in Chapter 1, respect and support for the client's resistance is a basic principle in integrative psychotherapy. One way in which this is accomplished is through awareness of the client's signal that he or she doesn't want or isn't ready to pursue a particular avenue. The timing may be wrong, or the "avenue" may be a dead end. The therapist must be willing both to explore hunches, and to give them up (at least temporarily) if they seem to go nowhere. In this interchange, Richard is curious about the possible significance of Conrad's word confusion. When he attempts to pursue this, though, Richard gets two denials in a row: First, Conrad "forgets" the distinction he has just made between "widdle" and "wiggle," and then he "doesn't know" what the experience means. Rather than continue in the face of this resistance, Richard respects it and shifts, allowing Conrad to approach his work on his own terms.

At any point in a piece of work, of course, there are many possible interventions. Richard could have stayed with Conrad's anger here, helping him to express and explore it more fully. During the course of his therapy, however, Conrad has gotten angry several times already, and has made little progress through that route. This time, Richard goes another way . . .

Richard: This was your mother calling up to you? Close your eyes right now. Be back up in the tree. Feel what it's like to sway, to wiggle a peach tree.

Conrad: It's great!

Going back to the topic that Conrad himself had introduced, Richard gains access to the feeling state associated with the content of the story. Again, a side effect of this choice is to send a subtle message that Conrad's way of doing his work is "good enough"; Richard will not insist on following his own agenda, but will attend to Conrad's signals.

Richard: Just feel that freedom. Climb higher and higher. Feel the power in the shape of those branches in that tree (*pause; Conrad's expression clearly indicates that he is reliving the experience*). And tell your friend down below what you're feeling.

Conrad: Oh, it's great up here! It's great! Shit, I'm even higher than the birds (*he is crying now*).

Richard: Do that, right now, look down at the birds. Tell your friend what it's like to be a master tree-climber.

A number of things are occurring here. First, Richard has invited Conrad into an age regression. He is to take himself back in time, back to the experience of a small boy, swaying in the top of a peach tree. Richard calls on several sensory modalities in order to heighten the intensity of the regression experience: the voice of Conrad's mother, the motion of the swaying tree, the kinesthetic sensations of climbing, the sight of the birds below him. By directing Conrad to talk to his friend, he adds the actual sound of Conrad's own voice; thus internal fantasy is augmented by here-and-now sensory experience. Moreover, as Conrad reports to his friend, he is forced to symbolize the feeling in words, thus integrating his emotional, motoric, and cognitive experience.

Finally, the description of himself as a "master tree-climber" is another assault on the "not good enough" script belief.

Conrad: (*whispers very softly*) It's great to look down at the birds.

Richard: Say that to him again: It's great to look down at the birds.

Conrad: There were no words. For me there were no words.

Richard: Can you do it in sign language?

Conrad: No. It's a feeling of . . .

Richard: Just reach out and grab the branches . . .

Conrad again signals that he's not ready to follow Richard's lead. He wants to do it his way, and in doing so he issues a subtle invitation to Richard to fight with him, and (again) prove that his way isn't right, isn't good enough. Richard declines the invitation, respecting the resistance and offering instead another way to move ahead. Conrad counters by beginning to pull out of the regression, to stand back and describe rather than actually to experience. The direction to "reach out and grab the branches" provides a sensory anchor, so that Conrad can move back into the age-regressed state.

Conrad: Just such a swelling up . . . that same feeling I talked about with the Chariots of Fire music; just a sense of being transported. So far . . . so full . . . complete, free and complete and fulfilled.

Richard: Tell that to that friend down below.

Conrad: Oh, Jimmy, it's so great! I'm free.

Richard: Shout it at him.

Conrad: (*crying*) I'M FREE!

Richard: Try shouting it at him again.

Richard: (*after a long pause*) Just say it again, then.

Conrad: (*pause*) What I was saying inside is, "I'm not."

Script is not easily changed; script messages are not easily defeated. Conrad momentarily allowed himself to experience the freedom and the autonomy of having climbed away from the constraints that held him down, but, as soon as he paused, his old cognitive habits reappeared to counter the emotional experience. The therapists want to strengthen the new, script-opposing feelings before dealing with the belief system, to avert the possibility that Conrad may still be able to use an "unsuccessful" piece of work to prove that he's "not good enough."

Richard: That's going to come next. For now, just stay with this. "I'm free . . ."

Conrad: I have one hell of a time separating those. Jimmy, I'm free.

The affective charge has dissipated, and Conrad's "I'm free" is flat and unconvincing. He is parroting Richard, adapting to Richard's directions (after all, to Conrad, the therapists know better) rather than experiencing himself in a genuine way. He's back in script. Again, Richard does not confront, but follows Conrad's lead: If the injunction to stay not-free and not good enough is foreground, then that's what Conrad needs to deal with. Hypothesizing that the script was originally developed out of Conrad's relationship with Mother, Richard focuses there. He keeps Conrad up in the tree, however, in the place where he had previously experienced the sensations of being free and autonomous.

Richard: Look at your mother, coming in through the yard.

Conrad: I didn't even see her.

Richard: She's standing down there.

Conrad: Just her voice, out of nowhere.

Richard: Standing down there, at the bottom of that tree . . . Listen to her voice. What do you hear her saying?

Mother's voice is remembered/fantasized as coming "out of nowhere," and this is re-created in Conrad's life as an adult. As he moves tentatively toward autonomy, the script message comes "out of nowhere" and urges him back into a one-down position. In the therapy, he is encouraged to keep the sound input as it was, but to couple it with a new and different sensory experience, the visual stimulus of Mother standing on the ground, below him, out of reach.

Conrad: "Conrad Stamfield, you come down out of that tree or I'll widdle you!"

Richard: Tell her what you'd like to say from your place.

Conrad: (*whispering*) Get lost, woman!

Richard: Louder.

Conrad: Get lost, woman!

Richard: Climb a little higher.

Richard is still using the spatial relationship of the fantasy to combat the symbolic one-downness that Conrad feels with his mother.

Conrad: Get lost, woman!

Richard: Before you tell her to get lost more, climb up higher. Get on a higher branch.

Conrad: Come and get me! (*the group cheers*)

Richard: C'mon, say something else to her. (*pause*) Say that— "Come and get me."

Hoping to build on the energy that is generating in the group, Richard urges Conrad to solidify and expand his feeling of power. He may have gone too fast, because Conrad doesn't respond; Richard comes back to Conrad's own words, and Conrad continues.

Conrad: (*laughing*) Come and get me!

The laughter is new, both as a behavior and a physiological response. Both in his therapy work and in his social interactions in the workshop setting, Conrad seldom relaxes in laughter. It is thus a signal that the script system may be changing.

Richard: Cause tell her what you know.

Conrad: You can't climb yourself.

Richard: And therefore . . .

Conrad: And you don't want me to climb.

Richard: Say that again.

We have now come to what may be a central part of the original scripting: Don't do what I can't do, don't go past me, let me stay superior. Having gotten here, Richard will stay with it, letting Conrad experience and expand upon its implications for him.

Conrad: You don't want me to climb. You don't want me to climb roofs, you don't want me to climb trees . . .

Richard: And the true reason is . . .

Conrad: You want me down there so that I'll be with you all your life.

Richard: You can't climb . . .

Conrad: You cannot climb.

Richard: Louder.

Conrad: You can't climb!

There are many ways to stay with a particular point in regression work. Here Richard uses two such techniques, the unfinished repetition ("You can't climb . . .") and a request to repeat the same words more loudly. Providing an open-ended sentence encourages elaboration of the message and thus invites cognitive input; "say it louder" invites greater affective involvement. Conrad may be somewhat stuck at this juncture, for he provides no further details and also doesn't appear to heighten his emotional response. Richard chooses to provide an interpretation:

Richard: Tell her what she's doing with her fear . . . With her fear about climbing.

Conrad: (*pause*) She can't climb.

Richard: She can't climb.

Conrad: She doesn't know how to climb.

Conrad doesn't pick up on the idea of Mother's being afraid, so Richard drops it in favor of another "explanation," this one closer to what Conrad has come up with himself.

Richard: Yeah. And tell her what she's doing with her climbing ignorance.

Conrad: You hold me down . . . Give me lip service . . .

Richard: You can't climb, yet you hold me down . . .

Conrad: You can't climb. You hold me down, and if anyone were to hear you, they'd say "Oh, you're helping him."

Richard: And the truth is . . .

Conrad: And the truth is, you're not.

Finally, an open door. Conrad is recognizing the double bind in which Mother appears to help, while she really holds him back. No longer simply adapting to the therapists, Conrad has constructed his own interpretation and elaboration: Cognition and affect are beginning to come together. Richard moves to prevent this beginning integration from sliding over into pure cognition, as has happened in Conrad's work in the past.

Richard: Now climb to a higher branch, Conrad. (*pause*) Now tell her what—

Conrad: I'm going to change the tree. To a taller tree.

Conrad actively cooperates in manipulating the fantasy to

heighten its emotional impact, a sign that the work is indeed going well. Apparently the kinesthetic cues are easily assimilated and used.

Richard: Just sort of swing, from the branch to something else. You know, like Tarzan.

Conrad: Got it. This is a pine tree, and they grow real tall, and they got nice branches to climb on.

Richard: (*chuckling*) I bet you've got a comment from the pine tree.

Conrad: (*laughing*) If you want me so fucking much, come and get me.

Richard: Say that word again. You want me so FUCKING much . . .

Conrad: You want me so fucking much, come and get me.

Richard: Tell her what you mean by that, five-year-old.

Is Conrad dealing with a sexual/Oedipal issue here, or is the word fucking *merely a culturally used expletive? Having tucked away the Oedipal question early in Conrad's therapy, Richard now judges that the momentum will carry Conrad into exploring a perhaps dangerous topic.*

Conrad: (*pause*) Five-year-old didn't know. (*pause*) You want me as your father, you want me as your husband . . . you're scared . . . you just want me there. By your side.

Rebecca: Tell her what that's like for you. When she wants you so much, as a husband and father.

Conrad: It's a safe prison. It feels safe in this prison.

Richard: And when I'm up in this pine tree . . .

Conrad: I'm not in a prison.

The sexual aspects of the relationship are not as salient for Conrad right now as the sense of being stifled, held back; when Rebecca probes for sexual implications, Conrad threatens to move back into the safe prison of his script. Richard quickly brings him back to the new experience, the freedom of being up in the pine tree, and begins to set up another framework within which redecision can occur.

Richard: Try this: I'm not your father. I'm not your father when I'm up here.

Conrad: I'm not your father. I'm not your father up here.

Richard: Louder.

Conrad: I'm not your father up here.

Richard: Scream it at her.

Conrad: I'M NOT YOUR FATHER UP HERE!

The emotional intensity is back, and Conrad appears ready to take another step. He demonstrates this by adding his own elaboration to Richard's suggestions.

Richard: Tell her who else . . .

Conrad: I'm not your father; I'm not your husband, I'm not your caretaker! I'm not your little baby!

Richard: Tell her who you are in the pine tree.

Conrad: (*pause*) She never knew . . . (*loudly*) I'm Conrad Stamfield!

Richard: And I'm not a baby.

Conrad: And I'm not a baby.

Richard: And tell her what you're doing, up in that pine tree.

Conrad: What I'm doing is weaving my way around the branches upward. Playing up here.

Rebecca: That's your turf. And where's Jimmy?

Having taken a major step in dealing with the one-down, not-good-enough issue with Mother, the therapists now come back to peer relationships. We'll see whether there's any movement here; if the work with Mother has "taken," Conrad should be able to deal with Jimmy in a different way.

Conrad: (*pause*) I don't know.

Richard: Pretty lonely up there, in that freedom?

Conrad: Yeah. (*pause*) Hey, c'mon up . . . (*pause*) I don't really want him to come up.

Richard: Tell him that.

Conrad: I don't really want you to come up; I want you to find another tree, and I want you to invite me over there.

Something is certainly different; Conrad is much clearer about what he wants from his friend. Not only does he know what he wants, he can say it directly. Again, Richard's next intervention is designed to heighten the emotional involvement, while at the same time clarifying Conrad's understanding.

Richard: Feel that longing, Conrad. For that invitation.

Conrad: (*long pause*) So important . . . so important, I so want people to, to invite me.

Richard: Talk to Jimmy again.

Conrad: Jimmy, I want you to, I want you to ask me to . . . you find a tree and play over there with you. And then we'll come back over here, and play in my tree.

Richard: If you invite me, Jimmy . . .

Conrad: I know I belong. (*pause*) If you invite me, I know I belong.

Conrad pauses, and then repeats his statement: He is experiencing the force of his old decision about not belonging. While this sort of pause-repeat pattern doesn't necessarily signal a redecision, it is certainly indicative that script is being understood and experienced in a new way. Conrad is realizing how he contributes to his sense of not belonging when he rules out the possibility of inviting himself. And what does this have to do with Mother, and Conrad's relationship with her? It's time to tie together the two major threads of this piece of work.

Richard: I want you to try a little experiment, and see what happens. Say that to your mother. "If you invite me as your son, instead of your father or your husband, or baby . . ."

Conrad: As you were saying it, I felt a . . . surge of energy, or strength.

The "surge of energy" is an indication of physiological involvement. While Conrad is borrowing from the therapists' strength here in demanding what he needs from Mother, he may internalize this response in his memory collection so that later he will be able to make those demands on his own.

Richard: Then I'll talk to your mom . . . Mom, you need to invite him as your son. You need to invite him down out of that tree, like—

Conrad: I don't want you to take care of me, I want you to share your strength with me.

While Conrad's comment here is addressed to his image of Mother, he may also be reacting to the therapist's caretaking. Having been energized by Richard's intervention on his behalf, he now no longer needs or wants it; he wants a different kind of working relationship.

Richard: Um-hm. Keep going.

Conrad: So that I can learn, and I can grow. You always knew what I should do, when I was in trouble. I'm flunking out of college, and you know exactly where I can go to get a job. It's all that you knew. If I was hurting, you were there for me. You were right there. And I needed you, I need you to be with me when I'm flying. And to say "Go, Conrad. Have a good life."

In regression work, feelings from past and present often flow together at the moment of redecision. Integration of then and now—of archaeopsychic and exteropsychic ego into the neopsychic ego—is a hallmark of integrative psychotherapy. At the end of Conrad's work, the confrontation of Mother's overprotectiveness flows from the tree-climbing child to the young adult college student. Here and in the two statements to follow, Conrad is processing feelings from many different times in his life, putting them together into a new way of responding to Mother—and, by extension, to the other important people in his life.

Richard: Talk to her, Conrad.

Conrad: You were left alone. I know you were scared, and hurt, and angry. (*crying*)

Richard: But I need . . .

Conrad: (*pause*) I need . . . I need you to let me know you're proud of me, and that you're with me. I need to know that you don't need me to hurt. (*pause*) I hear her voice, and she's saying, "I wanted so much . . . so much that the other, my brothers and sisters had, and I never got." And then she's saying, "Yeah, I do love you. And I want you to fly." And she does love me.

Richard: Respond to her. Tell her about that love.

Conrad: I do love you. And I want to share with you. I want you to be as excited as you can be about . . . things that I'm proud of. (*pause*) When I get a scholarship, and nobody said I could get it. And after I got it the whole high school changed their procedures because they were surprised that I got it, but I got it. I earned it. (*pause*) And I graduated from college. (*pause*) Got my master's, got my Ph.D. I want you to be proud of that. (*pause*) You gave me roots, all right; you didn't give me wings. That's it.

Conrad has summed up here, metaphorically, the whole relationship with Mother. He has been stuck because, were he to reject her smothering, he would also be rejecting the support and rootedness that he needed. Disconnecting those two aspects of Mother—support on the one hand, overprotection on the other—is Conrad's first step toward redecision.

The tie-in between Mother's stifling and Conrad's sense of "not good enough" has not yet been made completely clear. Following this work, Conrad did subsequent therapy in which he came to realize that by trying to take the place of the adult males in his mother's family, he set up a situation in which he could never measure up, could never be "good enough" to make up for their loss. He made a new decision: to be the son in the family, not the husband or the father; in that role he was competent and "good enough."

Conrad's work, of course, is not complete. He has yet to deal with the way in which he will relate to his peers, now that he has decided to be who he really is (his mother's son) rather than assuming a falsely superior role (the husband, the father) and then feeling incompetent and unwelcome.

This chapter of Conrad's work was, however, quite significant. Not only did he gain an important insight into the nature of his scripting, but he also allowed himself to experience the emotional and physiological significance of that script. Another important ingredient, his intent to change, allowed him to stay with the work even at moments when it was frightening or painful. It is this intent that will determine how the work affects his life in the days to come, whether he will integrate the new experiences into his ongoing behavior or sink back into his older and more familiar habits. Intent, cognition, emotion, physiology, and behavior: the vital elements of therapeutic change. We shall meet them again and again in the chapters to come.

3

CHRIS
Discovering a Self-Created Parent

Conrad's work, presented in Chapter 2, illustrated the weaving together of cognitive, affective, physiological, and behavioral components in the context of a will to change. As we have seen, alterations of script typically involve several—if not all—of these elements. The work can focus primarily on changing cognitions (beliefs about self, others, the nature of life), or on changing feelings (the sense of "having to" react emotionally in a certain way), or on changing actual overt behavior. Script changes can be made with regard to parental figures, peers, or stressful events in the client's life. Or the client may merely uncover and understand the early decision, and choose to process its implications for a while without making a new decision during the therapy session, saving the actual redecision for a later time.

The following piece of work is an example of the latter process: The client does not make a clear redecision in the work itself. Chris works early in the course of the workshop, and works exclusively with Richard. Chris knows that he will have ample opportunity for follow-up. Richard allows him to explore the thoughts, feelings, and behaviors that surrounded his early experiences, and ends the work in such a way as to encourage him to continue this process as the workshop progresses. The intent to change is clearly present, and it is this intent that will carry the impact of the therapeutic work into the structure of the client's everyday life. The work also introduces a number of themes, concepts, and techniques typical of integrative psychotherapy, and will further illustrate the way in which we conceptualize the structure of personality and the avenues through which change can be accomplished.

Chris is a man in his midthirties, well-versed in therapeutic theory and practice. He has worked with Richard before and he understands many of his own issues. While this sort of sophistication can be an advantage in that it cuts through a great deal of initial floundering, it also can contribute to a kind of layering of defenses, using cognitive understandings to protect oneself from actually feeling the emotional pain of early experiences. A major challenge for the therapist is to move past the well-established and thought-through cognitive structures into the raw experience out of which were generated Chris's early script decisions.

Chris begins his work by describing his habit of overcriticizing and being overdemanding of subordinates:

> It's real easy for me to just compartmentalize people, and then not have to deal with them. Once I put them in a box, and have a spot for them on the shelf, then I don't have to reach out and contact them. I know who they are, I know what they are, and that's that. They have no use for me. And I miss out on a lot of people.

He moves on to relate this behavior to his feelings toward his former wife, and then describes the frustration of trying to think his way out of these patterns. "I'm intelligent. I can learn theory and apply it to myself, it doesn't do a hell of a lot of good in freeing myself of this stuff."

The work proceeds at a leisurely pace; Chris is encouraged to talk through what he has figured out about his system. He talks of his early years, being brought up by his grandparents, and how important it was for him to find a way really to belong in that family. Chris was the first child of an inadequate mother and father who were "around" but unable or unwilling to accept parental responsibilities; Chris's younger siblings were reared in an orphanage. He describes his mother as "a nonentity in my life" about whom he has no particular feeling at all. His ideal was his Uncle Pete, who was his grandparents' "number-one son"; he, Chris, came to be very proud of being the Number Two Son of Grandma and Grandpa. Even so, many years later, the vague sense of not belonging, of not having a place of his own, still lingers.

After a long discussion of all this history, Richard introduces the idea of a fantasy parent, a parent figure invented by the child as a protective device. Richard's explanation is much the same as the description of the self-created or fantasy parent presented in Chapter 1:

Richard: Chris, you did have an early rejection; whether you experienced it biologically, you must certainly have begun to experience it psychologically and socially. To protect yourself from that trauma ever happening again, you created a Spook, who could reject you. Then you got to keep your grandparents as good folks, who would never be rejecting. As we create that Spook, it gets as tenacious as something that has been introjected. That's why I call it a self-generated parent. It functions like a Parent ego state; almost as an external voice. But it is so driving, so demanding—I think part of dealing with compulsion is to find that driving Spook, and know its early origin, as a child's frightened fantasy of what could have occurred.

Chris: Um-hm. When I am experiencing that drivenness, I also am aware that that's not me. When I'm that critical of myself, or the people around me, um, it's like when Paul was out at my house and we were driving down the highway, and he said something like, that guy's going to have a car accident, the way he's driving. And then right away he went like this (*waving his hand*), he said, "Wave that one off, God." And what he said was, "I don't want to wish any ill on that person, indirectly or directly." So he waved it off. It's like I borrow that, and when I come out that critical, you know, I wave it off, I don't really mean that. I don't really wish ill on that person; I waved that off.

Richard: We experience our boogeymen as external. Because to project, you have to deny.

Chris: Well, I can put that on people around me. And I don't understand, then why I do it so much myself, to myself.

Richard: In order not to be rejected. I think it's all going on in Child ego state. I'll bet it occurs when you're tired, when you're stressed, when you're under pressure, when you're lonely; does not occur when you're well rested, when things are functioning well.

Chris: That's right.

Richard: That's one of the diagnostic clues that it's in Child. Where is it in Child? I think it's the parent that the Child imagines. Either very good, or very bad. In your case, a bad parent, to keep you good. I think all four-year-olds do it. Most of us give it up midway through grade school. The other kids confront the reality of it, and we drop it. In your case, there was some lying, some unreality, about who you belonged to. So holding onto that Spook, that rejector, is going to be more tenacious.

Richard has dropped into an easy, conversational mode with Chris. The interaction sounds almost like two colleagues discussing an interesting clinical example. There is no doubt that Richard respects Chris's intelligence and knowledge, and that he is taking pains to inform Chris's Adult ego state about what he, Richard, believes to motivate the overcriticism that Chris complains of. By using this approach, Richard engages—almost automatically—two of the necessary components of script change. Thinking and theorizing are cognitive functions, and these are surely involved here. And Chris's intent to work, to change, is supported both by Richard's respectful attitude and by his implicit assumption that understanding can be a first step in the change process.

Throughout this early part of the work, Richard has been assessing the degree to which Chris is accepting these theoretical ideas. All the nonverbal signs—facial expression, posture, tone of voice—suggest that he is interested and intrigued, that the concepts make sense to him. Cognition and intent are present, and it is now time to move into affect. Richard invites him to do so, by means of totally recalling an earlier experience. The induction not only specifies the time to be reexperienced, but also anchors the setting, the emotional tone, the hopes and expectations of a small boy. The language is that of a child, with a child's pride in his own status and achievements:

Richard: Let me try something. Just close your eyes. Go back to that railroad flat. I want to talk to the little boy, want to talk to the little boy who knows that next year, in this coming September, he's going to start kindergarten. The little boy who's excited, maybe, about going to school. Maybe even first grade. But somebody who's still home all day long. Somebody who doesn't go to school yet. Somebody who's too big to take naps. So that the days are very long . . . Somebody who's playing alone . . . What are you feeling, little boy?

Chris: I'm feeling that I want to go to school. That I can go with my friends. Um, I'm feeling, like wow! I'm going to go to that big building, where all the big kids go.

Richard: Have you outgrown this apartment? Too big for this apartment now? I bet you know every little nook and cranny.

Chris: I think when I go to school then I get my own room.

Richard: That's exciting.

Chris: Yeah.

Richard: Where are you sleeping now?

Chris: Well, I have to share the big bedroom with my grandmother. Right off the kitchen.

Richard: You going to get Pete's room?

Chris: Yeah. That's the room I want.

Richard: Yeah. Up front, huh?

Chris: Well, it opens onto the porch. I'm not allowed to go out on the porch.

Richard: When you're big?

Chris: When you're big, you can go out on the porch. But I can't, cause I'm too little. Cause it's windows.

Richard: I bet you'd like to get big.

Chris: Oh, I go on the porch anyway, when nobody's around.

Chris is increasingly caught up in the regression; this whole interchange is essentially an extension of the original invitation to reexperience childhood. Chris's language has changed and he is now talking like a five-year-old boy. The conversation has established a relationship with the therapist as a trusted adult, a person who understands and is interested in a little boy's world. Indeed, Chris's last comment suggests that Richard is an ally, someone who can be trusted with secrets that other grown-ups can't share. With this trust established, Richard begins to focus the work.

Richard: What would happen, if somebody came around and caught you out there?

Chris: They'd beat me.

Richard: They'd beat you, huh?

Chris: No.

Here is an initial and partial confirmation of the hypothesis about the self-generated parent: The child Chris is confused about the consequences of misbehavior. His first response to "What would happen?" is that he would be beaten; but he immediately contradicts himself and says no, he wouldn't. The self-generated parent would beat him, and it is to this self-created parent that he goes first to make his prediction. Even as a five-year-old, however, his reality sense is strong enough to conflict with and contradict the fantasy.

Richard: Do you ever do bad things when nobody's around?

Chris: Yeah.

Richard: And what do you do when they come around?

Chris: I get good.

Richard: How come?

Chris: Cause I don't want to get in trouble. I get good.

While "getting good" is a common five-year-old reaction to the presence of a grown-up, in this case it may also be the response to the self-created parent. Certainly some children don't "get good" whenever parents are in the vicinity, and most children don't "get good" every time—does Chris? And, if so, why? Is he again responding to the fantasied harsh punishment of his self-generated parent, rather than to the reality of his grandparents' discipline?

Richard: What's the worst kind of trouble you get in?

Chris: The worst kind of trouble is my grandmother crying.

Richard: Uh-huh. And what would that be like for you? When Grandma cries?

Chris: It would be that maybe she's going to get sicker.

Richard: And if she gets real sick?

Chris: She's gonna die. It's gonna be my fault.

Richard: And if she dies, what happens to you?

Chris: I don't know.

A lingering but vague sense of omnipotence is natural at this developmental stage. The five-year-old Chris believes that he can cause his grandmother's death by rather trivial and commonplace naughtiness. Thus he has another reason for creating a threatening, punitive parent figure: to keep him in line, so that he won't be a danger to the person he loves.

Grandma's death is threatening not only in that Chris would lose her, but also because of the punishment he would incur. When Richard tries to explore this aspect of Chris's experience, he meets a defensive "I don't know." Although neither the adult Chris nor the little boy does literally know what would happen, this lack of factual information has not blocked the fantasy work up until now; so Richard persists in probing for the catastrophic expectation that is being guarded against.

Richard: Think about it, little boy.

Chris: (*pause, sighing*) I don't know. I don't know.

Richard: What happens to you if Grandma dies?

Chris: Well, I think everybody's gonna be mad at me. My aunts, my grandfather.

Richard: What happens inside of you if Grandma dies? And people are mad?

Chris: Then I have nothing.

Richard: Uh-huh. What's that going to be like, having nothing?

Chris: Scary!

Richard: And where do you feel it, in your body?

Chris: (*touching his midsection*) Right here.

In this interchange, Richard gathers information about the physiological aspects of Chris's scripting process: where he tightens his muscles in order not to feel an emotion fully. Chris stores his scare about Grandma's death (and his own related misbehavior) in his midsection. This information will allow

Richard to build and test hypotheses about possible psychosomatic implications in later life; it also gives him an entry point should he choose to work directly on the body tissues involved in Chris's script pattern. It is still too early for either of these interventions, however; more information is needed.

Richard: Uh-huh. So how can you be sure that nothing bad's going to happen like that?

Chris: Don't do nothing wrong. Or don't get caught doing nothing wrong.

Chris defines clearly the job—the function—of the self-created parent. It will keep him either blameless or very, very careful (or both) and thus keep him safe. Richard continues to work on this issue, solidifying Chris's identification with the Child ego state while gathering more data.

Richard: Why, cause you'll wind up with a dead grandma?

Chris: Yeah.

Richard: All alone? Cause you could cause her to go away to heaven, huh?

Chris: I could, I could do bad things. And she could get sicker. She's sick already.

Richard: Ummm. She have a heart attack, or what?

Chris: I don't know what's wrong with her. I know she's sick; I know she takes a lot of pills. I know she goes to see the doctor a lot.

Richard: So if you lost your Grandma, that would be a bad thing.

Chris: Yeah, everybody'd be mad at me.

Richard: Everybody?

Chris: Everybody.

Again, we see that it isn't just losing Grandma that must be prevented. That, while perhaps painful, could be tolerated. But losing everyone, having them all angry (and rejecting him) would be catastrophic.

Richard: So you gotta do all the right things. What kind of things do you do that are good things, so nobody gets mad?

Chris: I do lots of good things. I don't start trouble in the neighborhood. I don't throw rocks at houses.

Richard: Would you like to sometimes?

Chris: I like to throw rocks on garage roofs.

Richard: Um-hm. And watch 'em come down? Or are they flat roofs?

Chris: Flat roofs. See 'em roll.

Richard: Yeah.

Chris: I also like to get up on top of garage roofs, and then throw the rocks back down.

Richard: I remember doing that, that's fun (*laughs*). 'Cept we used to use bottles, and fill 'em half full of sand, and throw 'em, so they'd explode like hand grenades. And you could see that there'd be a big smoke cloud. Did you ever do that?

Little Chris has confessed to some naughtiness, and his scripting dictates that someone must now be disapproving. Richard refuses to follow the script, however, and even joins him in his naughtiness. Rapport is cemented, and Chris is encouraged to explore more deeply the feelings and sensations of this critical period in his life.

Chris: No. I used to say real smart things. I used to make funny statements and stuff like that, and say funny words, and everybody would laugh.

Is Chris shifting here from being naughty to being cute and entertaining? Or does "smart" mean sassy, smart aleck, and thus represent another step into forbidden territory? Richard needs to know whether things have moved too fast, throwing Chris into a hasty retreat, or whether he is in fact continuing on track.

Richard: Was that a good experience, or bad?

Chris: Well, each time I said something I didn't now whether they would laugh, or whether they would be mad.

Apparently Chris himself didn't always know what kinds of behavior were OK and what kinds were not. Trying to win approval and attention, he was unsure whether people would be pleased or angry. Saying nothing would lead to being ignored—and that would stimulate the old fears of abandonment—so he had to speak up, and run the risk of doing it wrong.

Richard: What if you said something real bad, and they got mad?

Chris: Then I'd get sent to my room. And then I'd get told, "Children should be seen and not heard."

Richard: So they would send you away.

Richard makes the obvious connection.

Chris: Yeah.

Richard: Did you like that?

Chris: Heck, no. I got it done to me once or twice, but I learned very very fast how not to do that.

Richard: You were determined never to be sent away again.

Chris: No way!

The hypothesis is now well supported: For Chris, the catastrophe of being sent away was to be avoided at all costs. There was "no way" that he would allow himself to risk that; it was too terrible. Richard now moves to establish the specific rules that Chris's self-created Parent established and enforced in order to be safe.

Richard: What'd you have to do, then, to make sure they wouldn't send you away?

Chris: Well, I'd either keep quiet, or I hadda say something that I knew would be OK.

Richard: Um-hm. Something that would please them.

Chris: Or do something that would please them.

Chris not only agrees, but embellishes—a good sign that the work is on track.

Richard: So if they're displeased, they get rid of you. And if you were really bad, and killed your grandmother, do you think they'd send you to the orphanage.

Chris: I don't know about orphanages. I just know that if I did anything that bad, I'd be in trouble. I would be in trouble.

It is possible that the baldness of Richard's question, stating openly both unmentionable fears (killing Grandma, and being sent to the orphanage), may have been too much for Chris. Or his response may be quite accurate: At the age to which he is regressed, the word orphanage is not meaningful. He may not have verbal understanding of the "trouble" he would be in, but rather a visceral and emotional sense of being left or cast out: Scripting at this early age is often rooted much more in affective and body sensations than in cognitions. Richard chooses not to pursue the cognitive aspects, but instead to clarify the protective rules that Chris is setting up for himself.

Richard: So what do you say inside your head to stay out of trouble?

Chris: Don't do anything wrong. Better figure out what's the right thing to do, and do it. Otherwise you're in trouble.

Richard: Um-hm. You're clever. How many times a day do you say that to yourself?

This child, with his great sensitivity to disapproval, might well have interpreted Richard's curiosity and persistence about his script behavior as a negative reaction, a "how odd of you to have done these things" kind of response. To avoid this, Richard strokes Chris for his cleverness, and then asks for more details. The details provide information both for the therapist, in terms of diagnosis and treatment planning, and for the observing Adult ego state of the client.

Chris: Whenever I'm around grown-ups. Cause I spend a lot of time out with my friends. As long as I come back.

Richard: Do you ever say it when you're out with your friends, too? Just in case they do things that would . . .

Chris: Only around the bigger kids.

Richard: Why do you do that?

Chris: Try to get liked by the bigger kids.

Richard: How do you manage that?

Chris: Well, I show them how good I am. And what we're doing. Figure out how to do what they're doing, so I'm one of the big guys. Whether it's climbing roofs, or . . .

Richard: Cause if you're bad at doing those things, what happens?

Chris: They're going to say, "You're a little kid, get out of here. We don't want you to hang around with us."

Richard: So they get rid of you too.

Chris: Yeah.

The rule is clear: Do it right, please people, don't make mistakes, push yourself to look smart and capable and grown-up. And if you do all this without a fumble, you won't be sent away. The self-created parent must be constantly vigilant, to make sure that Chris follows this rule at all times; with such a parent on duty, the Child ego state can enjoy at least the semblance of normal, age-appropriate behavior. Having the therapist understand is not enough, however; the Child Chris must also begin to make sense of the system.

Richard: That's a big thing for you. Being chased away. So you got a protector inside of your head that keeps you from getting chased away.

Chris: Figure out what they want, and give it to them. Don't tell them everything. What they don't know won't hurt them . . .

It seems pretty clear to Chris, as well—perhaps too clear. There is a strangely adultlike ring to his response, as if he is parroting what he has learned from someone else. Perhaps these rules are not all self-generated, after all, but are an introject from some significant other in his life. Richard needs to find out:

Richard: Um-hm. Somebody else tell you to do that, or did you figure that out?

Chris: My grandfather says that.

Richard: What does he say?

Chris: "Hey, what they don't know won't hurt them."

Richard: And what about the first part?

Chris: I figured that out. I figured that out myself.

Richard: Well, which one seems like a better message? The one from Grandfather, or the one you figured out?

We have both an introjected message (Grandfather's "what they don't know won't hurt them") and a self-generated message (give them what they want). The treatment of choice is quite different for an introject than it is for a self-generated image. Self-generated parent is a production of the child, and it is best worked with through the Child ego state. Introjects, in contrast, are accessed through the Parent ego state. Richard will need to make a choice about which to deal with first. He asks Chris which is more important, in order to stay with Chris's own energy and investment.

Chris: I don't know.

Richard: If you could only have one of those two, to help you in life, which one would you choose?

Chris: Well, I don't know. They both get me in trouble.

Does Chris anticipate where the work is going, or is he uncovering another facet of the script-forming environment?

Richard: What do you mean?

Chris: Well, people get mad at me when I don't tell them everything, cause then they think I'm lying to them. And I'm not lying to them, I'm just not telling them everything. I figure they don't need to know everything, so I don't tell them everything.

Richard: Um-hm. So that one gets you in trouble.

Chris: Well, sometimes when I get caught, it gets me in trouble.

Grandpa's introjected advice is a blind alley—it not only doesn't serve as a protection, but may even create the very situation it was supposed to avoid. Richard could easily have stayed right here, working at this spot. But there's a loose string: the other half of the rules.

Richard: And the other one?

Chris: Well, sometimes I can't do what they want me to do, or what I think they want me to do, and then I'm stuck. Cause if I do it, and I can't do it, then they know I can't do it; and if I say I can't do it, then they know I can't do it.

Obviously, there is energy here as well. Richard is ready to return to the task of prioritizing, when Chris introduces a new theme:

Richard: Um-hm. So both of those things are important. You're figuring out that it's better to be good to please them, and work real hard to please them; and Grandfather's statement not to tell people everything.

Chris: Well, he never told Grandma everything.

Richard: Are you sure? How do you know?

It's beginning to sound as if the "don't tell everything" rule, though partially an introjected one, may also have a decisional component. The little boy, watching Grandpa's behavior, was figuring out for himself just how to survive in the family, and may have decided that what he saw (or thought he saw) Grandpa doing would probably work for him, as well. Script beliefs of this sort—that is, those supported by both decision and introject—need to be dealt with at both levels; to do only the deconfusion or redecision work, or only the Parent ego state work, leaves a part of the script still intact. Richard probes to discover whether Chris did, in fact, make his own decision about how Grandpa operated and how well this might work for the little boy himself.

Chris: Cause I watched. He'd go out in his garden and go to sleep.

She'd say what'd you do, and he says, "Oh, I was out in the garden." He never told her he was sleeping, he just said he was out in the garden. And she thought he was working on the roses and stuff. (*laughs*) I knew he was sleeping.

Richard: And what did you conclude from that?

Chris: Hey, you could get away with some neat stuff by doing that.

Richard: Are you going to do that when you get big?

Chris: Oh, I do it already. I do it. My grandfather catches me, though.

Richard: Well, you got a voice inside your head that you made, too, that tells you that you have to do things to please people. So that they don't get rid of you.

Chris's introjected "don't tell everything" and the self-generated "please people" apparently create conflict for him: When he doesn't tell everything, and gets caught in his omissions, he discovers that people may be displeased. This activates the old fears of abandonment. To avert such a catastrophe, the self-created parent is activated and Chris flips into an exaggerated need to please other people. No matter which course he takes, the catastrophe may occur. It's time to begin to challenge the belief system, to reeducate the Child in him about the likely consequences of his behavior, as well as the inappropriate sternness of his rules. And Chris, like most children whose beliefs are challenged, resists:

Chris: I don't know about that.

Richard: Your real mama went away.

Chris: I don't know about that. I don't, I don't know what happened, or why, or how come, or . . .

A child who believes that his naughtiness may cause his Grandma to die is also likely to believe that similar naughtiness drove his mother away. The fact of her absence is an ongoing reinforcement of the script belief, consistently "proving" the need for the self-created parent to be stern and vigilant. Although Chris denies knowledge of what happened to his mother, his leap from not knowing what happened to speculation about why it happened can only suggest that he does, indeed, either know or believe something about his mother's leaving. Why else would he volunteer that he doesn't know why it happened? In fact, we may suspect (as does the therapist) that he has some pretty clear notions about both the "why" and the "what" of her departure.

Richard: Did you ever think that maybe it was cause you were a bad baby?

Chris: I don't, I don't let myself think that.

A possible verification—a thought must be present in order to be denied or retroflected.

Chris: (*continuing*) I just, I just try to pick up pieces of stuff when the grown-ups talk.

Richard: What are some of the things you heard about why your mama gave you away?

Chris: Oh, my father's bad.

Richard: Ah. So if somebody's bad, somebody gets given away.

Chris: Yeah. I heard my father was bad, and my mother couldn't stop him from being bad, and then my grandfather took me.

Richard: Um-hm.

Chris: And that my father drinks a lot.

Richard: So if you're bad they'll give you away.

Chris is drifting here into another issue, that of what his father (and, by extension, he himself) is like. While this is, of course, important, it is really another chapter, so the therapist attempts to draw him back.

Chris: Yeah. I guess. I don't know, I just don't know anything that went on with that whole stuff with my mother and father. I don't know. Nobody will tell me.

Richard: What do you think? What do you imagine?

Chris: I think I was a bad baby. I think I cried too much.

At last, like a piece dropping into a nearly completed jigsaw puzzle, comes the fantasy, in Chris's own words. In his world, people are sent away not when just "somebody" is bad, but when the banished one is bad. He was a bad baby because he cried too much; it was his own fault that he was abandoned. He didn't please the people who needed to be pleased. Richard will stay with this important bit, will explore the details, so that Chris himself can begin to understand the myth that he has created.

Richard: And if you cry too much, what happens to that kind of baby?

Chris: Well, then, they can't be taken care of, and somebody else has to take care of them.

Richard: Um-hm. And how does that feel to the baby? If it gets given away?

Chris: I don't know. I don't know.

Richard: But you don't want your Grandma to die.

Chris: No.

Richard: So you know that would feel bad.

Chris: Yeah, I know that. I know that.

Richard: Sometimes you think that maybe you were a bad baby, huh?

Chris: Yeah. Yeah. I don't listen to her so good. She yells a lot.

Richard: So it's going to be important for you not to be sent away again.

Chris: Yeah. I don't know where I'd go.

Richard: I don't either. Except I don't think Grandfather will let you be sent away.

Is Chris ready to reconsider the fantasy of being sent away? If the fear is less strong, then the need for protection is also less, and the rules that he has set up for himself can relax.

Chris: Well, I don't think so, either. I hope not.

Richard: But you're scared about it a bit, huh?

Chris: If I'm bad.

Richard: So that means?

Chris: Well, what it means is, be good. As long as I'm good, I don't have to worry about what'll happen if I'm bad. Cause if I'm bad, I'll get sent away, maybe. Don't know. Sort of like, I don't know, and I don't want to know, and I'll just, just not upset things. Not upset people, just keep things nice.

The frightened Child ego state is still in charge, and still in the grip of his nightmare fantasy. It's time to call up reinforcements: the Adult ego state, who has been observing the whole piece of work.

Richard: Listen to that decision, Chris. (*pause*) The whole paragraph you just said. Say it again, so you hear it.

Chris: So, if I make things nice, I don't upset things. (*long pause*) I don't remember it. I might say it wrong.

The Child ego state is quite frightened here. His protection has been challenged, and he feels vulnerable. The fear of displeasing and being left extends even to the therapist, who up to now has been a friend and ally. He needs support, and Richard is quick to offer it.

Richard: Just say it your way. Which will make it the right way.

Chris: (*pause*) I'm gonna do things good and nice and right, so I won't get sent away, because I don't want to be sent away, and I don't want people to get sick or die . . .

Richard now utilizes a technique called "disconnecting the rubber band," in which a client, while experiencing the world from a regressed, Child ego state, is asked to predict the consequences of an early decision. This procedure helps the client to understand what has happened both as a rational adult and from the perspective of an intuitive and emotional child.

Richard: Now imagine the future, when you're a grown-up man. And if you still keep that same rule, what's life going to be like when you're 35, thirty years from now?

Chris: That's a long time.

Richard: Yeah, but you can imagine into the future.

Chris: I don't know. I don't know what. I'll go to work, and I'll come home.

Richard: Do you think grown-ups have to worry about being sent away?

Chris: Grown-ups have to be worried about getting sent away? No.

Clearly, Chris is not ready to take this next step. He has taken in the information about his protective system, and he is processing this information. To push him further at this point, when he so obviously needs more time, would not be therapeutic. Richard ends the piece of work, therefore, stroking him for his risk-taking and his understanding, and promising to be available to continue the work later, when Chris has had time to think about what he has learned so far.

It would have been easy, in this example, for the therapist to have gotten so involved in Chris's unfolding story, so intrigued by the way in which Chris provided verification of the therapeutic hypotheses, that he would have continued the work past the point of real effectiveness. Too often, therapists continue to poke at clients after they have signaled that they have had enough, worrying at them like a dog with an old bone, demanding that they do more and more and just a little bit more. The result of this kind of treatment may be either an adaptive pseudocompliance or a rebuilding of the defenses that have been so painstakingly let down in the first part of the work. In either case, the poor work has to be undone before the next piece can be well begun, just as bad carpentry must be torn out before further remodeling can continue. It is much more appropriate to end a particular piece, and allow the client an opportunity to do his own integration, according to his own internal time schedule. When he is ready, Chris will be back to complete his work.

4

BEN
Therapy with the Parent Ego State

Central to script theory is the concept of the childhood decision. These decisions, often begun even before the individual has words to conceptualize what is being decided/experienced/understood, continue to shape our script throughout our lives. The early decision sets up expectations, which lead us to find and interpret new situations so as to strengthen or reinforce the decision, "proving" that the old way of thinking and feeling and being was indeed the only possible choice. Regression work is a major technique for dealing with this sort of script decision.

Not all script, however, is most usefully characterized as formed through a decision-making process. As was described in Chapter 1, the beliefs, attitudes, feelings, and behaviors of one's parents (or other primary caretakers) are taken in by the child, swallowed whole. The child has no choice about this kind of scripting; the thoughts and feelings and behaviors permeate the very atmosphere, and the child must breathe them in if he or she is to breathe at all. Such introjected material forms the Parent ego state, and when this ego state is cathected, it is as if the introjected parent(s) had psychologically replaced their now-grown-up offspring.

To summarize, script beliefs may arise out of early decisions, or they may be introjected—swallowed whole, as they come from influential figures in childhood. The chapters presented thus far have dealt primarily with the former type of scripting, in which the most common therapeutic remedy lies in regression and redecision work. In this chapter, we will deal with the latter, introjected variety.

In integrative psychotherapy, we move the Parent ego state itself into the arena of script change. Rather than inviting the client to leave the Parent ego state, and cathect Adult or Child ego states, in order to effect change, we continue to work with the introjection by conducting the therapy with the activated Parent ego state. Just as work with Child ego state sounds, to the casual listener, like a therapist working with a small child, so Parent therapy sounds like a therapist working with the client's parent. The client's Adult and Child ego states are, of course, passively attuned, listening in, and may derive additional benefit from the therapeutic exchange, but the primary target is the Parent ego state: that organized collection of thoughts, feelings, and behaviors that the client introjected without question over years of exposure.

Ben, the client, is working with these therapists for the first time, and the work contains elements of both diagnostic information-gathering and therapy proper. As we shall see, it eventually takes the form of Parent ego state work—the therapy of choice in dealing with introjected material. Ben is a 50-year-old man who has decided, relatively late in life, to change careers and become a psychotherapist. He appears to be significantly depressed (though, as we shall see, he is only partially aware of his depression). We are well into the second full day of the workshop when Ben requests an opportunity to work.

Ben: I'd like to work next. I've been feeling very calm, and relaxed all day yesterday. And I think it's a way of not doing my work. Sort of, I have to feel bad, in order to do my work. So I decided to do it even when I feel good. I go through life happy and active all the time. Active. Happy. And I know that underneath I feel depressed, and I most always succeed in fighting it off. I feel very tired. I'm tired of fighting it.

Ben certainly opens with a mixed message: I feel good, I feel bad, I'm usually depressed, I'm usually happy, I have to feel bad to work, but I'll work when I feel good, but I don't feel good, I feel tired. The unwary therapist might plunge eagerly into all of this, only to discover far down the road that he and Ben were working on a nonproblem. The therapists in this case decide to hold back a bit, to find out more about what Ben is experiencing right now.

Rebecca: What's been happening here when you're cutting down your activity and so forth?

Ben: I've made a conscious decision to just be quiet, to stay by myself. To not interact as much as I usually do. And I felt very calm and good about it.

Richard: What do you suppose would happen if you went ahead and got depressed here? And really wallowed in it?

Ben: Even the times that I've been depressed, I don't think I ever really wallow in it and let it wash over me. I think I, I keep it at a certain level, and all I need is one phone call, or one interaction with another person, and I can snap right out of it.

So far Ben has given one confused and self-contradictory statement, one half-answer to a question, and one nonanswer to a question. Is this a preview of some kind of power or control struggle in the work to come? What is the script issue that underlies this verbal slipperiness? Who, in Ben's background, was hard to pin down? And what purpose does the slipperiness serve in Ben's life today? These are the kinds of questions that run through the therapists' minds as the work begins to take shape.

Richard: That's what I mean. What if you make a decision—

Ben: To really go into it?

Richard: —that this was an environment where you could go ahead and be depressed without fighting it off. And let us take care of you.

This is the first major probe: How will Ben respond to the invitation that he give up some of this control and let himself be "taken care of" by someone else? From the little we have seen, we might predict that he will resist the idea.

Ben: It's the being taken care of that's a problem for me. I can take care of people, but . . .

Richard: And that'd be one of the first tasks. No more taking care of people.

Ben: That sounds scary to me. Cause if I don't take care of them, they're not going to like me. I have to take care of them in order for them to like me. I almost don't know any other way to relate to people. Except to take care of them. And certainly not to have them take care of me. I think there's an issue around . . . I think the sadness is that I'll never get what I want.

Ben talks here in a genuine-sounding way about feeling scared, about how he gives others what he would like for himself but doesn't know how to get. Then he backs away, puts "the issue" and "the sadness" outside of himself, probably as a way of maintaining control.

Rebecca: Umm. Feeling that right now.

Ben: I can guess . . . I feel that, that my father never loved me the way I wanted. (*pause*) I'm also angry that they'll never give me what I want. I gave them . . . I'm so confused as to past and present.

Richard: Are they still living?

Ben: My mother is; my father died two years ago . . . It feels like it's so far away, and so long, long ago.

Rebecca: Was your father depressed also?

Ben: No, on the contrary, he was very much like me. So, so perhaps underneath . . . certainly on the surface he was extremely gregarious and pleasant and was liked . . . he was a very nice guy.

Rebecca: So how was it that he missed you? . . . (*Ben makes an odd, almost self-negating gesture*) Just stay with what you're feeling, Ben, just go with that . . . want to tell us about it?

Ben: I just had the feeling that I wasn't what he wanted. And then he, then he caught himself. And all of my adult life he genuinely respected me. And looked up to me . . .

Clearly, Ben has invested a lot of energy in his relationship with his father, and it is that relationship that is in the foreground of his work right now. Knowing that he is a therapeutically sophisticated client, and suspecting that his need to be in control will seriously interfere with his ability to deal with emotional issues, however, Rebecca is wary of encouraging him to do any more speculating, theorizing, or storytelling about Father. She sets up a Parent interview instead—one that may or may not evolve into Parent therapy; and she is careful to enlist Ben's full cooperation in doing so. Deferring to the client's sense of what seems like a right direction not only defuses much of the resistance, but also reinforces the client's autonomy and self-respect.

Rebecca: Have you ever done a Parent interview with your father? That's what I'm feeling would be a good direction. How does that sound to you? How 'bout if we do that? All right with you?

Ben: Am I going to be my father, or am I going to talk to him?

Rebecca: No, you're going to be your father. We're going to talk to him.

Ben: I look like my father. My mother says I get more like him all the time.

Rebecca: Well, take on his characteristics right now, as fully as you can. Close your eyes. And first of all, get a good image of him. If you need to sit up on the couch, if that's the way he would sit, then go ahead and do that (*Ben has been seated on the mat, with the therapists*).

Ben: Yeah, he wouldn't be sitting on the floor. (*he moves up to sit on a couch*)

Rebecca: Most of our parents wouldn't. Where would you like to sit? Is that where he would sit? Where in this room would he be inclined to sit?

Ben: Well, the room is amorphous; I'll be all right here.

Rebecca: All right. Just close your eyes again, and tell me his name.

Ben: Max.

Rebecca: Will you just get yourself in the posture of Max? . . . Now acquire his facial expression . . . then move into his feelings . . . and the way he thinks . . .

Notice the preparation for the Parent interview. Ben is not instructed to play the role of Max; he is told to actually be Max, and the therapist helps him to do so by means of spatial, visual, kinesthetic, and cognitive anchors.

Rebecca: So, Max, are you here?

Ben (as Max): Yes.

Rebecca: I'd like to know a little bit about you. Will you tell me, like where you come from, Max?

Ben (as Max): Well, I come from a pretty poor background. But I've transcended that. I'm successful as an artist.

Rebecca: You're an artist. Quite a successful artist?

Ben (as Max): No, I'm moderately successful, but I'm quite happy with that.

Rebecca: Enough so that you don't feel poor any more.

Ben (as Max): No. Not poor any more.

Rebecca: Well, congratulations.

Ben (as Max): Thank you. I'm very proud of myself.

Rebecca: It must have been a lot of work, to get yourself out of that background.

Ben (as Max): Yes, it was. During the Depression. But I was very good.

As with any brand-new client, Rebecca begins by building rapport, using basic listening and questioning techniques to establish a foundation for relationship.

Rebecca: How old were you during the Depression?

Ben (as Max): I was in my twenties and thirties.

Rebecca: An artist, and that age?

Ben (as Max): I was a commercial artist. Everyone was out of work, but I was so good that I always had work. Then my union shared the work among the less good people, so I was working two days a week. So the other guys could get jobs. I was doing three times as much work as they. But that was OK.

This is a rather self-righteous statement, one that probably covers a good deal of resentment. In the interest of rapport-building, however, Rebecca takes it at face value.

Rebecca: So you're quite a moral man, too.

Ben (as Max): Yeah, I'm a nice guy.

Rebecca: How do you feel when you say that, Max? "I'm a nice guy."

Ben (as Max): I feel proud.

This interchange supports the wisdom of avoiding direct confrontation at this point: Given two chances to open up the issue of resentment, Max/Ben is clearly not interested. Richard reenters the interaction, going back to a more neutral process of history-taking.

Richard: Where are you from originally, Max?

Ben (as Max): I was born on the lower East side of New York. No, I'm sorry, I was born on the upper East side. But we were poor.

Richard: How'd you get to the lower East side?

Ben (as Max): Well, Jews, most of the Jews lived on the lower East side, but we actually lived on the upper East side, in a poor neighborhood.

Richard: It's interesting, though, that you made that slip. Is that significant?

Ben (as Max): Yeah. There's a part of me that still feels like a lower East Side Jew.

Richard: What does a lower East Side Jew feel like?

Ben (as Max): Discriminated against. Not wanted. An outsider.

Richard does not interpret the slip of the tongue himself, but invites Max/Ben to make the interpretation. And Max/Ben does so, providing the first clear indication of a script issue: Ben may have taken from Max the belief that, because he is Jewish, he is an unwanted outsider.

Richard: What does an outsider feel like?

Ben (as Max): Not OK. I've always fought to feel OK.

Richard: How come?

Ben (as Max): Cause I'm a Jew.

Richard: Was that true on the upper East Side, too?

Ben (as Max): Yeah, it was an Italian neighborhood.

Rebecca: So you were discriminated against there too? How did you happen to live up there, when all of the other Jews were down on the lower East Side?

Ben (as Max): Cause my parents chose it.

Richard: Do you know why? Tell us about your folks, Max.

Ben (as Max): My father was a very religious man.

Richard: Orthodox?

Ben (as Max): Orthodox.

Richard: Did you keep a Kosher household?

Ben (as Max): My father did. I mean, I certainly don't any more.

Richard: That would be a little hard, living in an Italian neighborhood.

Ben (as Max): I don't know why my father chose to live there. I never thought about that.

Richard: What business was your dad in, Max?

Ben (as Max): He just had a job. He was a rabbi back in the old country, but he worked as a tailor. A very demeaning job.

Again the flavor of resentment, of specialness, of "I/we deserve better"—and again the therapists choose to step over it. It's too soon; Ben hasn't had enough time to decide that these therapists can be trusted, and Max certainly hasn't.

The Parent interview proceeds as if the therapists were actually getting acquainted with that parent, a complete stranger who has agreed to be interviewed. Frequent use of the parent's first name helps keep Ben's Parent ego state cathected; in fact, this early phase of the Parent interview serves almost as an extended hypnotic induction, leading the client deeper and deeper into his experiencing of himself as the father he once knew. The pace is leisurely, allowing the client to settle into his new identity, and giving all participants plenty of time to get to know each other. It is not quite the same as a casual conversation, for the questions are more pointed and the direction more one-sided; yet it is different from an initial therapy session in that this "parent" has not requested any kind of help for himself. The therapists are interested, respectful—and alert to the possibility that this ego state may become open to a new kind of experiencing. At that point, the Parent interview becomes Parent therapy. But this is not yet the time.

Richard: Where'd he come from?

Ben (as Max): Russia.

Richard: But you were born here, Max?

Ben (as Max): Yeah. I was born in New York, 1908.

Richard: So you're 77 now, if you were still around . . . Well, Max, what was your family like?

Ben (as Max): My mother and father fought like cats and dogs. They hated each other.

Richard: How was that for you?

Ben (as Max): Not very good. My mother was a very vain and self-centered woman. And so is my father. So they didn't get along very well. My mother used to throw my father out of the house.

Richard: Were you an only child?

Ben (as Max): No, no. I have two older brothers, a younger sister and a younger brother.

Richard: You're right stuck in the middle.

Ben (as Max): Um-hm. But I'm the smartest one. I'm the one who got out of the, sort of, lower East Side mentality. I'm the only one who did.

Richard: Well, I'm surprised you say that. Cause a few minutes ago I had the opposite impression, that you were still there. And negatively paralyzed.

Yet a third time, Max indicates his sense of "specialness." This time Richard ventures a gentle confrontation, pointing out the inconsistency of this remark with what Max has said earlier. He then adds an interpretation, couching it in complicated polysyllables—tempting bait for Max, who almost certainly considers himself an intellectual.

Ben (as Max): That's maybe true. In 1939 we moved to a Christian neighborhood, brought up our kids in a Christian neighborhood.

Rebecca: What'd that signify to you, Max?

Ben (as Max): That I got out. Out of being a ghetto lower East Side Jew.

Rebecca: I wonder if that's what your dad was doing, too, by living with the Italians. Trying to get out. Think so?

Ben (as Max): He was too religious, no, he was too Jewish. I'm much less that.

Richard: How come you're not so Jewish?

Ben (as Max): There's a part of me that says it's not OK to be Jewish.

We have heard before that Max has taken in some anti-Semitic messages, and now he returns to the same theme. Again, he uses the phrase, "a part of me," which may reflect a leakage or contamination from Ben's psychologically trained Adult ego state, but nevertheless can also be a signal that he is ready to shift into a more therapeutic mode.

Richard: That's the part we'd like to know about, Max.

Ben (as Max): Well, shit, we all got beaten up when we were kids, for being Jewish. I learned how to fight back then.

Richard: Did you get beaten up?

Ben (as Max): No, I fought back.

Richard: What went on in your family, Max? You say your parents were fighting a lot. Did that feel like getting beaten up, when they mixed it up?

Ben (as Max): I don't know.

> *Max/Ben offers a superficially persuasive reason for his "not OK to be Jewish" feelings: Jews were persecuted in his neighborhood. But lots of Jews grow up in hostile neighborhoods, and not all of them feel uncomfortable with their Jewishness. What's different about Max's experience? Most often, a sense of not-OK-ness originates in the family, long before the child's awareness has graduated to the larger neighborhood; peer experiences tend to support and elaborate previously established script beliefs. "It's not good to be a Jew" may be a later elaboration of a more sweeping early decision that "There's something wrong with me." The therapists attempt to discover how Max's family set the stage for his feeling that being a Jew was not OK; and this time they persist, in spite of Max/Ben's first refusal to cooperate.*

Rebecca: Sounds like it must have been pretty scary, to have your dad tossed out of the house. Were you close to your father?

Ben (as Max): When I was married, and my mother used to throw my father out, he used to come live with us.

Rebecca: That's kind of a "yes," but it doesn't feel like it comes from your heart. Did you feel close to him from your heart?

Ben (as Max): I don't know.

> *It appears that Max/Ben will talk readily about things and events and feelings of his own choosing, but retreats into not knowing when asked to follow the therapist's lead. But the "induction" is holding; Max shows no signs of reverting back to being Ben. His posture, voice, and general demeanor remain as they were when Ben originally cathected the Max ego state. Richard decides to risk a stronger push:*

Richard: You know, Max, your son has implied that he thought that you were, underneath your gregariousness, depressed. What do you think deep inside, Max?

Ben (as Max): No, I'm not depressed. I'm scared.

Rebecca: Scared of what?

Ben (as Max): Scared of being beaten out by the Christians. Most of the time I thought I really would.

Rebecca: So what did you have to do?

Ben (as Max): I put on a good front. Placate them.

Rebecca: Look gregarious, and not be?

Ben (as Max): I moved into our neighborhood in 1939. The man across the street was a military man. Hated Jews. And he, he actually was a member of the Ku Klux Klan and the Nazi Bund. And three years ago when I died, he came to my funeral.

Max/Ben reverts back to storytelling—or is he really talking about feelings through metaphor? Richard assumes the latter, and asks for clarification.

Richard: What's that mean to you, Max?

Ben (as Max): It took 40 years to get him to accept me.

Rebecca: Boy, you surely go for the strong tests, don't you?

One way to stay depressed and not OK is to choose tasks and goals that are so difficult that they don't allow success. Failing such tasks, then, can be used as proof that one really is inferior, or mistreated, or that the world really is unfair, and thus the depressive position is maintained. Rebecca hints at this, leaving it up to Max/Ben whether to pick it up or not. Notice that, by now, the work with Max is more like therapy than like an informational interview. Were we to come in with no prior knowledge at this point, we would not know that the work is being done with a cathected Parent ego state; we would assume that Max was the original client.

Ben (as Max): Seems like I did it the hard way, didn't I? Tough on my kids, too.

Rebecca: How so?

Ben (as Max): They had to do it all over again. Cause it was a Christian neighborhood.

Richard: Same thing that happened to you as a kid. But you taught 'em to be survivors, huh? How to fight?

Ben (as Max): I wasn't so sure that Ben would make it. He was kind of a weak and scared kid, couldn't fight and couldn't play ball. And I was really disappointed in him. But he turned out to be so smart that he figured out a way of outsmarting them. So he was OK. Very proud of him now.

Rebecca: Were you scared for him?

Ben (as Max): No, I was angry with him.

Richard: Max, would you like Ben to be like those tough Italian kids? Would you like him to walk down the streets of New York, and everybody say, "Hey, he's Italian. Watch out!"

Along with doing therapy with the Parent ego state, the therapists are still searching for the script message that Max passed on to Ben—the rules about "this is how I am, this is how the world is, this is how you must be."

Ben (as Max): Yeah, I think so.

Richard: How come, Max?

Ben (as Max): Cause that's what I would have wanted to be.

Rebecca: Like him not to have to be scared like you are?

Rebecca goes back to Max's earlier description of himself as "scared." Even though he denies being scared for Ben, it's likely that the anger is a defense against an underlying scare for both him and his son, both Jews in a hostile environment.

Ben (as Max): He wasn't, he was more scared.

Richard: Oh, that must have been hard. You think he picked up your scare underneath, Max?

Ben (as Max): No, he wouldn't understand that.

Rebecca: Kid's smart. He knows.

If Max/Ben can recognize how he transmitted his own scare, in the form of a script belief, to his son, he may be able to give Ben's Adult ego state permission to reject it, to be himself rather than to be like Dad. This is the ultimate aim of Parent therapy: to decommission the Parent ego state, take away its power to interfere with the ongoing functioning of the client. Having planted the seed, the therapists continue to explore feelings:

Richard: You say you're scared, Max. But as you talk about that Nazi across the street, you have a deep sadness. That's what I'd like to know about, Max.

Ben (as Max): They were putting swastikas on the Jewish shops in 1939, in Queens. I was scared. Two blocks away from where I worked. Then the war came, and it changed. Then it was almost OK to be a Jew.

Rebecca: Almost. No one would dare to do it openly any more.

Ben (as Max): Right.

Richard: Why do I keep getting the sense that in spite of your father's religiousness there was something wrong with being a Jew for you too?

Ben (as Max): I guess if you're told it often enough you believe it.

Richard: Told what often enough?

Ben (as Max): That you're a dirty Jew.

Richard: That what your dad told you?

Ben (as Max): No, but that's what the neighborhood people would call . . .

Richard: And yet you continued to stay there and take that abuse.

Ben (as Max): I don't know why he did that; I never knew.

There is some apparent confusion here about who it was who chose to stay in the non-Jewish neighborhood. Max's father and Max both did so, both subjected their children to anti-Semitic abuse. Richard cuts through the confusion by making the parallel, simultaneously reinforcing the presence of the "Max" ego state.

Richard: Probably the same reason you moved to that Gentile neighborhood. In 1939.

Ben (as Max): It seemed like a way of having my own house.

Richard: There's something more significant than that, Max.

Ben (as Max): I think if I had it to do over again I wouldn't live there. I thought by moving to a Christian neighborhood, the kids would grow up to be educated and professional.

Richard: The point is, it sounds like you as kids in your neighborhood needed to fight pretty hard. One way or another. You had to stand up against some pretty tough odds.

We keep edging closer and closer to a direct statement of Max's denial of his Jewishness; Max/Ben is reluctant to deal with it head-on. Although we are fairly sure, at this point, that being a Jew is a highly charged issue for Ben, we still don't know what specific implications Jewishness has for him; this is what the therapists are probing for in Max. In Max/Ben's next response, we get at least part of it.

Ben (as Max): It's a tough world.

Richard: Say that again, Max.

Ben (as Max): It's a tough world out there.

Rebecca: So therefore, if it's a tough world, then . . .

Ben (as Max): It's a tough world, so you have to learn how to survive.

Richard: Quite a thing to teach a little boy before he goes to school. No wonder Ben was scared. You tell him, hey, Ben, I'm sending you off to school. And in the same breath you tell him it's a tough world out there. Goyim will get you.

Ben (as Max): He learned how to cope.

Richard: At what price?

Ben (as Max): I only wanted the best for him.

Max/Ben becomes defensive—a good sign that the therapy is on target, that the therapists are indeed approaching the heart of the script belief system. But they don't want to frighten Max away; it's time to ease off a bit.

Rebecca: I believe that. And most of all you wanted him to survive in this world.

Ben (as Max): I wanted him to be able to survive anything.

Richard: But listen to the double message, Max.

Ben (as Max): I wanted him to survive in a . . . I wanted him to survive as a Jew in a Christian world. That's what I wanted.

Richard: So you told him to go out there, do a good job, make it, go for excellence . . .

Ben (as Max): And learn how to fight. He never learned that.

Max/Ben returns again to the theme of having to fight. The world is difficult, things will be hard, people will be against you. This is the message that Ben was given, that he took in; this is still how he experiences his life. Max—the Max who still lives in Ben's head—needs to take another look at that belief, at how it has affected his own life and how it has affected Ben.

Richard: He's just a little boy.

Ben (as Max): The other kids are little kids too.

Richard: You teach him how to fight?

Ben (as Max): Tried to. He was too scared.

Richard: Scared of you, Max? Scared of your scare?

Ben (as Max): Yeah, he was scared of me.

Richard: Why, Max?

Ben (as Max): Cause I had to pretend to be strong.

Rebecca: And he knew it was pretend.

Ben (as Max): I don't think he knew that. Not when he was a little kid.

Richard: Ben knew something was wrong. By the time he was getting ready to go to kindergarten, Max. There was something wrong in your relationship.

Ben (as Max): I was afraid to get close to him.

Another piece falls into place. We would have predicted this, given Max's caution in talking about his feelings (and Ben's, as well), but now Max/Ben has owned it. Richard loses no time in capitalizing on the opening.

Richard: How come, Max?

Ben (as Max): I was scared of him.

Richard: Why?

Ben (as Max): I don't know. I've always been scared of him.

Richard: What was going on, Max?

Ben (as Max): Just easier to keep my distance. Cause I was scared.

This is is a crucial point in the work. Ben is deeply inducted; he "is" Max, the Max who is a part of him and who influences his whole way of being. Richard's intervention is aimed at a part of Max that is beyond Ben's conscious awareness, but is of central importance in Max's developing and maintaining the beliefs and expectations that he passed on to his son.

Richard: What would you have felt about the little boy in you, Max, if you got close to the little boy in him? (*long pause*) My guess, Max, is that you saw the scare in the little boy in Ben, who got scared when you told him the world was scary, and then it was a reminder of the little boy in you. That you did not want to feel.

Ben (as Max): No, that isn't true.

Richard: I suspect it's true, Max, because one of the things that I've done over my professional career is to keep track of grown-ups who cannot relate to certain age groups of children. And whatever age group that was, that was where many of these people would go back to in therapy, that would be exactly the age where they were stuck or had some problems. I first discovered that in doing therapy with teachers, who would come and talk about the age groups of kids they just couldn't stand. I wonder if that's true for you, Max? That little five-year-old boy inside of you, that Ben's a reminder of?

Ben (as Max): Yeah, I wouldn't want to have to go through that again.

Rebecca: What would you have to go through again?

Ben (as Max): I was scared of the other kids. Always having fights, not wanting them to see that I was scared. I wouldn't want for him to do that.

Richard: He didn't need to.

Ben (as Max): Yes he did. Kids will be human.

Richard: But not for the same reason, Max.

Expecting to have to fight, and being afraid to, was more painful to Max than the fighting itself. In passing these attitudes on to Ben, Max created for him the very situation he most wanted Ben to avoid. His eyes fill with tears as he begins really to take in what has happened.

Ben (as Max): For the same reason. It's no different. Why the shit I'd put him through that . . .

Rebecca: You wanted to teach him to be a survivor.

Ben (as Max): Like throwing a kid into a swimming pool and expecting him to swim. Supposed to be a nice guy. I wasn't so nice to my kid. I just thought that was the way you did it.

Richard: May be that you end up being like your own father. Was he going to make sure that no child of his would ever get muscled out of this country?

Ben (as Max): I see what you mean.

Richard: So he taught you to be a survivor. And you taught your son how to be a survivor. Good training. Every time Ben relaxes, he's expecting another herd of Cossacks. Ben is scared to relax. Scared to let go of that control. Somehow the Cossacks are going to come riding down.

Shifting back to Max's father helps Max/Ben to experience the current of this belief pattern, flowing down through the generations. It also highlights the nonrealistic quality of the expectations—there are no Cossacks in Max's or Ben's life. Max/Ben is not quite ready to let go of the script belief, however:

Ben (as Max): That's somewhat realistic, though.

Richard: What do you mean, Max?

Ben (as Max): Once in a while you hear something. Some undertone of anti-Semitism.

Rebecca: So the threat is always there.

Ben (as Max): That's really scary.

Richard: But the problem is that the threat is even worse when what's missing is a real close relationship with your father. I think that's what you missed, Max, and I think that's what Ben missed.

When there's so much focus on surviving, what's often missing is a good close relationship with Father.

This is a clear interpretation, in the psychoanalytic sense. Just as in traditional psychodynamic therapy, it is made at a moment when it will be taken in emotionally as well as cognitively. But it is even more impactful here, for it is heard by three ego states: the cathected Parent, Max, and the observing Adult and Child ego states of Ben. Each of these three is affected by that absence of closeness in his own unique way, and each will be uniquely affected by the interpretation.

Ben (as Max): I was scared to get close to him. Because I didn't get close to my boy . . . it's too late now. We had a nice relationship as adults. When he got to be thirty years old, we had a nice relationship. It was good. We didn't see each other a lot, we weren't that close. But we respected each other.

Rebecca: What are you feeling now, Max? Will you tell us about that?

Ben (as Max): I feel sad that I never got close to him. (*pause*) I feel sad that he had to go through what I had to go through, as a kid. I did the best I could.

Richard: I imagine you spend most of the time denying that sadness, Max.

Ben (as Max): I never should have mentioned it. I'm considered a very happy guy.

The new behavior, the new openness, is uncomfortable to Max/Ben, and he starts to close up, to put his "happy guy" mask back on. Rather than go back to the old facade, he needs to stay with what has been happening in order for it really to penetrate those tough, well-established defenses. Richard brings him back to the unfinished business:

Richard: You were missing something you needed: a real, loving, contactful relationship with Dad. You passed that right on to your own boy.

Ben (as Max): I think he pushed me away.

Richard: I bet he didn't at first.

Ben (as Max): (*pause*) He pushed me away. I think he really wanted to be close to my wife.

Rebecca: Kids will go where the contact's available. And he still needed you. He needed you there; he needed you to keep reaching out.

Ben (as Max): I gave him everything I could.

Richard: I don't believe that.

Ben (as Max): There was a competition for my wife.

Throughout these last few exchanges, Max/Ben has been hinting at a new element: a kind of resentful blaming of Ben. Is this resentment the poison that tainted the father-son relationship? If so, encouraging Ben and "Max" to be open with each other just increases the toxicity of what Ben takes in. Even though it's time to begin to close the piece of work, this must be checked out.

Rebecca: He take her away from you?

Ben (as Max): Yeah, for a while.

Rebecca: How did he do that?

Ben (as Max): When he was first born, she spent a lot of time with him. Inordinate.

Rebecca: Did you resent that?

Ben (as Max): (*pause*) But after a while it was OK again.

Rebecca: How did you get her back?

Ben (as Max): I don't know. Just did. In fact it was really us against the kids. We had a very tight and a very good marriage. Twenty-nine and a half years. (*begins to cry*)

Richard: Let it come, Max. I won't tell any of the neighbors that you cried.

Ben: Max's not going to cry. He never did.

Ben/Max's last defense is to go away, to decathect, leaving Ben's Adult ego state to talk to the therapists. But Max is not far away, and can be called back.

Richard: (*very softly*) Go ahead and cry, Max. So Ben doesn't have to bear your sorrows. (*pause*) Your wife is very important to you, isn't she, Max? (*he nods*) So sad . . .

Ben (as Max): She took care of me.

Richard: More than just taking care of you, Max.

Ben (as Max): She took care of me, and she pretended that I took care of her. She made me feel strong.

Richard: Ben's birth must have been a real threat to that which you held precious.

Ben (as Max): Well, I wanted, I wanted a son. I wanted a child.

Richard: No, but did you know how much time she'd spend with him? How much you'd be ignored for a period of time? So even though you wanted him, you must have also had some resentment at the same time, huh? He was a real threat to you. Since that woman was so precious.

Resentment and envy of a son, particularly in the Jewish culture, is an unacceptable response (though, out of awareness, it may be quite common). It's important to support and normalize these feelings for Max, so that he will be able to continue his exploration rather than closing up and retreating into denial.

Ben (as Max): Well, the problem was I didn't really have any, it didn't seem like it was my kid. I wanted this kid, and yet she kept him all to herself.

Richard: How was that for you, Max? That she kept your son all to herself?

Ben (as Max): I was angry.

Richard: And then what did you do with that anger, Max?

Ben (as Max): Maybe took it out on the kid. Took it out on Ben . . .

Richard: Is that a question or a statement?

Ben (as Max): Yeah, I was angry with Ben. I was angry cause he couldn't play ball.

Richard: That's the social excuse.

Ben (as Max): I was angry because, because I was jealous.

Richard: Max, I have a good respect for you. That takes a lot of balls to say that.

This is the first clear, genuine statement of Max's deep conflict around his relationship to Ben. Richard reinforces—strokes—the statement. And hidden in the crudity of the language is another message: One can be masculine, and respected by men, and still talk about feelings.

Ben (as Max): Wish I'd done it sooner. (*he weeps*)

Richard: What would you do differently, Max? If you could turn the clock back?

Ben (as Max): I could love my wife, and I could love Ben too.

Richard: So in losing her, you gave up on Ben, huh? Turned against him?

Ben (as Max): I didn't mean to.

Richard: I know. I believe that, Max. I think that underneath that facade you must be very, very decent.

Ben (as Max): I was afraid I was going to lose my wife. Seemed like she was drifting away from me.

Rebecca: Was she your stability?

Ben (as Max): Yeah, she was.

Richard: In that strange neighborhood, she was close. She was one of you. (*pause*) Many, many marriages have been shook up by the birth of the first child. Particularly those marriages that have been very close. And dependent on each other, before . . . Anything else you want to tell us, Max, before we say good-bye for this session?

Both time constraints—Ben has been working for more than an hour—and the therapists' sense that he may have accomplished as much as he can in a single piece of work lead Richard to invite closure at this point. Ben needs some time to be alone, to process, to integrate what he has discovered in himself. Closing will require a delicate touch; the therapists must avoid leaving Ben/Max with a feeling of being criticized or rejected for his new behaviors.

Ben (as Max): I'm finding it very hard to say that I love Ben.

Richard: Well, Max, something's still in your way.

Ben (as Max): I must have loved him; a father's supposed to love him.

Richard: "Must of" and "supposed to" aren't the same as the fact that you were jealous.

Ben (as Max): He was only a little kid!

Richard: And he took your wife away.

Ben (as Max): (*still weeping*) I needed her!

Richard: Yes, you did, Max. In some ways you were like her little kid, weren't you?

Ben (as Max): For fifty years. Forty-nine and a half. I killed myself before fifty. I crossed that street every day for forty years. And one day I just got hit by a car. I didn't want to get old.

Richard: (*pause*) You know, your marriage worked out after all, Max. Even though you were scared by Ben's birth.

Ben: I have a very strong desire to say good-bye to him. I don't want to be him any more.

While part of Ben's shift into his own persona and out of the role of Max may be a response to Richard's invitation to wind up the work, he also seems to be making a genuine choice to deal with his father in a brand-new way, with a new kind of connectedness. Often, the spontaneous return of Adult or Child ego state does signal a closing point in the work of Parent therapy, a point at which the client experiences the need to process, evaluate, and integrate. With his request to say good-bye to Max, Ben closes the Parent interview and readies himself for the next chapter of therapeutic growth.

In these pages, we have seen Ben deal with a whole series of issues. In a real sense, it would be more accurate to say that we have seen Max deal with them. The adult Ben was present in the work only as an onlooker; the real client was Max-as-known-and-experienced-by-Ben. It is unlikely that Ben could have "known" all of the things that he revealed as Max; nor is it particularly important whether those revelations are historically accurate. They are Max as Ben experienced him, in and out of awareness, Max as he influenced and shaped that young boy.

Indeed, Ben in an ordinary state of consciousness would probably not have been able to tell us all of this material. Most of it has been out of Adult awareness, hidden away in his Parent ego state, yet deeply influencing his life as an adult—just as Max, long ago, deeply influenced the growing up of his son.

Working with Ben cannot, of course, change what really went on between that father and that little boy. We cannot go back and redo a relationship of 50 years ago. But we can change the ongoing relationship *within* a client: through healing the Parent ego state, we can block off or open up or make nourishing that which has been punishing or toxic internally. When the restrictive and destructive Parent ego state messages are withdrawn, the Child ego state is then free to make the redecisions it needs; with this accomplished, all of the ego states are available to be integrated into a functioning whole.

5

FRANKIE
The Absent Father

By far the most common occurrence in therapeutic regression work is that a client works through conflicts with one or both parents. We have seen Conrad dealing with his mother in Chapter 2, and Chris preparing for a confrontation and decommissioning a self-created Parent in Chapter 3. In the piece of work presented in this chapter, the client is also dealing with a parent, but it is an *absent* parent who is the focus of the work.

Frankie's father died when Frankie was an infant. His mother, herself highly dependent, was overbearing and abusive of Frankie, using him to deal with her own needs rather than providing him with clear limits and appropriate nurturance. Frankie grew into his teens as an obese, socially isolated adolescent. With no effective male models, he failed to develop an adequate gender identity and experienced himself as nonsexual. In his early twenties, he began intensive psychotherapy, and was able to resolve much of the conflict around his dealings with his mother. At 33, he looks 23: a now slim, quiet, adaptive young man who is beginning to experiment with both homosexual and heterosexual relationships. Father, however, has remained an important though shadowy influence throughout his life.

Early in his developmental history, Frankie created a fantasy father. Much of his life script has been built up around this fantasy father, around his imaginings of what his father was like and how life might have been had his father lived. Unlike Chris's self-created Parent, which was totally created by Chris during childhood and manifested itself years later through a harshly critical and perfection-demanding attitude toward himself (and others), Frankie's father did have a real existence. The fantasy father is an elaboration, a building onto, of what once was—or what, in Frankie's imagination, might have been. As is typical of young children, Frankie first denied that his father was really dead. In adulthood, with this denial shifted underground and out of awareness, Frankie experiences himself as a psychological orphan, needing the support and "specialness" that a child gets from a good and loving parent.

Frankie's work in this segment is of interest not only because it illustrates another facet of the therapeutic treatment of parent-child issues, but also because Frankie can be seen to be dealing with his fantasy father from several distinctly different developmental stages. The shift from one stage to another is abrupt and clearly distinguishable. By following these shifts and responding to Frankie in an age-appropriate way, the therapist is able to help him move past the early denial.

In this piece, as in the work with Chris, Richard is the only therapist. The work begins with a relaxation exercise, in which Frankie is directed to first tighten and then let go of successive muscle groups. This process allows Frankie to access the intense emotion that he has blocked from awareness, literally holding it in by means of muscular tension. As the muscle tension decreases, and the feelings begin to emerge, Richard directs Frankie to cry out his rage and frustration, and to let his body express that rage by pounding and kicking at the mat on which he is working. Frankie kicks, pounds, and thrashes; the wordless cries gradually take shape as a desperate scream of "Help me!"

Frankie: Help me! Help me! Help! I can't breathe! I can't—please!

Richard: You're doing fine . . .

Richard: Help! Help! I can't breathe! I can't breathe! You're squashing me! Help! Ohhh! God, help me! Help me! No—I'm suffocating! I'm suffocating!

In this early stage of the work, both Frankie and Richard expect that Frankie will continue on from a previous segment, in which Frankie dealt with his physically abusive mother. The imagery of being squashed and unable to breathe is certainly consistent with Frankie's old relationship with Mother. To intensify this imagery, Richard has moved over to Frankie and is holding his shoulders against the mat, physically re-creating the held-down, smothering situation that Frankie experienced socially and psychologically during his childhood. In order for him to experience himself as powerful, able to fight back against a suffocating environment, he needs to free himself from being held down. Rather than be helpless and get someone else to rescue him, he needs to know that he can do it for himself, can fight and win his own battles.

Richard: Kick with your feet, you'll do fine . . .

Frankie: No! No! I'm suffocating! I'm suffocating!

Richard: Frankie, you're just reliving that old experience. So stay in it, feel the suffocation; push.

Frankie: I'm suffocating! I can't straighten up! Ohh! My chest! Ohh! I can't! Get up, get up, get up! Get away! Get up! Get up! (*he continues to struggle ineffectually, demanding to be rescued*) Don't you understand you're killing me? I can't go on. Ohh! Let me go! Let me die! I just can't fight any more!

Richard: Listen to that little boy's decision.

Frankie: Let me die! I can't fight you! Ohh!

Richard: Don't give up, Frankie.

Frankie: I can't! You're much bigger than me. You're so much bigger . . .

Richard: Tell her how you died.

Frankie: I'm dying inside. I don't want to live no more. I can't take . . . I can't . . . God, let me go! Out! Out! God, help me! PLEASE take me!

Richard's use of the word "her" acknowledges that Frankie is still dealing with Mother. The work is, in a sense, a recap of work he has done before, in which he struggles with Mother but finds her too big and too strong to overcome. Not wanting to continue trampling in an already well-muddied field, Richard decides to invite an abrupt switch:

Richard: Try something. Talk to your daddy.

Frankie: Dad—Dad, I know you're . . . Dad, help me! Please, Dad . . .

Richard: Call the daddy that wasn't there.

Frankie: Oh, God . . . Dad! Dad, she's killing me! Oh, God! Dad! Dad!

Richard: If you were alive . . .

Frankie: Dad! If you had lived, I wouldn't be in this mess. Dad! Why? Why? Why did you do this? Dad! Dad! Daddy!

Richard: Tell him what this little boy needs.

Frankie: Daddy! I need some love. Dad! Dad, I need you to hold me! Please! Please!

Richard: Tell him what to do with her.

Remember, Richard is still holding Frankie's shoulders down on the mat as all this conversation is going on, and Frankie is still struggling (though not with much energy) to escape. Although he seems unable to summon the resources he needs to fight effectively against that which holds him down, he may be able to call upon the imagined resources of his father for the strength he can't find in himself. As he tells Dad about the love he needs, however, Frankie begins to collapse even further; the work threatens to reinforce his self-perception of helpless weakness. Richard moves to block the collapse by focusing Frankie's attention on what Dad must do to counter Mother's stranglehold.

Richard: Tell him what to do with her.

Frankie: Get her off my back. Get her off my back! My back! Ohh, God! My back is breaking! Dad! Dad!

Richard: Get up!

Frankie: Dad! Hear me! Don't let me die! Daddy! Daddy! She's killing me! She's killing me! Daaaad! Dad! I'm dying! Dad!

Richard: And without you . . .

Frankie: Without you I'll never make it. I'll never be a man. I'll never be a man! Dad, I'll never be a man! I'll always be little! Dad! Dad! She won't make me a man! Dad! Dad!

Richard: Listen to that decision.

Frankie: Dad!

Richard: Without you . . .

Frankie: I want you. To help . . . Dad, she's suffocating me.

Apparently, Frankie is not yet ready to win the struggle with his therapist/mother. He has, however, identified an important new fragment of script: Frankie cannot be a man unless Dad is there for him. Richard decides to abandon temporarily his attempts to get Frankie to empower himself, and to deal directly with the script decision. He moves away from Frankie, who remains huddled on the mat. The work continues:

Richard: Say that, "I want you to help."

Frankie: Dad! I want your help! Dad! Dad! Where are you?

Richard: Tell him where he's not.

Frankie: Dad! You gotta be here! You gotta be here, Dad!

Richard: Cause without you . . .

Frankie: Dad, without you I'm dying! I can't go on! Dad! I need support! Dad! Dad! Dad! Why won't you come? Dad, why won't you come?

Richard: Frankie, make that a statement.

Notice that Frankie's demands to "get her off my back" and to keep him from being suffocated have now changed to a plea for support. Even though he is no longer being held down by Richard, he is unable to pick himself up, and cries to be rescued. Changing his question into a statement will not only provide Richard with information about his belief system, but will also be a shift in the direction of self-assertion and control. At first, Frankie resists making the shift:

Frankie: Why don't you come? Dad, please come!

Richard: You don't come because . . .

Frankie: Dad! Dad, you don't come because you're frightened of her. You're frightened of her! She killed you, I know! You're frightened of her, you chicken! Chicken! Chicken!

At last, some power! Frankie moves out of helplessness as he expresses his anger at Dad.

Richard: And if I'm a man like you . . .

Frankie: Chicken! No, I'm not gonna be like you! You died! You died! Dad! Dad! Don't let her kill me! (*he has relapsed into his earlier helplessness, and continues to beg Dad for help*)

Richard: Cause if you don't help . . .

Frankie: If you don't help, I just can't make it.

Richard: Tell him about when you were in high school, if you'd had a daddy, what it would have been like.

Frankie moved briefly out of his helplessness, but was unable to sustain the shift. Focusing on high school will access an older Child ego state, one that has more available resources, and thus may be better able to support himself and deal with Mother.

Frankie: I wouldn't have been 200 pounds.

Richard: Yeah, say that to him again.

Frankie: If you'd been alive, you would have been able to straighten up this mess.

Richard: Cause what you would have told me . . .

Frankie: He would have told me it was HIS fault and not mine. You would have told me what young kids don't know about that. You would have told me what I needed to know. So I wouldn't be feeling bad all this time. You and Mom could have talked about it. Would have told me I wasn't so bad. And I might have been living all those years . . . Stead of stuffing . . . The way every good Catholic should. Where are you now, Dad?

Frankie threatens to slide back into helplessness, and Richard counters.

Richard: Make that a statement, Frankie.

Frankie: Wherever you are now, Dad, I'm gonna live. I'm living, Dad! I'm living! Found some good people, Dad. I'm living. I ain't copping out like you did, Dad. You died to avoid all this. You died to avoid all this pain in life. But not me. I'm grown up, and I can take it. I'm not folding up the way you did. AIN'T PACKING IT IN, DAD! Staying right here.

There's a lot of energy in this long statement. The affective component of script change is clearly present. Cognition, behavior, and intent—the understanding and will actually to make observable changes—are less obvious. Richard begins to probe for them.

Richard: Tell him what life would be like if he had been alive.

Frankie: Well, I wouldn't have got the shit beat out of me, that's for sure. I wouldn't have to walk around scared to death. I wouldn't have had to get beat with a strap. I wouldn't of got welts on my body.

Richard: Cause what you'd of done, Dad . . .

Frankie: Cause you would have stopped it, Dad. She went nuts. She was nuts. The woman was crazy, Dad. The only thing she knew was a good beating.

Richard: Tell Dad what you decided about women during that early time.

Frankie: Oooh. They're all screwed up, Dad. All nuts. All out to hurt men. All out to get me. All going to screw me up, somehow.

Richard: So what I'll do is . . .

Frankie: I'll avoid them. I'll stay away from them. I'll like men.

Here is the adolescent script decision, the decision to act out his pain at Dad's absence and Mother's abuse by being homosexual. Richard underlines it:

Richard: Say that again.

Frankie: I'll avoid women and I'll like men.

Richard: Tell him what you'd like most of all, with him.

The phrase "with him" brings Frankie back to the original unmet need—the fixed gestalt, which his homosexual experimentation could never fully satisfy.

Frankie: I want your love, so bad.

Richard: And if I can't get yours . . .

Frankie: If I can't get yours, I'll just go out and look for some other man. Just did. How was I supposed to know? I just wanted a body. To make things right.

Richard pauses here to allow Frankie to hear and digest what he has said. Frankie begins to sob.

Richard: Would your dad have made things right? Put your dad right there and talk to him. Do that now, and say that. I need a daddy . . .

Frankie: I need (*he is sobbing too hard to talk*) . . .

Richard: Keep going, Frankie. Look at that face. Say it again, only louder.

Frankie: Needed you, and I kept trying to take care of it—

Richard: Come on, Frankie, look at your dad . . .

Frankie: To tell me what to do . . .

Richard: Tell him what it would be like if he'd been around when you were a baby.

Frankie: Well, the first thing, Dad, is I wouldn't have gotten given away early. Had to go live with somebody . . . and I woulda had my own parents.

Richard: Yeah. If you'd come home to me every night after work . . .

Frankie: You woulda come home and held me. I wouldn't have had to go out and get some other men to hold me. Dad, there just wouldn't have been this mess.

Richard: Tell him how you've been looking for him all this time. Inside and outside.

From Frankie's return to the theme of finding men who could substitute for Dad, Richard hypothesizes that Frankie has been very invested in the search for a father. From early childhood, Frankie had no adult male in his life from whom he could receive love and support. He had no opportunity to internalize these qualities as a part of his masculine identity, and so the searching (and not finding) was internal as well as external.

Frankie: It's been a long time. Hoping, at night . . . it's ridiculous, I'm looking for you. Some stupid fantasy that you were going to appear. You were still living! Oh, God, how could I! I still hoped that you were living! I wasn't even . . . Ohhh! I was nuts!

Richard: You're not nuts.

Frankie: Thirty-three years of thinking he's gonna come back.

Richard: That's real normal if you haven't grieved.

Frankie: (*crying*) Thirty-three years! I thought you were gonna walk down the steps some day! I watched the steps all the time! I must be nuts.

Richard: No, you're not nuts, Frankie.

Frankie: I watch the steps!

Richard: Instead of saying "I'm nuts," say "I'm wanting."

Frankie, in his recollecting of how he used to watch the steps for Dad, is already beginning to slip back to an earlier ego state. Richard's instruction to say "I'm wanting" instead of the more adolescent "I'm nuts" precipitates another regression, and suddenly we are listening to a five- or six-year-old boy.

Frankie: Ahhhh, I want you!

Richard: Yeah, say that again.

Frankie: I want you to come down the steps!

Richard: I WANT you, Dad . . .

Frankie: Ohhhh! I want you come down the steps!

Richard: Cause if you don't . . .

Frankie: I don't know . . . COME DOWN THE STEPS CAUSE IF YOU DON'T I'LL . . . Ohhh . . .

Richard: Yeah, say that: "If you don't, I'm gonna . . ."

Frankie: I'm so confused! I'm gonna have to face that you're dead.

At this level, Frankie has not experienced or accepted his father's death. The little boy denied it, and created a fantasy of Father who was gone but might return at any time. Having denied the reality of Father's being dead, Frankie did not complete his grieving. The loss is still an open wound, crusted over in the present but still bleeding in the past. Here, regressed to that early denial stage, Frankie begins to face the truth.

Richard: Say that again.

Frankie: (*shouting angrily*) If you don't come down those steps I'm gonna have to face that you're dead!

Richard: And if I do that . . .

Frankie: I'll . . . I'll have to let go of this fantasy that you're coming back. (*he shouts again*) Dad, come down those steps! Get down! Get down those steps! Get down! Dad! Dad, get down those steps! (*he continues to demand that Dad respond; he sounds like a thwarted child having a temper tantrum*)

Richard: I won't recognize that you're dead, Dad.

Frankie: Oh, NO! NO! You're not dead! Come down those steps! Come-down-those-steps! You are not dead! You are not dead! Come-down-those-steps!

Richard: If I admit you're dead . . .

Frankie: No! No! No! No! Come-down-those-steps! Down! Down! Down those steps!

Richard: Cause if I admit you're dead . . .

Frankie continues to shout "No" and demand that Dad "come down those steps." He is deeply regressed, and using the tantrum behavior of a child to maintain the denial. Believing that Dad would someday return was, at that early age, his way of surviving an intolerable situation; needing to hang on to the denial, he has been unable to move on, to grow past this age emotionally. He must break through, somehow, but alone he simply hasn't the strength to do so. Richard shifts tactics here, pulling Frankie out of the fruitless struggle with a dad who will never answer, and making contact himself as a nurturing, caring adult who nevertheless insists that Frankie accept what is real.

Richard: Frankie, your daddy's dead.

Frankie: No! No! No! Nooooo!

Richard: He was just a young man, but he died.

Frankie: No! He's too young to die!

Richard: Yes, that's true.

Frankie: No! No, he's not dead. Ohhh, he's too young to die! (*he begins to sob*) He's not, he was too young!

Richard: Say, "I'm too young for him to die."

Frankie begins to break through his denial and experience the pain of losing Dad; Richard now will help him to stay with the grief work, countering Frankie's repeated attempts to slide back into denial.

Frankie: I'm too young for him to die! Noooo! (*crying*)

Richard: Say, "I'm too young."

Frankie: Dad, I'm too young for you to die . . . Ohhh! Look at me! Dad, look at me! Ohh, Daddy, look at me! Ohhh! Ohhh! Daddy, look at me!

Richard: He's dead, Frankie.

Frankie: Let him look at me! Ohh, Daddy, look at me!

Richard: They buried him in the cemetery.

Frankie: No, don't let them do that! Ohhh, I see it coming down! Ohhh!

Richard: Your mama already lit candles in the church.

Frankie: (*sobbing hard*) Daddy's dead! Ohhh! In the ground. I'll never get a chance to see him!

Richard: Tell him what you wanted, Frankie.

Frankie: (*more quietly*) See me. Just see me.

Richard: Repeat that.

Frankie: See me, just see me.

Richard: Tell him what else. Bet there's more than "just." "See me and . . .

Frankie: Be with me.

Richard: And . . .

Frankie: Be with me and love me. So impossible. Useless! (*he begins to pound the mat with his fist, harder and harder*)

As Frankie lets go of the little boy's denial, he experiences the true extent of his loss, and what he really wanted from the father he never had. His body relaxes; his "be with me" has a ring of authenticity that was absent from the tantrumlike screaming. And as he relaxes, another shift occurs: like peeling an onion, he moves to a yet earlier, younger stage. His face changes, his posture changes; he's angry again but it's a toddler's weak, frustrated anger now. His head moves up and down, jerkily, as though he were butting his head against something.

Richard: Try banging your head, Frankie. Bang your head. Say "useless." Try it, bang your head and say "useless."

Richard, aware of the shift, suggests a physical movement that will emphasize the age-typical behavior of a three-year-old. We don't yet know the significance of useless, *but by acting out the very early frustration, and repeating the word, Frankie will find his own meaning.*

Frankie: (*bangs his head on the mat, repeating the word* useless *several times*) You don't get up; you don't get up; you never get up; you get up, you—get—up!

Richard: Doesn't help to bang your head, does it? Or to beat your fists.

Frankie: No, it doesn't, it doesn't, it doesn't, it doesn't, cause he just doesn't get up. He just doesn't get up! He doesn't get up!

Richard: Do that with your head again.

Frankie: (*banging his head*) It's useless, useless, useless, useless, useless, useless. Useless!

Richard: For a three-year-old, having a temper tantrum doesn't change things, but it feels so good.

Frankie: Useless! Useless! I'm not, you are! You're useless, not me!

Richard: Not useless, Frankie. He's dead.

Here we are again, dealing with denial. While the six-year-old Frankie may have accepted Dad's death, the three-year-old hasn't. It's easier to be angry with a "useless" father than to mourn a dead one. And again, the denial must be overcome, the grief experienced, before Frankie can move on emotionally.

Richard: Not useless, Frankie. He's dead.
Frankie: But he doesn't do anything!
Richard: He's dead.
Frankie: He doesn't do anything! So what!
Richard: He would have.
Frankie: If he would just get up.
Richard: He can't, he's dead.
Frankie: If he just would get up!
Richard: He's dead, Frankie.
Frankie: He just won't get up.
Richard: His spirit's gone.
Frankie: No, he just doesn't want to get up. Get up, get up, get up!
Richard: Why doesn't he want to get up, Frankie?
Frankie: Get up! Getupgetupgetup!
Richard: Why doesn't he want to get up, little boy?
Frankie: Don't know.
Richard: Well, take a guess. You just said he wasn't dead . . .
Frankie: (*sulkily*) He's not.
Richard: Just being stubborn. Why?
Frankie: Doesn't want to look at me.
Richard: Why?
Frankie: Cause.
Richard: What'd you do?
Frankie: I don't know. Didn't do nuthin.
Richard: Didn't do nuthin?
Frankie: No. I was just born.
Richard: You didn't do nuthin?
Frankie: No, I was just born, that's all.
Richard: Oh. Then why doesn't he want to get up and help?
Frankie: I don't know, he's useless!
Richard: He's just dead.

Patiently staying with the process, making contact with an angrily sad little boy, talking and repeating and listening over and over again—this is an excellent example of work with a deeply regressed client. An adult would not talk as Frankie is doing here, nor would an adult tolerate being talked to as Richard is doing.

Frankie is psychologically only a few years old at this point, and the therapy is child therapy. And, working just as he would with someone who was chronologically quite young, Richard now introduces a new idea:

Richard: Did Mama say Daddy was useless?

Frankie: (*pause*) I don't know.

Richard: Did Mama say he's no good and useless?

Frankie: No, she said he was wonderful.

Dad's "uselessness" might have been introjected from Mother's comments about him; this hypothesis needed to be tested. But Frankie says no; Mother said that Dad was wonderful. Was the "useless" notion, then, the child's own decision, his way of making sense out of Dad's absence?

Richard: What do you say he is?

Frankie: Useless.

Richard: Wasn't wonderful to you, was he?

Frankie: No.

Richard: Why not?

Frankie: He went away.

Richard: Yukky thing to do.

Frankie: Sure was.

Richard: So if he went away, either he's gotta be bad or you gotta be bad.

Frankie: Not me. Him.

The three-year-old child lives in a world of either/or. There are few shades of gray; discriminations are crude and categories are limited. Something bad has happened, therefore, someone bad made it happen. The logic of the child forces a choice: either he's bad, or I'm bad. Richard is preparing to offer a third possibility, one that will break the impasse; again, he does so in language that a very young child can understand.

Richard: Frankie?

Frankie: What?

Richard: God wanted him.

Frankie: I wanted him! (*bursts into tears*) I wanted him! Who's God, anyway? It was my right, not his!

Frankie's denial gives a little. He has worked hard, and is obviously tiring; the session needs to begin to wind down.

Richard now begins to search for a way to end the piece without closing Frankie off from the emotional impact of what he has accomplished, and also to provide him with a new cognitive frame of reference within which he can integrate the affective work.

Richard: You're correct. It was your right to have a daddy.

Frankie: It was my right!

Richard: And for some reason, it wasn't supposed to happen. Maybe there's something very important for you to learn about being a man in this world. All by yourself.

Frankie: (*sulky again*) That's just tough.

Richard: Sure is. What do you think of that? Having to learn to be a man all by yourself, without the help of a daddy?

Notice how the question points Frankie back toward being an adult, while still addressing the little boy. In his next four short responses, Frankie literally grows up before our eyes.

Frankie: It's awful. Didn't have all the information, so I had to figure it out.

Richard: Well, how've you done? Did you pass the test?

Frankie: Think so.

Richard: What if I told you there was this big master plan, that called for your father to stay alive for one purpose only. And that was so he could give you his genes. And then his purpose was finished. And the real purpose is what you do with those genes.

Frankie: Oh, that's hard to take.

Richard: What about that, Frankie? If there was some master plan, whose purpose was to sire you? To give you life? To give you the genes that you have. And then he was finished with his purpose for living. And part of your task is to see what kind of a man you will become without a biological father in the house.

Frankie: It's a hell of a trip.

Richard: Yeah. Thirty-three-year trip.

Frankie: Whew.

Richard: What have you learned along the way?

Frankie: Well, I didn't do that bad.

Richard: No, I don't think so! For a while I had my doubts, but I don't think so any more.

Frankie: Thanks to you.

Richard: And I can't be your dad. I can be your therapist, help you learn how to be a good professional; I can even be your friend. (*pause*) And you miss *him*.

Frankie: Very much. Every day. Every damn day.

As the work ended, Frankie was experiencing his loss in an adult-appropriate, here-and-now way. He was sad, and he missed his father. There was an almost surprised quality to his last remark, lending support to the idea that he had not consciously realized, until now, just how much he had been missing his father, or how large a part that missing Dad had played in his life as an adult. He had more grieving to do—indeed, for several days after this at the workshop he appeared sad—but the grieving did not have the stuck, sulky, going nowhere quality that had been his trademark.

One of the things that made this piece of work possible is Richard's sensitivity to the emotional age level—the developmental stage of the cathected ego state—of the client at each stage of the work. Not only did the quality of Frankie's responses change, but Richard's interventions changed too. As Frankie grew younger, Richard's comments and questions grew shorter and grammatically simpler, and the vocabulary more restricted. Responding to Frankie in an age-appropriate way allowed him to maintain the regression, just as shifting to a more adult way of speaking, at the end of the work, helped him to recathect his Adult ego state.

One last word needs to be said about the pace of the work. Books of theory, articles in which therapists talk about their work, seldom capture the endless repetition, the retracing of a path again and again, which is so necessary when working with a deeply regressed person. We have chosen to present entire pieces of work verbatim, so that the reader can experience the slowness, the patience, the way in which the therapist needs to sit down and simply "be" with a client as he works away at an early issue. To move faster might give the illusion of progress, but it would be only illusion; there is no substitute for time and patience if the work is to be done well.

6

ROBERT
Challenging a Cultural Script

In dealing with introjected script material, we typically work with a personification of one or both of the client's actual parents. Occasionally, though, an introjected ego state had its origins not with the actual parents, but with some other person or people. Other family members (older siblings, grandparents, aunts and uncles), neighbors, teachers, clergy—all can be sources of introjection. Whether the scripting comes from an actual parent, or from some other influential individual, working with this kind of introject tends to follow the same general procedure.

There is another kind of Parent ego state content, though, that is not introjected from a single person. Cultural scripting consists of introjected thoughts, feelings, attitudes, and behaviors that are taken in from a multitude of sources. Cultural scripting often determines the kind of music we enjoy, the foods we refuse to eat, our attitudes toward people of different races or religions. This sort of scripting is not always a negative influence: a fondness for Beethoven, or spoon bread, or a sense of comfort derived from the sound of ocean waves crashing on the beach can be sources of great pleasure. It is when these attitudes and expectations limit our options and interrupt our ability to be flexible and creative that they may become a focus of therapy.

Robert, the client whose work is presented in this chapter, is dealing with a cultural script. Robert is gay, and at a neopsychic ego level has adapted his sexual orientation quite comfortably into his ongoing personality and sense of self. He also, however, experiences some negative attitudes toward homosexuality, attitudes that cause him discomfort. There is no single person who can be pinpointed as the source of these attitudes; they were acquired from a variety of sources. In the work presented here, Robert begins with the image of a specific person from his past. Soon, however, the image begins to take on a symbolic, generalized quality. "Lance," the young man whom Robert role-plays, becomes a screen for the attitudes and values prevalent throughout Robert's social milieu. Robert creates a symbolic source, a composite of the many people whose behaviors contributed to his internalized rejection of his gay orientation. It is this symbolic, constructed Parent fragment that Robert confronts at the conclusion of the therapeutic session.

Robert begins his session by describing his reactions to a piece of work done the day before by another member of the group.

Robert: Jerry's work made me aware of some things that I hadn't thought of for quite a while. And that is, at home, in San Francisco, I'm quite comfortable with being gay. I'm "out" to my family, my friends, at work. It's not something that I think of, hardly at all. It's just not an issue. And when Jerry said something like, "I've been going through a lot of changes," what I immediately thought to myself was, "Boy, there's a euphemism for somebody who's 'coming out.'" I was almost sure of it. And then I started getting uptight about that, and—

Rebecca: About what?

Robert: Because it wasn't, because he wasn't being open about it. And then he said "sexual orientation." And, not "gay." And, again like he wasn't being open about it. And I started getting more and more uptight. And felt like I wanted to hide, and didn't want anybody to notice me; I felt really uncomfortable. Sort of squirmy. And I was just . . . I was really interested in that, because that is not something that's happened for a long time . . . So I started thinking about it afterwards. And what I realized was that it was exactly like I was being the target. Like I was being this taboo topic. It was just like, "I'm a taboo subject, and I want to hide, and I don't want to be seen." And I thought, wow! And that is really familiar, it was so natural . . . What I realized was that, I think I've always done that. I think probably most gay people do that. Like when you become an adolescent, there's no one around to identify with. There's no role models, at all. And so there's nothing to identify with, to take in. And it's like you identify with a concept, which is totally negative. Like you hear nothing, it's just totally bad news, it's a taboo . . .

Robert is quite articulate about his feelings; he has obviously done a lot of thinking about what is going on for him internally. He recognizes the discomfort as Adult ego-dystonic: the sense of not-OK-ness that he feels doesn't fit with his overall beliefs and attitudes, but it is nevertheless real and lasting. He identifies it as coming from the absence of a positive model. The negative introject is fuzzier for him; he alludes to the "taboo subject," the feeling of "wanting to hide," but at this point is less clear about having taken in those values from an external source.

The therapists' first concern is to help Robert to connect more solidly with his own emotional response. By externalizing and intellectualizing, Robert protects himself from the pain of his internal conflict. While this can be a useful technique to provide clear thinking and problem solving, it is less useful in therapeutic work. The Parent ego state, and the Child ego state's response to cultural or peer group messages, are usually not clear and logical, nor can they be detached from feelings.

Richard: Will you say these things in the first person, and see if they make a different impact? Your statements are "you, you, you" which is a pushing outside of experience by generalizing. See what happens if you take it, say "I" and make it a statement of your own experience.

Robert: OK. I wasn't aware I was doing that. All the time I was saying "you"? Hmm. OK.

Richard: It's partly a disowning process. Part of it may be general publicly learned speaking. That's what I'm asking you to experiment with, saying it in "I." Go back to the adolescent stuff.

Robert: OK. So, I didn't have any role models, and so what I did is, I identified with a concept, which was really negative. I took on an uncomfortableness that is a societal thing. And I'm sort of excited about that, because I realize it's like a parental introject, that isn't me. Like, I really got a sense when I thought about it, of "I feel comfortable, Robert feels comfortable, but I've taken on an uncomfortableness that belongs to a lot of other people, like other adolescents. And, like what I want to do is to get rid of that. I want to realize that I'm comfortable, and I'm not going to take on other people's . . .

Here is a fine demonstration of the way in which understanding, intellectual knowing about, does not resolve a script issue. Robert is an intelligent, psychologically sophisticated man, a competent therapist in his own right. He understands the theoretical basis of introjects, and has correctly diagnosed his issue. Yet, even though he understands what is going on, his emotional response remains unchanged. If therapy is to be effective, he must somehow break past the cognitive and into the affective domain.

Rebecca: Notice what you're feeling. Just be aware of your emotions.

Robert: I feel worked up.

Rebecca: Your eyes started suddenly to fill with tears.

Robert: I don't feel sad. I, I feel energized.

Richard: I have an idea about doing an experiment. Would you like to do it?

Robert: Well, tell me what it is first.

Robert translates his specific feelings into a general "worked up," which again serves to defend him from truly experiencing them. Richard recognizes that Robert can probably intellectualize his way through a whole piece of work if he is allowed to continue "talking about," and so suggests an "experiment," and Robert immediately asks for information that will allow him to structure it cognitively ahead of time. Notice the respectful way in which Richard refuses to give this information:

Richard: I'd rather take you into it. I just want your permission to do the experiment. If I tell you what it is, I think I'll ruin it.

Robert: OK. Is it a long one?

Richard: I don't know. I have no idea.

Robert: All right.

Richard begins the process of helping Robert to access the visual, auditory, kinesthetic, and olfactory cues that will help him cathect his adolescent ego state. Notice the leisurely, matter-of-fact style that is used: Robert is allowed to proceed at a pace that is comfortable and safe for him.

Richard: Just close your eyes. Go back to the home town you lived in as an adolescent. (*pause*) And go to your high school. (*pause*) Walk the corridors; perhaps there's a favorite teacher whose face comes to mind. And I want you to think of one of the guys in that high school who's Mr. Outstanding. Either a football hero, basketball hero, perhaps the class president. Somebody who really represented the spirit of that school. When you do, I want you to tell me his name. (*pause*) Got his name? Or a face?

Robert: No, I don't yet. I'm there in the school, but I'm having difficulty remembering. I can remember my close friends, but I can't remember sort of outside that circle.

Richard: He'd be the kind of person that'd have more photographs in the yearbook than anybody. And would really represent the spirit of the school. (*pause*) If you don't find him, who among those close friends was really the psychological leader? Who set the tone of what you were going to do?

The actual identity of the person Robert chooses is relatively unimportant. Because of the way Robert has "primed himself" for the work, he is very likely to choose someone who exemplifies the nonacceptance that he's been talking about, or who is important in some other way in the context of that nonacceptance. In either event, his choice will not be random or accidental. Richard trusts Robert's out-of-awareness processes to find or create an appropriate symbolic figure for the work he needs to do.

Robert: (*pause*) That's hard to say. Like we all did, in different ways.

Richard: Go back to Mr. Big Shot on Campus. Might be a composite image.

Robert: It's really funny that I can't . . . (*pause*) cause I didn't place a high value on athletics, particularly. So I can't even remember who, who was involved with it. OK. Yeah, OK, yeah, yeah, I got somebody now.

Richard: What's his name?

Robert: Lance.

Richard: (*pause*) Well, Lance, I want to talk to you as the representative of the school. Of the outstanding person who represents the norms. Lance, we've invited you here today to represent your high school. To make sure that you keep your high school's standards at all times. I know that there are things that get bent a little bit at parties, but I'm talking about the moral standards of the school. And I know that you're probably the best one to do it. Right, Lance?

Robert (as Lance): Uh-hm.

Richard: I want you to tell me what you think the standards are, or what they should be.

Robert (as Lance): Hmm. Well, you mean, for the men or for the women?

Richard: Well, both, they interact.

Robert (as Lance): OK. Well, the men should be involved in sports, should like sports. The women should—

Richard: Is there a sport that's better to like than any others?

In this piece of work, there was less of a formal "induction" process than usual to make contact with the introjected figure. In part, the induction process had occurred during Robert's mental search for Lance; in part, the induction is a two-way process carried out through the initial interaction between therapist and this created figure. Richard and Lance/Robert continue to chat for several more minutes about sports, before coming back to the introductory theme; we pick up the work again as Richard says:

Richard: I want to know about being the high school hero. What are the kinds of things you have to do to be a hero?

Robert (as Lance): I don't know, I never really thought about it.

Richard: Mean it comes so easy to you?

Robert (as Lance): Yeah, kind of, right. Right. Yeah.

Richard: Well, how do you make it with the teachers when you're a hero?

Robert (as Lance): Well, I mean, I'm kind of friendly, easy to get along with. I'm not a great student, but, I'm just an average student.

Richard: Well, you don't have to be if you're a hero, do you? How are you in with the other students? All the boys and girls in this high school?

Robert (as Lance): Oh, they like me. Yeah, they, um, think that I'm a pretty good guy.

Richard: What is the moral standard of the student body? Describe that to me?

Robert (as Lance): Moral standard . . .

Richard: Yeah. Since you're the representative and represent this moral standard, I'd like to know about it.

Robert (as Lance): Right. Well, you kinda, you don't look at anything in depth at all. I mean, you just, you're kind of shallow and you, um, just accept things for the way they are, and you don't think about things much. You just sort of . . .

Rebecca: Have a good time.

In his response to Richard's question about moral standards, Lance/Robert shows signs of sliding too far into Robert's own adolescent disdain for the Lances of this world. While Robert may eventually need to reject Lance's opinions, feelings, and attitudes, it is important at this point to keep Lance around; thus Rebecca reframes Lance/Robert's response into a less disparaging one, one that would be more in line with how Lance himself might have described the "rules" for getting along in high school. The maneuver is successful, in that Lance/Robert's next response is more relaxed and in keeping with Lance's, rather than Robert's, typical style.

Robert (as Lance): Yeah, and you, you know, you take on the values of the community. So guys are supposed to drink a bit before they go to dances on Friday night, but not get really boozed, just . . .

Richard: A little beer, a little whiskey . . .

Robert (as Lance): Yeah, that kind of thing, right.

Richard: You guys into smoking dope in those days, or . . .

Robert (as Lance): No.

Richard: Just drinking, huh?

Robert (as Lance): Just drinking.

Richard: More manly?

Robert (as Lance): Yeah, right. So, let's see, what else. Moral values, umm . . .

Richard: What'd you do at the parties?

Robert (as Lance): Oh, you know, try to make it with the girls. Feel them up. I mean, there's not many that'll put out, so you gotta just, you know, be content with, uh, you know, trying to feel them up necking. And bragging about it to the other guys.

Richard: What do you mean, bragging about it?

Robert (as Lance): Well, I mean, sometimes you exaggerate.

Richard: Little tit becomes a whole screw?

Robert (as Lance): Yeah, right. You got it.

Richard has established his credentials with Lance/Robert—he's an OK guy, who understands this kind of talk. It's interesting how quickly the conversation has turned to sexual matters. This may be in part simply a function of a general adolescent preoccupation with sex; it may also reflect Robert's need and willingness to deal with his own sexuality at this age. At any rate, Richard knows there will be no problem introducing the subject. He chooses not to pursue it at this point, but to go back to the question of general behavioral norms.

Richard: What else about being a good American citizen in your high school?

Robert (as Lance): Well, let's see. Oh, you probably shouldn't really excel at school. Not, not be real brainy. That's kinda, that's not really masculine.

Far from having trouble introducing the topic of sexuality, we seem to be unable to avoid it. Because Lance/Robert comes right back to it, we may assume that it's foreground for him—this is where his energy is focused. The invitation is clear, and Richard accepts:

Richard: Masculine, huh.

Robert (as Lance): Yup.

Richard: What's masculine?

Robert (as Lance): Well, it's more towards the, um, average. It's sort of like the outstanding average.

Richard: Um-hm. The outstanding average is masculine. So if somebody is ordinary or not so outstanding, or not sporty, what are they?

Robert (as Lance): Uh, let's see . . .

Richard: Are they sissies?

Robert (as Lance): Um, I suppose, I suppose so.

Richard: What do you think of Robert?

Robert (as Lance): Oh, he's a, he's a nice guy. He's friendly, um, he's easy to get along with. Um, I don't know a lot about him.

Lance/Robert is not ready to address the "sissy" issue specifically with relation to Robert, but backs off into socially acceptable generalities. He has indicated, though, that he's willing to get into possibly uncomfortable areas, and so can tolerate some gentle pushing.

Richard: You certainly see him.

Robert (as Lance): Um-hm.

Richard: What do you think of when you see him walking down the hall?

Robert (as Lance): Oh, I don't think I think anything.

Richard: Why not?

By refusing to accept Lance/Robert's unspoken assumptions that his own kind of thinking or feeling or behaving is so natural that there's nothing to say about it, Richard forces him to examine what he has always taken for granted. Immediately, we discover an adolescent homophobia: Above all, Lance/Robert must avoid anything that might hint at homosexual interests. His voice rises, and his manner is decidedly agitated.

Robert (as Lance): Well, Christ, I mean, why would I? I mean, I look at the girls.

Richard: Why would you not look at Robert?

Robert (as Lance): Well, I, I don't have any interest in looking at guys, paying attention to the guys.

Richard: Why not?

Robert (as Lance): Well, I mean, that's just weird. I mean, you know . . .

Richard: What do you mean, weird?

Robert (as Lance): Well, it's just, I, I can't understand why would anybody want to look at a guy? Or pay any attention to him?

Richard: He's a human being.

Robert (as Lance): Yeah, but I'm interested in the female human beings.

Richard: Why?

Richard is being deliberately obtuse here, deliberately refusing to understand what Lance/Robert means and thus forcing him to spell out his prejudice plainly and unmistakably. As the exchange continues, Lance/Robert becomes more and more agitated.

Robert (as Lance): Well, cause that, that's the way it is. I mean, that's what you're s'posed to be. You know, not queer or anything.

Richard: What?

Robert (as Lance): I'm not queer or anything.

Richard: What does that mean?

Robert (as Lance): Well, I don't, I don't know. I mean, God, that's something you don't talk about.

Richard: Why not?

Robert (as Lance): Well, cause it's a, I don't . . .

Richard: Sure getting uncomfortable, Lance.

Robert (as Lance): You just don't talk about that. I mean, it's revolting, disgusting.

Richard: What's disgusting about you talking about the fact that I asked you if you recognized Robert in the hall?

Robert (as Lance): (*pause*) I don't know, it just is.

Richard: Suddenly you're worried about being queer.

Robert (as Lance): Well, yeah, I mean, if I'm going around noticing guys, then that seems . . .

Richard: I didn't ask you to crotch-watch.

Richard capitalizes on Lance/Robert's discomfort to confuse and agitate him further. Robert's intellectualizing defense has been quite thoroughly dissolved by this time; he is experiencing the world through the acutely uncomfortable eyes of a self-confident high school athlete whose values are being strongly challenged. Keeping Lance/Robert off balance here allows us to probe more deeply into those unaware values, and into the fears and concerns that even Lance has experienced, but that he is so careful not to acknowledge.

Robert (as Lance): Yeah, I know. But I mean . . .

Richard: I was thinking mostly of his face.

Robert (as Lance): Hm. Oh, well, I guess . . .

Richard: Do you ever crotch-watch?

Robert (as Lance): Are you kidding?

Richard: But you tit-watch.

Robert (as Lance): Yeah.

Richard: How come you don't crotch-watch?

Robert (as Lance): Oh, cause I'm not, you know. I'm not interested. Oh, you know, I, in the showers or whatever, I look at the guys to see how I stack up with the others, but . . .

Richard: How do you do?

Robert (as Lance): Oh, OK.

Richard: Sure seem squirmy, Lance.

Robert (as Lance): Well, yeah, I mean, it's a, what a stupid thing to be talking about. It's revolting.

Richard: What's revolting about my questioning you if you know Robert?

By again deliberately misunderstanding Lance/Robert's comment, Richard points to a deeper truth: That, for Lance, Robert himself (that is, what Robert represents) is revolting and disgusting. The conversation is not unlike a fencing match; Richard darts in under the defenses and scores, then backs off and awaits another opening, feinting and weaving to keep his "opponent," Lance, off guard, and thereby aligning himself with Robert.

Robert (as Lance): Yeah, but I mean, you were talking about crotch-watching, really sick stuff.

Richard: When did you decide it was sick?

Robert (as Lance): Well, good God, everybody knows that.

Richard: How did you know it?

Robert (as Lance): Well, I don't know—

Richard: I mean, certainly at four or five you must have played doctor with your friends.

Robert (as Lance): Oh, yeah, but I mean, I'm not five now.

Richard: What happened between five and now?

Robert (as Lance): Well, I grew up.

Richard: Hm. Cause there's a couple guys in your high school that find you attractive.

Another probe, another score: Lance/Robert responds to this thrust with predictable homophobic anger.

Robert (as Lance): Well, all I can say is, they better not let me know about it.

Richard: Why not?

Robert (as Lance): Well, just that. I sure don't want to—

Richard: What would you do about it if Robert told you he thought you were cute?

Robert (as Lance): Well, I'd probably deck him.

Richard: That's one of the reasons why Robert avoids you.

Robert (as Lance): Well, could be.

Richard: What do you mean, you'd deck him?

Robert (as Lance): Oh, I'd like, smash him.

Richard: What do you mean, smash him? You've gotten from decking him to smashing him . . .

Robert (as Lance): Not, no, by decking him I mean, like, you know—

Richard: Like breaking his jaw, or his nose?

Robert (as Lance): I don't know if I'd go that far, but I'd . . . you know, I'd hit him.

Richard: What would you hit him for? Some girl comes up to you and says she thinks you're cute, or well hung, or something, would like to go out with you, you'd probably get all flattered.

Robert (as Lance): Well, that's right. I would.

Richard: Then why you gonna beat up Robert?

Robert (as Lance): Well, that's just something that's, I mean something that's really unnatural, something you don't even talk about.

Richard: How do you know it's unnatural?

Robert (as Lance): Well, I mean, that's what everybody said. I mean, they don't even talk about it. They don't talk about it, so therefore it must mean it's really bad.

Here is the first hint of yielding in Lance/Robert's previously unshakable prejudice. He is beginning, reluctantly, to look at the origins of his attitudes. If something has an origin, then there must have been a time before it was around—and the unthinkable becomes thinkable. Having made this step, Richard decides not to push any farther here and risk Lance/Robert's closing up again. Instead, he takes another tack:

Richard: Which is exactly what you're trying to get me to do, is not talk about it.

Robert (as Lance): Well, yeah, that's right.

Richard: Then we'll keep it bad.

Robert (as Lance): Pardon?

Richard: Then we'll keep it bad.

Robert (as Lance): Well yeah, sure, that's fine with me. I want to keep it bad.

Richard: Why?

Robert (as Lance): Well, good God, I mean, if you didn't, who knows what would happen.

Richard: That's what I want to find out.

Robert (as Lance): Well, I don't want, I don't want guys coming up to me in the hall, and, and coming on to me.

Richard: Why not?

Richard's refusal to accept Lance/Robert's attitudes as reasons in and of themselves finally pays off, as Lance/Robert admits to his own bisexual interests.

Robert (as Lance): Well, I mean, you want me to be really honest?

Richard: Um-hm.

Robert (as Lance): Well, it might be, I don't know, it might be kinda interesting.

Richard: Hmm.

Robert (as Lance): But don't tell anybody else I said that.

Rebecca: That scares you, that that might be interesting to you?

Robert (as Lance): Well, yeah.

Richard: So you create a norm that makes it uncomfortable for guys like Robert.

Robert (as Lance): (*very firmly*) That's right!

Richard: Say that again. "That's right!" So I can hear that tone again.

Robert (as Lance): That's right!

Something unexpected has happened here. Instead of continuing along the path of increased awareness of his own feelings, Lance/Robert snapped closed again; his tone of voice signaled a definite shift in energy. Richard asks him to repeat it, both to check out whether he really heard what he thought he heard, and to let the observing Robert hear it too. He then goes on to explore what the shift is all about.

Richard: What do you mean by "That's right!"?

Robert (as Lance): Well, you hit the nail on the head. I mean, that's why you gotta have rules and taboos.

Richard: Why?

Robert (as Lance): Well, cause things would get out of hand.

Richard: You see Robert acting out of hand?

Robert (as Lance): Um, no. But that's cause he knows what the rules are.

Richard: And the rule is . . .

Robert (as Lance): Well, guys are interested in girls, and vice versa, and guys aren't supposed to be interested in guys.

One could hardly ask for a clearer statement of the cultural script message!

Richard: What happens to those exceptions to that rule? Where there is a guy interested in a guy, or there is a girl interested in a girl?

Robert (as Lance): I don't even know. I don't even know anyone like that. I mean, it just, I just hear about, read about that. I haven't a clue what . . . it's something awful, I'm sure.

Richard: Cause you called him a queer.

Robert (as Lance): Well, I didn't say he was, but I said he'd be queer if he was interested in another guy.

Richard: And I said he might be interested in you.

Robert (as Lance): Oh, right, yeah. Well, that would make him a queer, then.

Lance/Robert's defenses are in place again. His slight glimpse of his own bisexuality was more than he was willing to tolerate for long. To belabor the point would probably only further solidify those defenses; in addition, the observing Robert has been given much fuel for thought here. Richard moves to another aspect of Lance/Robert's behavior:

Richard: So you set the rules, huh? You're part of the rule-making crowd.

Robert (as Lance): Um-hm.

Richard: And what do you think of having a rule that really takes away psychological freedom from someone?

Robert (as Lance): Say that again?

Richard: What do you think of rules that take away psychological freedom?

Robert (as Lance): Oh, I don't care about things like that.

Richard: You don't.

Robert (as Lance): No.

Richard: I thought you were a full, red-blooded American.

Robert (as Lance): Um-hm.

Richard: I thought Americans believed in freedom.

Robert (as Lance): Yeah, but I mean what's this "psychological freedom" bullshit?

Richard: Course if there was a Hitler in America, you'd want rid of him, wouldn't you?

Robert (as Lance): Sure.

Richard: Why?

Robert (as Lance): Well, cause he was bad.

Richard: Why?

Robert (as Lance): Well, he started a war, and killed all sorts of Jews.

Richard: You know how he did that?

Robert (as Lance): How he did it? Well, yeah, he had a big army, and . . .

Richard: He mostly did it by passing rules, that became the legal law of the land. Everything he did was legal. (*pause*) So you want to have a rule that limits people's sexual interest.

Robert (as Lance): Oh, yeah, for sure.

Richard: For security's sake.

Robert (as Lance): Um-hm. That would make me real uncomfortable. I mean, you know, if guys were openly affectionate, and women were, I'd just be really uncomfortable.

Lance/Robert is now much more in touch with his internal, emotional reaction to same-sex demonstrativeness than he was earlier, when his objections were made in a moralistic, self-righteous way. The next few exchanges serve to consolidate this gain, to ensure that Lance/Robert continues to operate from and be aware of his feelings.

Richard: Just affectionate openly. I mean, I'm not talking about dicking somebody.

Robert (as Lance): Well, no, I mean I don't think there should be any of that kind of stuff. I, it just makes me really uncomfortable.

Richard: So what are you going to do to make sure that this high school is run according to those rules?

Robert (as Lance): The best way to deal with it is to, to totally ignore it, pretend it doesn't exist.

Richard: So social isolation . . .

Robert (as Lance): Um-hm.

Richard: . . . dissolves the problem. You're very bright kids. Very clever.

Social isolation does *dissolve the problem for the Lances, who don't have to deal with it or be uncomfortable with it (or with their own hidden feelings about it) because for them it simply doesn't exist. For the Roberts, however, isolation means that they must live with a disapproval that is pervasive, but that can never be argued or even confronted because it is never acknowledged. Robert's expression at this point suggests that he is finally understanding, and feeling, how this mechanism works. He is ready to confront his symbolic internalized Lance—the introjected high school norm.*

Richard: Well, there is somebody here who wants to talk to you about it, Lance.

Robert (as Lance): Um-hm?

Richard: And I think you might find it very interesting to have a conversation with this young man.

Robert (as Lance): Hmm. OK.

Richard: Robert, move over here (*Robert moves to a spot on the* *mat across from where he sat as Lance*). Go back to high school, and talk to Lance. But I'm going to be here, so he doesn't deck you.

Switching positions is a technique designed to highlight the internal conflict. The internal conflict is externalized and the repressed reactions can be expressed fully and consciously. This two-chair technique also allows the therapist to make use of his or her own spatial relationship to the client. Robert's confrontation of Lance needs to be done from the emotional age at which the original introjection occurred. There is still some danger, in spite of all the work that has been done, that the teenage Robert may be too threatened by Lance, and collapse back into his old position. To prevent this, the therapist throws his own strength and protection on Robert's side by offering to "be here," backing him up; being seated just behind Robert provides a kinesthetic reminder of his support.

Robert: OK.

Richard: So you talk freely this time.

Robert: OK. I think I just want to start out by saying I think you're an asshole. You—

Richard: You want to say it louder?

Robert: (*louder*) I think you're an asshole.

Robert's voice is still quite controlled, and Richard's concern is that he not confront Lance from a controlled, cognitive place. Robert has "known" all along that Lance's position makes no sense. Rather, Robert needs to tap into his emotional response to Lance, and use that emotional energy to deal with the introject. Richard's request for more volume is intended to help him maintain and increase his emotional intensity.

Richard: You want to say it even louder?

Robert: (*shouting*) You're an asshole! I don't think you've got a brain in your head! I don't think you've ever thought about anything seriously. The world is much more complicated than you would like to think. And you can't, you can't make the world simple. It's not simple.

Richard: Explain, simply, what you mean by that, Robert. Because he thinks in simple terms.

It's not just that Lance thinks in simple terms: Robert's early response to Lance, and all that Lance symbolizes, is also a simple, adolescentlike reaction. Both the "simple" Lance and the Child ego state who reacts to Lance need to hear the confrontation in language that they can understand.

Robert: Well . . .

Robert's volume level has gone down, and his expression and posture suggest that he may, again, be shutting down emotionally.

Richard: Don't swallow those feelings, Robert. I'm not gonna let him punch you out, smash you. Even though he's taller than you.

Robert: (*pause*) I, I don't know what I want to say to you. I guess I want to, one of the things I want to say to you is, I don't care what you believe.

Richard: But he sets the standards, Robert.

Robert: Oh, well maybe I'm just going to have to set my own standards. (*pause*) His standards don't, don't account for how complicated the world is.

One incautious remark directly to Robert pulls him immediately away from his confrontation with Lance and into a discussion with the therapist. Richard quickly removes himself from the dialogue, directing Robert back to the business at hand.

Richard: Tell that to Lance.

Robert: Lance, you don't, you don't know. You don't know anything. You don't know anything. You can't set rules unless you know how complicated things are. I mean, you're like a five-year-old. I don't know if I want to listen to rules that are set by a five-year-old.

Richard: Tell him what your life was like under those rules.

Robert: Well, as I think about it, it's awful.

Richard: Think about it. And tell him.

Robert: Oh, it's . . . it's so stupid. Oh, God, it's stupid. I, cause I have no respect for you. And here I'm living, trying to conform to some idiotic rule, made by somebody I don't really have any respect for. Boy, what a . . . I'm a real dope.

At this moment, Robert seems to achieve a truly new kind of emotional awareness. For the first time, he can experience the world in a different way, free from a set of stifling rules imposed by a group of naive kids. Up to this point, although Robert "knew" that the rules made no sense, he was unable to let go of them. Now, suddenly, he does let go.

Richard: Go back to that previous statement, "I don't respect your rules."

Robert: Well I, I suppose I've been, I've been afraid of them. Up until now. But now I've decided I don't respect them, I'm not going to pay any attention to them.

Richard: Louder.

Robert: I'm not going to pay any attention to them.

Richard: Shout it now.

Robert: (*shouting*) I'm not going to pay any attention to them!

Richard: And furthermore . . .

Robert: Well, I don't now if there's any "furthermore." (*pause*) I guess, what I want to, I don't know what I want to say. I wish that there was somebody around who . . . who what? . . . Who was more mature than you. Somebody our age. Somebody who felt free to be sexual with guys and girls, and felt OK about it. If there was somebody around like that, then I think I could openly let you know what I think of you.

Robert asks for exactly what he himself may be able to provide, a peer who will understand, will be a model for openness about sexual feelings and behavior. It is important that Robert learn to be his own "backup," so that he can stand up for himself outside the therapy situation. Richard won't speak for him, but will support his speaking for himself; thus the "backup" can gradually be withdrawn as Robert begins to experience his own potency.

Richard: Openly do it now. I'll back you up.

Robert: Well, I just think you're a real stink: You're just a peabrain.

Richard: Tell him how you been following him all these years.

Robert: Oh, it's, I can't believe it. Oh, I can't believe it!

Rebecca: Say the whole thing, Robert. I can't believe . . .

Robert: I just can't believe that I would have . . . I mean, I did the same thing as you did, I took in these stupid rules without even thinking about them. I guess we're both kinda dumb. But it was, it was just easier to go along with what everybody else thought, and not think for myself.

Richard: And right here, today?

Robert: Well, today I am thinking for myself. And I really want to, I'm really going to. I'm not going to feel uncomfortable because you did. I'm not going to, you can have your uncomfortableness back. That's not going to be a part of me.

This is the decision that the teenage Robert needs to make. How will his introjected ego respond—how stubbornly will that part cling to its condemnation of Robert's choice?

Rebecca: Switch, and see what he says, Robert. (*Robert moves to the "Lance" spot*) Respond, Lance.

Robert (as Lance): Hm. Well, that's fine; you can do your own thing, but just don't bother me.

Richard: Now tell him the psychological message underneath that. That's a nice social message, and the meaning . . .

Robert (as Lance): (*pause*) Well, that's fine if you want to do that, but I don't want to know about it. Don't bother me with it. I don't, yeah, I don't want to know about it.

The introjected attitude has shifted significantly, from being disgusted and revolted at the very idea of homosexuality, to a willingness to look the other way. But does this mean that Robert must still live with a quietly disapproving part of himself? If so, his teenage Child will need firm and unmistakable support and acceptance from his Adult ego state, so that over time the introjected self-condemnation can be dissipated. Strengthening the self-confidence and approval of his Adult ego state, his sense of the irrationality of the introjected position, will allow the process of integration that was begun there to continue.

Rebecca: Sounds like you're saying "Go live in your separate world, Robert."

Robert (as Lance): Oh, yeah, I am. Um-hm.

Richard: Tell him that: "That's what I'm asking you to do, Robert. To get psychologically gone."

Robert (as Lance): Oh, yeah, go live in your own world.

Richard: "You don't belong here."

Robert (as Lance): Yeah. That's right. You don't belong here.

By heightening the intensity of the impasse between what was an introjected norm and the rest of the personality, Robert can be helped to experience the unreasonableness, the impossibility, of the Lance position. Seeing that position as unmistakably irrational, he can again refuse to buy into it, cognitively or emotionally.

Richard: Now switch. Respond to Lance, at the psychological level.

Robert: (*moving to the other place on the mat*) I don't know what you mean by "belong here." I mean, I belong in the world.

Richard: Louder.

Robert: I belong in the world, and I'm going to be the way I am. And if you don't like it, that is just tough shit. I don't care. I just, I don't care.

Richard: Is that true, that you don't care?

Robert: Yeah. Yeah. (*pause*) If, if he's willing to be my friend, that's fine. If he doesn't want to, it doesn't really matter, there're a lot more interesting, worthwhile people around. (*pause*) Yeah.

Richard: Anything more you want to say to Lance before you say good-bye to him? The standard-bearer of the high school? Imagine him with a big American flag right behind him, standing in front of the school.

Robert: I feel sorry for you. I really feel sorry for you.

Richard: Band's playing in the background . . .

Robert: Yeah, I feel sorry for you. (*pause*) Because I think, you know, I think you're going to miss a lot in life, by limiting yourself. If you want to stay in your rigid little straitjacket, go ahead. Yeah, go ahead. (*pause*) Yeah, I don't think I need to say any more . . . Yeah, I'm finished with him.

Robert really does seem to be finished. His face is smooth, his posture relaxed. Lance's attitudes and values have become ego alien; they are no longer a part of Robert's own self. There are, and always will be, people like Lance in the world, but Robert no longer needs to experience a part of himself allied with them. He can feel sorry for them, but he no longer needs to fear them.

There is no magic in this kind of therapy of the exteropsyche, although it often looks and sounds magical. Robert has experienced a very real shift in his deeply held perceptions, perceptions and expectations acquired years ago and held out of awareness ever since. By bringing them to awareness, and allowing him to react to them emotionally as well as cognitively, the therapy has given him an opportunity to reject them—something that could not happen as long as the whole package of disapproval and guilt was kept underground. But self-acceptance is a process, not a thing: Robert will need to continue to nurture his sense of OK-ness, and to disown the introjected disapproval. Like a seedling, his new experiencing of himself must be tended, fed, and protected so that it can grow into a strong, firmly rooted, and integrated aspect of his total person.

7

EMILY
From Dream to Script

In ordinary clinical practice, clients seldom walk into the office, sit down, and begin to deal with their basic conflicts. Many new clients present the symptoms of their problem, and do not understand that the roots of their present discomfort are deeply buried and out of awareness. The therapist needs to respect the presented problem, while at the same time focusing on the deeper issues.

Workshop and intensive group participants, too, are often unaware of where their work will take them. Although these clients are frequently sophisticated in the area of psychotherapy, they may be quite unaware of their own personal dynamics. It is always easier to see the forest when you're not lost among the trees!

There are many ways in which therapist and client can work together to open a path into the introjections or childhood decisions that will eventually need to be explored. Dream work is one such avenue. Working with dreams has a long and respectable history: Even before the landmark work of Freud in the late 1800s, physicians and philosophers had studied and speculated about the implications of dreams. Dream analysis today takes many forms, from the traditional psychoanalytic approach to the more active approaches of Gestalt therapy.

Emily's work, presented in this chapter, begins with a Gestalt treatment of dream material. Emily anticipates working with both Richard and Rebecca; as we shall see, the dream directly involves both of these individuals. As the meaning of the dream becomes clear, the therapists shift to the style with which we have become more familiar in previous chapters, helping Emily to deal with Parental introjects. We join the work as Emily begins to relate the contents of a dream from the previous night:

Emily: (*speaking to Richard*) Rebecca had asked me for a padlock, and I said sure, I have a padlock. And I gave it to you. And I had the combination to go with it. And then you came in into the room downstairs, and said to me, Emily, we can't use the padlock, because we can't find the combination. And I said, well I gave you the combination. Well, we don't have it, we can't find it, so we can't use it. And I said, well I don't remember the combination. And you said, well, look in your yearbook, and you'll find it there. And I said, I don't, even in the dream I was thinking, it wouldn't be in my yearbook. But I looked in my yearbook, and there was a combination in there, and I told you that there was a combination there. And it was my measurements. I mean, the combination number was what my measurements were.

Richard: You mean, like (*makes an hourglass shape with his hands*) . . .

Emily: Yes. And I said, here are three numbers, but I don't think it's the combination. And you took the numbers, and that was the end of the dream.

Richard: Fascinating dream. You want to work with it?

Emily: Sure.

The first step in working with the dream involves teasing out the meaning of the various symbols. Unlike the psychoanalytic and Jungian approaches, in which dream symbols are assumed to have universal meanings, Gestalt dream work encourages the client to discover his or her own idiosyncratic symbolism. Emily's manner, up to this point, has been tense, fearful, "locked in," and it is likely that the lock in the dream is significantly connected to her internal experience of herself. Richard chooses the lock, therefore, as a starting place.

Richard: Just close your eyes. Put yourself back into the mood of that dream . . . Describe yourself as that padlock. Do it all in the first person: "I am a padlock," and describe all the characteristics of being a lock. (*pause*) Do it out loud. What I'm looking for more is what catches you by surprise, than what you say. Close your eyes, and go ahead: "I'm a padlock . . ."

Emily (as the lock): I'm a padlock, uh . . . locked shut. Piece of steel, can't get open without the correct combination.

When parts of the self are fragmented, the function of dreaming is often integration of those parts. Each part of the dream is a projection of some aspect of the dreamer; each statement about something in the dream is a statement about the dreamer. In order to experience the full impact of these statements, Emily needs to own them, to bring them back to herself rather than talking about an "out there" object.

Richard: Start each sentence with "I" . . . say all those again, with "I am."

Emily (as the lock): I can't, OK, I, I'm a padlock. I feel like steel. Feel locked shut. Feel that I don't have the correct combination to get open.

Richard: Say that sentence again.

Repeating a particular sentence or phrase tends to emphasize it, to set it out in mental italics.

Emily (as the lock): I feel like I don't have the correct combination to get open.

Richard: Keep going, padlock. Describe your function.

Emily (as the lock): My function is to keep things locked up so nobody can get at them. To keep things protected.

Richard: Keep going, padlock.

Emily (as the lock): Once I, once I click locked, there's no way to open me up without the correct combination.

Richard: Switch, and be the combination, and describe yourself.

Emily (as the combination): I'm the combination. I am three correct numbers, and only three. Have to go to the right, to the left around past the number and back to the number, and then to the right. Exactly that way in order to have me open the lock. If I'm not doing it exactly that way, nothing will work.

Richard could have stayed with the combination, exploring the way in which "it" functions, or could have gone back to the lock, and the relationship between the two. But he wants a better sense of the overall meaning of the dream, so he moves on.

Richard: Now be the Rebecca in the dream, and describe yourself.

Emily (as Rebecca): I'm very frustrated that I don't have the combination to open the lock so that I can use it. It's not any good to me unless I can have the combination. It's a piece of trash, the lock is a piece of trash without the combination. I need to have the combination.

Each new elaboration brings out more information about Emily's feelings, experience, expectations. It is still early, and much remains unclear; Richard is still concerned with allowing Emily to uncover her own meanings. He is careful to keep his comments neutral, so as not to intrude his own hypotheses into the picture that is emerging. His task is to keep the work moving, without prematurely closing off possible avenues for later exploration.

Richard: Keep going, Rebecca. Say that to Emily.

Emily (as Rebecca): Emily, I need to have the combination in order to work the lock. The lock is worthless to me without the combination. I need the lock to protect my things, but it's no good to me if I can't open it up and get at my things.

Richard: Tell her what you mean by the word "trash."

Emily (as Rebecca): What good is a lock that stays locked?

Richard: Now be the lock, and respond. (*pause*) Just make a response, lock.

Emily (as the lock): You're right, I'm no good without the combination. And I just will be thrown away, without the combination. I'm worthless without the combination. Totally worthless.

Richard: Now be Rebecca and respond.

Emily (as Rebecca): You're right, you are worthless without the combination. A lock is no good unless it can be opened.

Richard: Repeat that sentence.

Emily: A lock is not good unless it can be opened. A lock that stays locked is a piece of trash.

Richard: Describe yourself again, lock.

Emily (as the lock): I'm a piece of trash unless I can be opened. I'm no good if I stay locked.

Here is a clear existential statement. In addition to wanting additional professional training, Emily has come to the workshop to learn about herself, to deal with her internal pain. She doesn't know how to get into her out-of-awareness issues; they (and she) are locked up. And as long as she stays locked, she is no good, a "piece of trash." Richard decides to look further, to discover what the other parts of the dream are saying:

Richard: Now be the yearbook and describe yourself.

Emily: (*speaking in a shaky, breathless tone*) I'm no good unless I have perfect measurements. 34, 24, 34. Has to be maintained at all times.

The statement that she is no good without her perfect measurements is something new for Emily; it had not been in her awareness before. It is frightening to her, and yet compelling. For the first time, she fails to follow the directions of the therapist. Instead of shifting, as he requests, Emily continues to talk about the importance of those measurements. She is like a bird transfixed by a cobra: terrified, yet unable to move away.

Richard: And maintaining it protects you from . . .

Emily: Being a real person, with feeling.

Richard: (*very softly*) A real person, with feeling.

Emily: Very scared of that.

Richard: A real person, with feeling, or a shapely, closed-up piece of steel.

Emily: (*her voice is very frightened*) It's like I'm no good without the correct measurements.

Emily's words and voice both attest to her fright; she looks ready to bolt from the room. In order to plan for the pacing of her work, Richard needs a better sense of how well grounded she is, of how much scare she can tolerate. The content of the dream gives him a fine opportunity to look for this information without changing his overall approach. The old inn in which the workshop is held has a ground floor dormitory room, still partially under construction; it is this room in which Emily has chosen to sleep, and to which she referred in the dream. Allowing her to experience herself as that room (remember, every part of a dream is a projection of some unintegrated part of the dreamer) will help her to find her solid, grounded aspect, and it will also give the therapists an opportunity to see just how well grounded she is.

Richard: Switch, and be the downstairs room.

Emily: Be what?

Richard: That downstairs room, and describe yourself. (*pause*) Describe yourself, room.

Emily (as the room): I'm a brand-new room. Everything there seems new, even the people. I feel like a stranger in there. I don't understand why Richard's coming into the room, except that I know he wants to get the combination for the lock.

Richard: Say your next idea.

Emily: (*pause*) The room feels cold.

Richard: Say that in the first person, room.

Emily (as the room): I feel cold.

Richard: Describe more of yourself. "I'm cold; I'm . . ."

Emily (as the room): (*pause*) Damp and unfriendly. Distant. Unfamiliar. Brand new.

The strategy has been successful. Emily is back with the dream, and no longer sounds terrified. She does have a solid, dependable base that she can use for grounding and protection. Having determined this, Richard moves on:

Richard: Now be Richard. Describe yourself.

Emily (as Richard): I'm in a hurry, cause I need something real bad. And I want to be quick about it, and not take a lot of time. (*pause*) Guess that's it.

Richard: Now talk to the Emily in the room, Richard.

Emily (as Richard): Emily, if you look in the yearbook, I think you'll find the combination there.

Richard: Tell her what you mean, Richard.

Emily (as Richard): You know where to look for things, uh . . . (*her voice sounds frightened again*) and . . . if you get the kind of coaching on where to look, you can find what you're looking for.

Everybody needs some help on where to look. And I would suggest that you look there.

As Richard in the dream, she offers help and suggests that the key to the lock—to her own dilemma—is hidden in the yearbook.

Richard: Tell her about your suggestion, Richard. What kind of wisdom went into suggesting the yearbook?

Emily (as Richard): (*sighing*) I don't know. I'm not coming up with anything.

Richard: Well, be Emily and respond to Richard.

Emily: I just don't know how you know that that's where I need to look for the combination. How come I don't know where to look for the combination?

Richard: Be Richard and respond.

Notice that we have now gone well beyond the actual events of the dream. Emily is creating new dialogue, through which the dream characters and objects will be able to tell their story even more clearly.

Emily (as Richard): I'm not saying, Emily, that that's where you're going to find it; I'm just suggesting that you might look there as a possibility.

Richard: Be Emily and respond to Richard. With what you discovered in the yearbook.

Emily: Richard, I found three numbers in the yearbook that look like the combination to the lock. You'll have to try those numbers out on the lock, and see if they'll open the lock. I don't know if they will. But I did find three numbers in the book, as you suggested that I look there.

Rebecca: What about those numbers?

Emily: The numbers were 34-24-34.

Richard: Tell him what those numbers mean.

Emily: And those numbers are the measurements that I always try very hard to maintain, no matter what.

Richard: Now look at the year on the yearbook. What's the date?

Emily: 1957.

Richard: And take the dream further. Look at that yearbook even further. To find the important inscription in that yearbook.

Because it is a yearbook, it must have a year. It is likely that the year she chooses will be the year in which some traumatic event occurred, an event that is connected to her decision to lock herself away. Emily comes up with this information easily, so Richard decides to find out how much more she will be able to "read" from the yearbook.

Emily: (*pause*) Under my name it says, "Thou Swell." I don't know who put it there, or why I wound up with that.

Richard: Describe what it means.

Emily: (*very frightened, almost unable to speak*) Ahh . . .

Richard: Say it again, several times.

Emily: Thou Swell.

Richard: Say it with the meaning.

Emily: (*pause*) I think, um, I think I just tried to be perfect in so many ways that it just came across that way. To whoever was writing those captions under the pictures.

Richard: Now, finish the dream, as you look into the 1957 yearbook. You've given Richard the combination. It's your dream; now finish it. Out loud.

Emily: I, um, to finish the dream I would, at this point in my life I'd like a happy ending. I would like the combination to work.

Richard: Tell that to Richard and Rebecca.

Emily: Richard, I want this combination to work for me. Please do what you can to make it work.

Richard: Now respond, Richard.

Emily (as Richard): I'll do whatever I can, Emily, to make it work. And if this one doesn't work, we'll find another one. Until one of them works. Because you don't have to stay locked up for the rest of your life. I know that, and I want you to know that too.

Rebecca: Be Emily again, and tell Richard how those numbers are going to be perfect for unlocking that lock. How they're just the right numbers.

Emily: I don't, I don't know if they're just the right numbers. Those are the numbers I saw in the book. I don't know, Richard, if they will work. Those are the three numbers in the book that I found. And you asked—

Richard: Trust in your intuition, what they represent.

Emily: (*pause*) I don't know if they're the combination to the lock, or if they're my measurements . . . I'm just uh, asking Richard to try them to see if they will unlock the padlock. I don't know, if they will. And I don't know if I'm answering the question. Am I?

Emily has pulled away from the dream experience, and addresses a direct question to the therapists. The initial work contract has been met: She has explored the dream, and experienced its message for her. Rather than take her back into more dream work, and run the risk of pushing her farther and faster than she is ready to go, Richard chooses to engage her Adult ego state as a full, cooperating partner in deciding what to do next.

Richard: What do you make of all this, Emily? Will you look at us? Obviously a profound experience for you.

Emily: I think all of the parts you had me talk from, it's the lock, that stays locked. That I won't believe I will ever have the combination to.

Richard: What did you lock up in 1957?

Emily: Me.

Richard: How come?

Emily: Cause I was scared.

Rebecca: At 17 years old? Scared of . . .

Emily: (*sounding frightened again*) I just think I made a decision then that no one would ever take advantage of me again.

Richard: The significant word was "again." Who was taking advantage of you?

Emily: Uh, when I was 12 I was taking accordion lessons, and, uh, my accordion teacher locked me into his practice room and started to try a few things on me. And I tried to get out, and I told him that I wanted to get out now, and, uh, and he tried to pull me away from the door, and I, uh, I remember I scratched him, not real bad, just a little bit. And I remember he opened the door and let me out. And that's, uh . . .

Richard: Your 34-24-34 body . . .

Emily: No, not at 12. Although I was overdeveloped for my age.

Richard: I watched you get very tense last night. The reason I turned to you during Jean's work was that you seemed to be resonating off of what she was doing.

The previous evening, one of the other workshop participants had done a very intense piece of work dealing with the experience of being sexually abused by her father.

Emily: She was working with six-year-old stuff. I wasn't that young. Six is a little different.

Richard: The experience of being molested is the same at any age. It's violation. That's what you're getting, is a violation. How did you make that decision at 17?

We now have at least two and possibly three Child ego states in the picture (all of whom were frightened by the incest work of another group member the previous evening, and may be identifying with her): The 17-year-old whose decision to stay locked up was symbolized by her high school yearbook; the 12-year-old who was molested by a teacher; and possibly an even younger child. It's likely that the later two points served to reinforce an earlier decision or belief, or that even those memories are connected to a still earlier situation in which the original scripting occurred. The therapists need more information, and will continue to work with Emily to sort all of this out.

Emily: Well, um, I just seemed to have a series of events after that, with different guys, that, um, brought me to that conclusion.

Richard: All of them wanting to get their hands on your body? How come you decided to have a perfect body? How come you didn't make the decision to have a very skinny, or a very fat body?

Emily: I, later on I got anorexic, got very skinny. After I made the decision I went down to about 88 pounds.

The therapists continue to probe for material around the script decision, and how Emily acted it out through her anorexia. They discover that she has made a more overt suicide attempt, in addition to the self-starvation, and that it was the caring attention of a friend who helped her to pull out of the self-destructive spiral. All of these later events appear to be directly tied to the molestation experience, and it is here that Richard chooses to move in. We pick up the work again as Richard invites Emily into an age regression:

Richard: Just close your eyes. Just go back, and take a moment to look at your accordion. How your fingers would feel on those keys; and as you do that, remember what it was like as your breasts began to develop. Now look at that accordion teacher, and look at that locked door in his little room . . . And look at him starting to come at you. And you put him out there, and you talk to him. I'll be here with you, Emily, to back you up. (*there is a long silence; Richard moves closer to Emily and continues*) I'm right here. You just talk to him. You tell him the things you wanted to say.

Emily: (*very long pause*) I have a . . . I think before I start on that I think the thing that's popping into my mind right now is what really bothered me, uh, more than him, touching my breasts, was, um, when it was time to go for my next lesson I wouldn't go. And then finally my mother wanted to know how come I didn't want to go any more. And I told her what happened and she screamed at me at the top of her lungs not to tell Dad because he would go down there and kill the man.

As traumatic as the molestation experience itself may have been, Mother's reaction to it was even more painful. This is where Emily's energy is, and Richard follows her lead.

Richard: Talk to Mom.

Emily: And I really got scared. (*her voice shakes*) That I had done something really bad.

Richard: Say that to Mom.

Emily: And so (*her voice is terrified*) I knew right then and there I could never leave the house again. That I was dangerous or something.

Emily's voice is that of a child; she sounds much younger now than she has previously. Richard, responding to this shift, uses language more appropriate to a little girl.

Richard: You put your mama right there, and tell her how. Just start with what you know about.

Emily: (*sighs*)

Richard: Want me to do it for you?

Emily: I have a lot of problem with doing that because, uh . . . another incident that I had with her, she went crazy on me, and uh . . .

Richard: So you're in a real double bind. When you're needing something and your mom goes crazy. (*Richard turns slightly to address an imaginary mom*) Mom, Emily's gotta tell you something. About what happened, and how it really happened. And don't go crazy. You sit there and you listen to her. No, don't shake your head "no," Mom. You're not going to go crazy. Your daughter was in a difficult situation and you just sit there and listen. She's gotta tell you exactly how it happened, Mom, so she can grow up healthy. (*shouting*) Sit down, Mom, and listen. No hysterics!

Emily, overwhelmed by her fear of Mother's craziness, cannot confront her and thus close the gestalt of her (Emily's) unmet need. The power scales of that relationship are strongly tilted in Mother's favor. Richard comes in on Emily's side, evening the balance. He uses his strength and authority to nullify Mother's threat to go crazy (and thus abandon Emily), so that Emily can finish what was begun and left unfinished for so many years. As we shall see, Emily continues to be afraid to deal with Mother; she talks about Mother to Richard, who in turn continues to direct her back to the confrontation.

Emily: You see, the thing that happened was, she wanted me to say the Lord's prayer over and over (*Emily can barely force the words out*), and that's what keeps running through my mind, is that I have to do that.

Richard: Tell her what you really need, Emily, from inside.

Emily: I can see that, at this other level I know that she's not going to be able to handle it.

Rebecca: We'll take care of your mom. Just start with saying, "Mom, I need you to hear me. I need you to understand."

Emily: Ahhh . . . This is really hard for me, because she was never there for me.

Rebecca: Tell her that. "Hard for me to tell you . . . " (*pause*) "I need you there for me, Mom. I need you to be in tune with me."

Emily: I wish you could just listen and, uh, and be with me instead of going crazy.

At last, Emily finds the strength to address Mother directly. Rather than ask her to elaborate, the therapists choose to stay with this simple request, strengthening it, and letting Emily pick up momentum in the process.

Richard: Say that same thing again. And say it a little louder.

Emily: I wish you could listen and be with me instead of just screaming and going crazy.

Richard: Try it once more, now, as a demand.

Emily: (*shouting, through tears*) I want you to listen and be with me instead of just screaming and going crazy!

Rebecca: (*softly*) Good, Emily, you're doing fine. Just keep going. Let those feelings come. (*louder*) "Cause when you go crazy . . ."

Emily: When you go crazy that scares the living shit right out of me.

Rebecca: Cause tell her what you start thinking about yourself.

Having noted Emily's earlier comment that she couldn't go out of the house because she was "dangerous," Rebecca wants to check out whether this self-concept is connected to a belief that she is responsible for her mother's craziness.

Emily: What I start thinking about myself is there's something really wrong with me.

Richard: Say it again. If you're crazy . . .

Emily: When you went crazy listening to me and what I was trying to say to you, it made me feel like there was something wrong with me. And so what I did was make sure that I would fix it so that I would never ever do anything wrong again.

Rebecca: And tell her what you really need, Emily.

Emily: What I really need is somebody to listen, be with me, so that I can breathe and be real.

Rebecca: Right now, just take that breath. And feel all those feelings.

Richard: (*placing his hand on her diaphragm*) Breathe right down in there.

Rebecca: Now tell her about that hurt, deep inside.

By making physical contact, Richard accomplishes several things. First, he provides support for the Child Emily at a tactile level, support that she can take in and use even when she cannot completely handle the verbal interchange. Second, he coaches her breathing, both with the verbal-tactile combination ("breathe to here") and by using pressure and release to pace the breathing pattern. Finally, the touch is diagnostic: He can monitor the spontaneous breathing rhythm as well as the degree of muscle tension in her midsection, and use this to guide his interventions.

Emily: (*crying hard*) The hurt is so bad, it's prevented me from ever having my own k—, k— (*the sobs are choking off her words*) from ever having my own kids.

Richard: Tell Mom what you decided, Emily.

Emily: I decided I would never allow myself to live again.

Rebecca: That's it, breathe right into that. And tell your Mama that decision you made. If you go crazy, Mom . . .

Emily: I made a very bad decision for myself . . . I've been able to do a lot of things anyway, but I've missed out on a lot of things I really wanted to do.

Richard: Tell her about the living you stopped yourself from doing.

Emily: I stopped myself from living. Really regret that now.

Richard: Tell her how you did that.

Emily: I didn't live because I never let anybody close to me again.

Richard: 'Cause when you don't listen to me, Mom . . .

Emily: (*pause*) What I did, Mom, was that I went out and I looked for some "mother" people. To find some kind of direction and get somebody to listen to me. And then I remember that when you got out of the hospital, how you hated that, how I was spending too much time at somebody else's house.

Rebecca: Tell her what you did then.

Emily: (*pause*) I find it very difficult to tell her what I was doing then, because . . . (*her fist is clenching on the mat*)

Richard: But your hand is talking. There's tension in that fist.

Emily: My mother was incapable of hearing anything about sex.

Richard: (*holding his hand up to her fist, so that she can push against it*) Push here. Push against her, instead of against you, and say it again. "You are incapable." (*pause*) Say that again to her. Feel the tension in your fist.

Emily tends to get lost in the words, or in the need to find words for what she feels; she then either breaks away from the emotional contact with Mother, or becomes mute and terrified. By encouraging her to push out against Mother, the therapists provide a way for her to express herself without having to find words. As the emotional expression and release come, the words will follow more easily.

Emily: (*she pushes, hard, saying nothing*)

Rebecca: Just push; let yourself feel all of that.

Emily: You're incapable of hearing anything about sex!

Rebecca: Keep going.

Emily: And sometimes I think you want me to be sexless or something.

Rebecca: And tell her how you feel about that, that she wanted you to be sexless.

Emily: (*shouting*) But how can you want me to be sexless in a real world? I don't know where you're coming from! I never understood you anyway!

Being "sexless" may mean a variety of things. What's important here is what it means to Emily, and what she did about dealing with that demand from Mother. Rather than assume that they understand what Emily means, Richard asks her to define it; he is careful to do so in the context of her encounter with Mother.

Richard: And if you want me to be sexless, that means . . .

Emily: That means I lock myself up. And I've done enough of it!

Rebecca: Yeah, say that again to her.

Emily: (*screaming*) I've done enough of it!

Richard: Just open your mouth, and scream it! "No!"

Emily: No, I'm not going to be sexless! (*she is pounding a pillow with the clenched fist*) I'm not going to lock myself up for you! I can't believe you wanted that for me!

To say "no" to the unreasonable demands, real or imagined, of a parent is a major recurring developmental task. Most children receive explicit instruction in how to say "yes"—that is, how to adapt to the rules of the family and the larger society—but seldom are supported in saying "no." Those who don't learn on their own are forced to go through life as Emily has done, threading their way through a mine field of forbidden thoughts, feelings, and behaviors. In this last statement, Emily begins to experience the strength of her own "no," but quickly backs off, redefining the relationship with Mother as one in which Mother didn't make the unreasonable demand after all. Rebecca, noting the danger of readaptation, supports Emily's expressing her "no" even more intensely.

Rebecca: Try it with both hands, Emily. (*Emily sighs, and buries her head in her hands*) You don't have to hide, Emily. What you're doing is just right. You need to say a lot of those things.

Emily: (*weeping*) I can't believe my life turned out like this!

Rebecca: Tell her, "I'm angry that my life turned out like this."

Again, Rebecca moves to counter Emily's tendency to readapt and shut down. Rather than swallow the anger, she is directed to put it out where it belongs. Because she is well into the work, and has allowed herself to experience the angry feelings, she is able to comply with the directions, to pick up the thread and continue to work.

Emily: (*pounding the pillow*) I'm so angry with you that when I see you, I want to choke you. I know I would never do it, but . . . I want to shake you, real bad!

Rebecca: Go ahead and do it. Grab the pillow. Go ahead and shake it, so you're not locking up your arms, too. And scream at her, at the same time. Open up your mouth, Emily, and let it come.

Emily: (*shaking pillow violently*) You were bringing up a girl, you had to teach me something! You couldn't stay in your depression forever and a day! (*screams*) And you're still in it!

Rebecca: Yeah, scream it at her. "Get out of your depression!"

Emily: You're still in that goddamn depression! I hate you for that!

Rebecca: Yeah. (*shouts*) "Listen to me! Get out of your depression and listen to me!"

Emily: Just get out of it for one second! I can tell you in one second!

Richard: So tell her now. Just shake her out of it, and tell her.

Emily: I can't believe you wanted me to be sexless! I just can't believe it, it's so hard to believe it! (*sobs*)

Rebecca: Yeah, you do believe it, though. Tell her what you're feeling.

Emily: Just last year I said to her, I really am thinking seriously about adopting a child. And she says, "Well why didn't you have one when you were supposed to?"

Rebecca: Tell her, Emily.

Emily: (*sobs, unable to speak*)

Rebecca: Tell her the answer to that, the real answer.

Emily: I can't do it. I've thought about it so many times, but it's just like I'd be doing it to, to get back at her or something.

Richard: Then do it here. Tell her the real reason. So you don't carry that Spook around inside your head.

Richard refers directly here to the Parent ego state, the introjected values and perceptions and expectations of Emily's "crazy" mother, which Emily has been responding to, out of awareness, as if they were a part of her. In order to "de-Spook" herself, Emily needs openly to renounce these introjects, both cognitively and emotionally—to defy and say "no" to the craziness, thus clearing the way for a new decision about how she will live her life.

Emily: I haven't been able to have kids because I learned how to be phobic. And it's been my whole life.

Richard: In order to . . .

Emily: (*still sobbing*) In order to protect myself and to be sexless.

Richard: Listen to that adolescent decision.

Emily: So I wouldn't ever, ever do anything that would cause you to go crazy.

Richard: Tell her what life is going to be like in the future, if you continue to live this way.

Emily: (*pause*) If I continue this way, there is a part of me that doesn't want to be here.

The suicide theme recurs. It is as if Emily is warning the therapists that these are indeed deep waters, that if she is to continue her process she needs to finish, go all the way through it; she will not tolerate being left in the middle, aware but unresolved.

Rebecca: Emily, tell her how you protected her. By being phobic.

Emily's phobias (she had revealed earlier in the workshop that she had once counted more than 30 objects or situations about which she was phobic) served to protect her from having to deal with the terror and pain of her early experiences; they may also have provided her with some tangible secondary gains. More important in this piece of work, however, is the way in which the whole phobic pattern protects Emily's introjected Parent ego state: By maintaining her own script system through phobic responses, Emily avoids dealing with Mother. In the shadow logic of childhood, Mother will be kept sane only if Emily is good, agreeable, adaptive—and sexless. Being phobic guards her against her natural sexuality, and thus ensures less conflict with the intrapsychic influence of the introjected mother.

Emily: (*sigh*) I did. I'm still doing it.

Richard: Tell her that. By being phobic . . .

Emily: Can't believe how you went crazy right in front of me.

Richard: You believed what you were seeing.

Emily: And I've always been afraid it was going to happen to me. Every time I had an anxiety attack, of course, it was the proof. This was it.

Richard: Now tell her what you were truly anxious about.

Emily: What I am truly anxious about with her?

Richard: Yeah. Like what it's like to have a mama you can't rely on. Who's not solid and dependable.

Emily: It's always felt like one great big discount. Like she wanted a daughter, but she didn't really want a real daughter. She wanted my hair to be pretty, she wanted everything about me to be pretty. But she didn't want me to be me.

Richard: Say it to her: "You wanted . . ."

Emily: You wanted me to be real pretty, and to be able to say when I walked out of the house, there goes my beautiful daughter, isn't she beautiful? But you never wanted me to be real. That's what blew your mind. I was some kind of a Barbie doll. Real kids are real kids!

The energy level ebbs and flows, as Emily moves into confronting Mother and then pulls back to talk to the therapists about what Mother did to her. Again and again the therapists redirect her, encouraging her to deal directly with Mother. And with each return to the confrontation, Emily appears to gain both strength and insight into how she adapted, compromised, set into operation the maladaptive responses that eventually developed into a constricted and phobic life-style. Cognition, emotion, and intent to change are all present in this work. Piece by piece, Emily is laying the foundation for a new way of relating to Mother, and to the world that she has (up to now) been experiencing in the context of the old catastrophic fears.

Rebecca: And that means . . .

Emily: That means you don't just dress 'em up.

Rebecca: "Don't dress me up, Mom."

Emily: (*pounding*) The biggest thrill of your life was to see me in the Rainbow Girls, dressed up in those frilly gowns. That's what you thought it was all about. Meanwhile I was encountering all these other experiences in the real world, and I needed you to talk to, and you just weren't there.

Richard: Tell her now, all about your real experiences.

Emily: I'm still protecting her.

Richard: Tell her.

Emily: I'm still protecting you, Mom.

Richard: Tell her what a good mother you are to her.

Emily: I'm really good. I'm a mom to you.

Emily is encouraged to look at her own behavior with Mom in terms of its strength, its purpose. As she begins to experience her actions as choices, rather than as something she was forced into, she will be able to recognize that there were (and are) other options as well.

Richard: Cause as long as I protect you . . .

Emily: As long as I protect you, I'll be protected myself.

Richard: Say that again, and listen to it carefully.

Emily: (*long pause*) As long as I keep protecting her, I can still hang on to it myself.

Richard: Now tell her about the experiences in the real world . . . Too soon?

As soon as she is invited to deal directly with Mother about those loaded, real-world issues, Emily begins to collapse again. Her face looks terrified and she seems almost to shrink physically. Richard's "Too soon?" is a recognition of this; it also plants the seed that, even though now may be too soon, Emily will eventually do this work. With this introduction, Emily begins to deal with the question of how to get ready to move into the next phase of her work.

Emily: Yeah. I don't know what it would take to do that.

Richard: A willingness to lose protection? Her protection of you?

Emily: A willingness to lose her protection of me?

Rebecca: A protection which was false, anyway. The myth that if you don't tell her anything, she won't go crazy, and she'll be there for you.

Emily: The myth that if I don't tell her anything, she'll be there for me?

Rebecca: Yes. Cause she won't go crazy. The fear is that if you tell her about what's real, she'll go crazy, and then you'll lose your mother. Is that right? By locking yourself inside, at least you can pretend that she's there for you... You want to come back and look at me, Emily? You understand what I'm saying?

Emily has been staring down at her hands, locked together in her lap. She is beginning to withdraw, to close down on her contact with the therapist, and may be reexperiencing the old sense of aloneness and abandonment. To forestall this, Rebecca invites her to "come back" and make contact with her again.

Emily: That I pretend that she's there for me, but I know that, uh, she just isn't, she's never been. She's always been a very depressed person.

Rebecca: And what are you scared of when you think of really telling her what went on?

Emily: Well, the other thing that I really feel bad about for her is that two years before I was born she had a very handicapped child, that died, when he was nine. And all the while she was trying to take care of me, and trying to get care for him, and find out if he could even be helped, she felt that God had punished her for having that baby. And so, I just . . . I always . . . when I think about it on an intellectual level I think, why should I add to the sadness that's already gone on for her? So I know I protect her. I know I do that.

Emily has moved out of the regression, into an Adult consideration of her relationship with Mother. But there is a contamination: She is unable to separate her need to protect herself (by locking herself up, keeping Mother sane, and thus avoiding abandonment) from her desire to protect Mother from additional distress. Emily's Child ego state is overwhelmed by the strength, the craziness, the unpredictability of the intrapsychic influence of her introjected mother. Even with the support of the therapists, she has been unable to confront that Parent directly and follow the confrontation through to a new and healthier decision. Something needs to be done to upset the balance of power.

Rebecca: You said before, "I don't know what it would take for me to be able to tell her." I think the next therapy piece we need to do with you is for us to talk to the mother inside of you. And if we take care of her, at least somewhat, then I think that Child in you will have the safety and permission to go ahead and be real. But I think we need to adjust the Parent first. Then the ideal is, when we take care of the Parent and take care of that Child then you will experience yourself as being whole, today. You won't have those two infringing on who you are today.

Emily: I don't think I've ever made a clear separation from my mom. She was scared of everything, and still does that . . .

Rebecca: Yeah. I think a lot of your phobias are her. You took on her scare. With some clear traumatic events to support your taking on those scares, to validate the "Mom really had a reason to be scared, and I should be like . . ." whatever you decided. That protects you, and it protects her. But it keeps you two hooked. That's why I think the next step is for us to work with the Parent, and unhook that end of the hook. Then you'll be able to unhook the rest yourself.

Emily and the therapists continue to talk for a few more minutes, bringing the work to a close. Emily ends by saying that she wants to leave the group now, to go and be by herself, but recognizes that this is her old pattern of locking herself away; the therapists agree and advise her to stay in the group—which she does.

Emily's script has been built both out of introjections—pieces swallowed whole—from Mother (and perhaps from others as well; we've not explored those avenues) and out of decisions that Emily herself made. This is typical of most script patterns. Most of us introject bits and pieces from the significant adults in our lives, and we also (often unconsciously) make decisions about what we have to do in order to get along with those adults. Then we spend our lives, as Emily has done, playing out variations of the internal dialogue—the Parent stimulus/Child response pattern. In Emily's work, the therapists recognized that both of these elements were significant in the segment of script that determined Emily's compulsion to lock herself up. It was also clear, from the initial dream work, that Emily was intellectually and emotionally invested in breaking that compulsion, and wanted help from the therapists in doing so—that is, she had formed a strong therapeutic alliance.

A number of gains were made in the course of this work. First, Emily was able to experience her own dynamics, the conflict between Child and Parent ego states, in a new way. She has new cognitive as well as emotional information that she can integrate and use to understand and modify her own behavior. The therapists have also learned a great deal, and are now in a position to plan Emily's future treatment; in fact, the final portion of the work consisted of mutual treatment planning and contracting.

Finally, a major outcome was Emily's non-script-bound behavior during the work itself. With the support and direction of the therapists, she *did* begin to confront Mother, and she *did* reveal parts of herself that had been locked up. Furthermore, nobody went crazy or abandoned her as a result of that behavior. Her Child ego state thus had the opportunity to experience new and previously forbidden behavior, and to have that behavior reinforced rather than punished.

Emily did several more pieces of work during the workshop, including a focus on her suicidal decision, with immediate cessation of many of the phobic reactions. She continues in treatment with a therapist in her home community. Her script pattern is deeply entrenched, and Emily will need to renew these therapeutic experiences in a variety of contexts before she will be free of it. But she has made a significant beginning: There is a chink in the wall, and she no longer sits alone in the darkness of her self-imposed prison.

8

SARAH
The Emerging Plan

Integrative psychotherapy maintains that the client frequently knows, better than anyone else, what he or she needs to do. The client is—when not hampered by his or her own denial—the world's greatest expert on him- or herself, because he or she is the only one who lives inside that particular skin. As the client's awareness unfolds, he or she will let the therapist know what step is next in the intricate therapeutic dance. At the same time, however, integrative psychotherapists are trained to think in terms of defense mechanisms, diagnosis, and treatment planning. We expect ourselves to recognize our clients' script issues, to look beyond their confusion and scare and resistance, to plan interventions that will help them to go where they cannot go on their own. They know best what they need—but we must know better than they. It feels like a paradox, a contradiction, which demands resolution if we are not to become paralyzed in our efforts to be both therapeutic and respectful of our clients' inner wisdom. How can this paradox be resolved?

Actually, the paradox is more apparent than real. Diagnosis in integrative psychotherapy has to do with identifying the ways in which a client interrupts and distorts contact, both internally and externally. Internally, the therapist looks for splits (in which one or more aspect of the self is experienced as separated out and in conflict with the others), for introjects (some "foreign body," some thought/feeling/behavior configuration that has been borrowed from another person and not integrated into the self), and for any fixations from the past that may interfere with or disrupt the natural flow of assimilation and accommodation processes within the client. Externally, patterns of communication with others and the transferring of old reactive patterns of behavior into the current environment are the focus of diagnosis. Treatment planning, logically, grows out of the diagnosis of these distortions and interruptions: It is a series of hypotheses about what is occurring for this person, what needs to be shifted or strengthened or sorted out, and how such changes may best be accomplished.

If we keep in mind that diagnosis and treatment planning are, in fact, hypotheses—subject to validation or rejection by the data provided by the client—then the paradox between "respecting the client's wisdom" and treatment planning is dissolved. We have tended to think of both *diagnosis* and *treatment plan* as nouns. In integrative psychotherapy, they are verbs—they are processes, changing and evolving through the course of therapy. The treatment plan leads the therapist to pay particular attention to one aspect of what the client says and does, to ask this rather than that question, to set up a particular exercise or experiment. If the client does not respond in the expected way, the therapeutic hypothesis may be disconfirmed; the unexpected behavior stimulates a new wave of hypothesizing, or encourages the therapist to consider a different theoretical perspective. Gradually the pieces begin to fit together, the percentage of disconfirmations grows smaller and smaller; client and therapist are both aware of the treatment plan and are both invested in implementing it.

The work presented in this chapter provides an example of this kind of unfolding, developing treatment plan. At the outset, the therapist focuses on what is apparent to both him and the client: the feelings the client has toward him. The transferential aspects of these feelings are immediately obvious, and the work appears to be proceeding in a predictable, if dramatic, fashion. Later, however, the work takes a new and rather unexpected turn: Though the contact disruption remains clear, the underlying cause (and that which demands remediation) is not as it initially appeared.

Sarah is a quiet, rather stern looking woman in her midfifties. Throughout the workshop, she has become increasingly agitated. With the cooperation and support of both therapists, she has allowed herself to experience a great deal of painful affect: she has wept, screamed, huddled; at times her whole body has seemed to be in spasm. Because she is ordinarily a highly cognitive person, who tends to cut off her feelings (and thus an important avenue to awareness) by overanalyzing them, she has been encouraged to move into these affective experiences without attempting to understand them but rather simply to experience what her body is demanding. It is now late in the workshop, and time to put together some of the pieces that have emerged from this strategy—this treatment plan.

Richard: What's on your mind, Sarah?

Sarah: (*whispering*) It's in my body, Richard.

Richard: What's in your body?

Sarah: (*whispering even more softly*) Fear. I mean, you said it the first time—the love and the hate.

Richard: Wait, I can't hear you. And you're this close . . .

Already, Sarah is showing her ambivalence both verbally and nonverbally. Her words, "the love and the hate," are echoed in her almost inaudible speech: I want to make contact, and I want to stay away. By confronting the nonverbal message, Richard engages Sarah's healthier aspect in an agreement to be present for the work.

Sarah: (*pause*) I don't know what to say . . .

Richard: I just heard you say the word "hate" a moment ago; give me the first part of that sentence.

Sarah: It was what you said, the first day, it's love and hate.

Richard: Ah. What do *you* experience?

It is unclear, and for that matter relatively unimportant, whether

Richard remembers the context of the remark attributed to him, or understands what Sarah wants him to remember. Instead, Richard focuses on what Sarah is experiencing in the here and now. This is a direct outgrowth of the current treatment plan(ning), in which Sarah has been invited to feel, rather than analyze, her situation.

Sarah: I go back and forth.

Richard: Will you tell me more about that going back and forth?

Sarah: It's easy for me to hate you. And when I see you being soft and gentle, I can feel myself wanting to love you, and that terrifies me. And so I go back to hate.

Richard: And what do you use to hate me with?

Again, the intervention is designed to help Sarah to focus on her current internal state, and to take responsibility for that state. Rather than experiencing the "hating" as something that happens to her, out of her control, she is asked to attend to how she achieves that feeling—what she "uses" to accomplish it.

Sarah: Stay away.

Richard: What do you mean—my staying away, or your staying away?

Sarah: No, I do.

Richard: I asked you what you use to hate me with: What is there in my behavior that you're using as the focal point to hate me?

Sarah: Tenderness.

Richard: So you hate me because I'm tender. And you love me because I'm tender.

Richard points out the essential contradiction in Sarah's position. The very thing that draws her toward him is also what she finds hateful about him. Rather than exploring the contradiction further, though, she uses it to label and discount herself.

Sarah: And it's crazy.

Richard: What do you mean, it's crazy?

At this point, Rebecca moves in; she has worked with Sarah in a separate small group session, and thus has access to information not shared by Richard.

Rebecca: (*after a pause*) What if you substituted the word "scare" for "hate"?

Richard: (*after a pause*) Do you agree with her?

Sarah: I guess the hate is the way not to feel the scare.

Richard: Um. Now what's scary about my being tender with you?

Having taken Sarah's somewhat tangential response as confirmation of Rebecca's interpretation, Richard continues to help Sarah to go more deeply into the internal meaning of her experience.

Sarah: (*pause*) Cause it makes me feel.

Richard: And what memory will you have if you feel?

Sarah: (*crying*) Of hate.

Richard: What *memory* will you have?

Sarah: You're asking me what conscious memory, what things come to mind . . .

Richard: You won't tell me?

Sarah: Right now, right now I can't tell.

Sarah's nonverbal behaviors contradict her verbalizations. She says that she "can't tell" of her memories (and, by extension, her thoughts and feelings), but her weeping, her facial expression, and her gestures indicate that something important is going on internally. Richard calls attention to that contradiction, just as he earlier called attention to the conflict around loving and hating.

Richard: You just did, Sarah. You just had a memory. Starting to cry, that's a signal of an emotional memory. I didn't particularly ask you what pictures, or what conversation you recall . . . What memory comes to mind, as you focus on that fear?

Sarah: I have the feeling that if I say anything, something will . . .

As Richard gently but persistently redirects Sarah's attention to her ongoing experience, she uncovers a new awareness: She resists talking about her feelings and memories out of fear. Something bad will happen if she tells. This sense of foreboding is, in itself, the emotional memory. Sarah's nonverbal behavior has been suggesting that she is responding to some sort of prohibition, some sense of "I mustn't talk about it," and now she confirms the hypothesis. With the confirmation, Richard moves more strongly to deal with the resistance itself.

Richard: What happens if you talk about my tenderness with you? (*she begins to cry again and her hand moves to her throat*) Be aware of how you're squeezing your throat tight. Just feel those two forces: the desire to squeeze your throat so tight that you can't talk; and also, inside, the desire that's wanting to come through, to tell me. So squeeze tighter; feel that squeeze. Also pay attention to the desire to tell me about the tenderness . . . there's a memory about the tenderness . . .

Throughout this long intervention, Sarah continues to cry and clutch at her throat. Although Richard is the only one who is actually talking in words, there is really a dialogue here: Sarah is communicating nonverbally, and Richard speaks to those messages. He monitors her responses, timing each statement so that it either reflects or paces the ongoing process.

Richard: (*continuing*) There's a feeling in addition to the scare about telling me. Squeeze that throat tighter, so you feel the two forces . . . the desire to tell me about the tenderness and its effect on you, and the desire—the demand—not to speak out . . . Rebecca is right there behind you, for support . . . Now feel that defense in that hand, more . . . squeezing off the voice box . . . squeezing tighter, holding it in. Holding in all that which wants to come out . . . hold it even tighter now, so you feel how much energy goes into holding back . . . Now do the opposite—just drop the hand, and see what comes.

Sarah drops her hand to her side, and her sobs come more deeply. Her face and throat relax, and she seems to be experiencing herself through her whole body.

Richard: (*continuing*) Um-hm, let the shake come. My guess is that there's some significant punishment for telling. Or some painful memory that you're anxious about. (*long pause*) Sarah, you're wanting to tell me something about the tenderness.

Sarah: I want to, and I don't.

Richard: Well, if you don't do it we're going to run out of time, and then you're going to be real depressed about not having done what you wanted to do. So you're in a real double bind.

Sarah has indicated that the resistance she feels is now conscious; she is clearly aware that she is making a choice about whether or not to talk. Richard's response acknowledges this awareness, and reminds her of what she already knows: that she will be disappointed if she chooses to stay closed. Leaving the decision up to her, he is nevertheless respectful of the difficulty she experiences, and (in his next response, below) willing to help the frightened and confused part of her.

Sarah: I don't know what to do.

Richard: That's my job, is to know what to do. Your job is simply to talk to me about your inner experience.

Sarah: I, I, words don't come. I don't know what you want me to say.

Richard: I don't have a want . . . but listen to all of what you do. How you expect me to have a want for you to adapt to.

Rebecca: Also think about what you did yesterday. How it was so much easier, and the way you could be close with your dad, was when you looked for what he wanted, so you could match it, in order to be close. But not asking him to be close with what you wanted. You fit into him, without asking him to fit into you.

Rebecca, who worked with Sarah the day before, offers her a cognitive explanation. Perhaps, recognizing what she is doing now as an old pattern, she will be able to find new options in this situation.

Sarah: Well, I guess that's what he just said. I'm waiting for him to say something so I could please him.

Richard: Well, I'm not going to do that.

Sarah: (*in a despairing tone*) But then I have nothing.

Richard: No. You've got you. (*he holds out his hand to her, and she flinches away*) Just feel that recoil, Sarah.

Sarah, deeply reliving an old emotional pattern, responds with fear to the hand held out to her in support. What is the symbolic meaning of Richard's gesture, within her old framework? Sarah's response prompts a hypothesis, which is tested—and that she immediately rejects.

Sarah: (*sobbing*) It's just a hand: Why does it . . . Why do I see it as a threat? It's just a hand. Just a hand. Just a hand. I feel like it's reaching out to suck me in, and then I won't have anything; I'll have nothing. And I don't have anything if I don't . . .

Richard: It's not your mother's hand. That's the difference. It's not your mother's hand.

Sarah: It's my father's hand. It's not my mother's hand . . . It just looks like his hand. (*crying*) Richard, take it away! Take it away, take it away! (*sobs loudly*)

So the issue is not with Mother, but with Father. Father's hand is threatening—of what? The kind of ambivalence Sarah has been expressing: The "tenderness is good, tenderness is frightening," and the fear of telling (a secret?) are often found among children who have been sexually abused. The therapists do not want to program this idea, especially with a client who adapts and agrees as easily as Sarah does, but they do need to be alert to the possibility so that they can help her to deal with it clearly and openly. Here is a hypothesis they will keep to themselves, checking it against the data that emerge in the therapeutic process.

Richard: Now say that to Dad: "Take it away."

Sarah: Take it away.

Richard: Look at his face. Close your eyes, and look at your father's face. Say that to him: "Take it away."

Sarah: Take it away.

Richard: Louder.

Sarah: Take it away.

Sarah's "take it away" has been quiet, mechanical. She is obeying Richard's directions, but has withdrawn herself from her earlier emotional response. This is a familiar protective mechanism for her, one that allows (and allowed) her to overcome her distress and get along in her daily life. But it is not useful now, when she needs to access that frightened child part of herself and learn some new and different way to respond to her father. Richard continues to nudge her into a more affectively impactful experience.

Richard: Now feel all the emotions, like you felt with my hand, and say it to him: "Take it away."

Sarah: Take it away!

Richard: Louder.

Sarah: Take it away, take it away!

Richard: Don't hold it back now; just open this throat. Say "take it away."

Sarah: (*crying loudly now*) Take it away!

Richard: Louder.

Sarah: Take it away!

Richard: Scream it at him!

Sarah: (*screaming*) TAKE IT AWAY!

Richard: (*holding his hand out to be pushed against*) Push it away. Push on him. Push on it.

Even with her full verbal involvement, Sarah is still holding back. Her body is tense; she has not completely released the intense emotion of the earlier scene she is working through. By giving her his hand literally to push against, Richard offers her a chance to do physically what she needed to do as a child: take care of herself by rejecting that which was not wanted. Sarah responds by pushing the hand away and flinching back at the same time, as she screams in terror; she then begins beating on her knees with her clenched fists.

Richard: Push on it. Keep going, Sarah. This way. Not against you; out here. (*he guides her hands away from the self-beating, toward himself*) Out here, Sarah. Come on. Out here.

Rebecca: It's all right; you're not going to kill anybody. Go ahead.

Often, when a person is experiencing strong feelings of anger and fear, and acts out those feelings in gestures against the self, the underlying concern is that the feelings will go out of control and that someone else will be hurt or even killed. This fear relates to the grandiosity of the young child, who experiences her anger as so intense and so enormous that, if not held in check, she really might kill the (also loved) object of her rage. It is this hypothesis that guided Rebecca in her intervention.

Richard: Push against me!

Sarah continues to scream, and try to beat on herself, while both therapists redirect her movements against Richard's hands.

Rebecca: You're not going to kill him, Sarah. Just go ahead and push.

Sarah: (*her screams gradually become words*) . . . No! No! No! No!

Richard: (*shouting*) Yes! (*Sarah sobs, and then begins screaming NO! again*) Yes! Yes, yes, YES! (*suddenly, Sarah stops screaming and pushing, and seems to collapse in on herself*)

If Sarah is to learn to fight for herself, for her identity and her right to think and feel, she needs something to fight against. Pushing allows her to enact this scenario physically; countering her "No" with a "Yes" provides a verbal counterpart of the same struggle. Sarah, however, is unable to sustain the experience; her collapse is a sudden retreat into the old, "give up" pattern that she has been trying to replace.

Rebecca: Push, Sarah. Don't go dead inside. Stay here . . . Sarah . . . (*to Richard*) She's gone . . . Sarah, come back here. Sarah. Come back; you need to feel what you're feeling. Don't go away. You need to feel your body again. Come back and feel your body . . . Tell me what's happening.

Another typical characteristic of abused children is that they learn to dissociate—literally to turn off their physical sensations, and not-know what is happening to them. If this is indeed what happened to Sarah, her collapse is probably a response to the re-creation of that early family environment. She needs encouragement and support now, to bring her back from the dissociation. Rebecca takes the supportive role, while Richard's temporary role as antagonist is preserved.

Sarah: (*after a pause*) I don't know.

Rebecca: (*kindly and supportively*) Yeah, you do. Come on back.

Sarah: He isn't my father.

Rebecca: Um-hm. Look at him.

Richard: (*still holding out his hand*) Say "take it away."

As soon as Sarah is "back," she is encouraged to return to the unfinished business; it's important that she not end her work having simply reinforced the old pattern of giving up and believing that her own needs won't be attended to.

Sarah: Take it away.

Richard: Push.

Sarah: Take it away.

Richard: Get your hands out here and push; push out here. Push against me. Use me as him. Push. Say "take it away."

Sarah is sobbing and crying again, and begins again to pound her knees.

Rebecca: Sarah, don't hurt yourself.

Sarah: I don't want to hurt him.

Rebecca: Just push. Push.

Richard: "Take it away!"

Sarah: Take it away.

Richard: Louder.

Sarah: Take it away. (*screaming*) TAKE IT AWAY!

She moves back into the scene more easily this time, and appears to have more energy available to fight for herself. Richard decides to escalate—remember, he is still evaluating the hypothesis of sexual abuse.

Richard: Here comes the hand—the hand is coming—(*moving his hand closer and closer to her*)

Sarah: (*screaming*) NOOOOO! NO! NO!

Rebecca: Keep going, Sarah; push!

Richard: Here comes the hand . . .

The form of the drama has emerged clearly now: Richard is the "bad parent" while Rebecca is the supportive "good parent" from whom Sarah can borrow courage and energy to do the work.

Sarah: (*continues to scream "No!" as she fends off Richard's hand*)

Rebecca: Push! Let them hear your scream!

Richard: Here comes the hand . . . (*Sarah screams and sobs as she tries to fend off the intrusive hand*) Here it comes . . .

Rebecca: Push, Sarah. That's it, push!

Sarah's sobs are more and more deep and totally involving; she begins to make gagging noises. While this may be simply a physiological effect of the deep sobbing, it also may be connected to early sexual abuse; the gagging reflex is a common response to forced oral sex.

Rebecca: Keep pushing, Sarah.

Richard: And bite. Here. (*he offers her a folded towel to bite on*)

Sarah: (*bites down hard on the towel, as she continues to push and scream*)

Rebecca: With all that energy; that's good. (*her hand is on Sarah's diaphragm, to support and guide her breathing*) Let it right out of there, Sarah.

Richard: Bite. Here comes the hand!

Rebecca: Go ahead and bite!

Sarah bites, screams, and then quiets down, breathing heavily. Unlike her earlier collapse, this seems a natural and gradual transition from the intense effort she has been making.

Rebecca: Now be aware of the next feeling. (*Sarah begins to pound her knees again*) Don't hurt yourself. Just be aware of that next feeling.

Sarah: Ohhhh . . . it's an awful kettle of worms.

Richard: Let me . . . I know how to handle worms. Come on. What just happened, Sarah? (*She has begun sobbing again*) What just happened? What's in that kettle of worms?

Sarah: Oh, dear . . .

Richard: You know, Sarah. You know. You just saw it. You know about the kettle of worms. Tell us about that kettle of worms.

Is the "kettle of worms" the emerging conscious awareness of early abuse? If Sarah verbalizes this, the therapists can address it directly. But her answer is still ambiguous; the hypothesis remains to be validated:

Sarah: I keep saying he was never there and he never touched me. And yet I saw a picture of him reaching out to touch me.

Rebecca: What was with that reaching out?

Sarah: I don't know what was with it. It was just his hands.

Richard: You know what those hands can do.

Rebecca: Let yourself know, Sarah. You're very frightened about something.

Richard: What do those hands do? (*again, moving his hand closer to Sarah*) Here comes the hand . . . here it comes . . . Look at it, Sarah . . . here comes the hand . . . (*Sarah pushes the hand away, but her gesture is halfhearted; she is staring at the floor, and seems to be on the verge of dissociating again*) . . . Sarah, you gotta look at it. You said you were going to do this work . . . you gotta look at that hand, so you know what it's going to do to you.

Sarah: Should I look at it inside with him, or outside with you?

Richard's abrupt shift from the role he has been playing to a more cognitive appeal to Sarah's "observing self" has accomplished its purpose: She abandons the dissociation, and again commits herself to deal with the issue.

Richard: Inside.

Sarah: (*breathlessly*) I'm seeing it.

Richard: OK. It's coming closer . . . now push it away. Push it.

Sarah: I want it . . . I want it!

A major change: Sarah, having allowed herself to experience fully her need to get away from the hand, is now able to feel the opposite. Love and tenderness, as she said at the beginning of this work, are the other side of her hatred.

Rebecca: OK, feel that. Reach out for it. Do that feeling; reach out for it.

Sarah: Ohhh, ohhh . . . (*after only a second or two of softness, she suddenly begins to scream and sob again*)

Rebecca: Let yourself feel that—(*the screams almost drown out her voice*)—you want it, and you don't want it. (*Sarah's cries are becoming more infantlike*) All right, go with it, Sarah. Don't bite yourself.

Richard: There's something with your mouth, that's important.

Rebecca: Pay attention to that hand, Sarah.

Richard: It's coming for you. Take the hand, that you said you wanted. It's coming closer now. (*Sarah screams and pushes herself away*)

Rebecca: Sarah, let yourself know. Go with it. Let your hands move.

Richard: Push, push it away.

Sarah: (*Sarah is now screaming and pushing against a pillow that Richard holds up. Gradually, words emerge*) . . . I hate you! I HATE YOU! (*slowly, the screams subside*)

Rebecca: Be aware of what's going on inside. Don't worry about taking care of Richard.

Still careful not to program their own interpretation of the work—though everything that Sarah has done is consistent with the sexual abuse hypothesis—the therapists continue to follow the ebb and flow of Sarah's work. The therapy has taken on an almost rhythmic pattern, with each new surge moving further into unknown territory.

Sarah: (*beginning to push again, and to scream; the next few moments are hectic—Sarah is screaming and struggling with Richard, who talks about "the hand" coming closer, while Rebecca coaches her to "push"; after some time, she appears to tire, and the struggles stop*) . . . I don't know why I feel like that.

Richard: The "why" at this moment is premature. Just that you do know. It comes from inside of you, and your experience.

Sarah, after a brief rest, is ready to work again. She begins to push against Richard, who asks for a mattress so that she can use her whole body to express the pushing away. After some encouragement, she moves again into the screaming and struggling; finally words come:

Sarah: I want to kill you! I want to hurt you! Don't want to hurt you.

Rebecca: Yes, you do. Of course you do, for a good reason. That energy is good energy. It's going to help you know. (*Sarah continues to scream and fight against the pillow*) Push! Push, Sarah, and just say No.

Sarah: Noooo!

All three are active again; Rebecca is coaching Sarah, who screams "No!" as she fights against the mattress; Richard yells "Yes!" in counterpoint.

Richard: Yes! Do it my way! Do it my way!

Rebecca: Keep going, Sarah! Don't give in, just push!

Richard: My way's the only way!

Rebecca: Push! Tell him, "I want to kill you!"

Richard: My way!

Sarah: (*sinking down, panting for breath*) I have to rest . . .

Rebecca: You want to stop it here for now? Or do you need to keep on?

Sarah has been working very hard for some time, and her physical reserves must be significantly depleted. While the work is clearly not finished (and the sexual abuse hypothesis remains neither confirmed nor rejected), she has not caved in nor has she dissociated in these later rounds of activity. The work could end here, leaving her with the experience of having fought rather than given up, a significant therapeutic advance. Indeed, it may be this new experience that prompts Sarah's determination to continue:

Sarah: (*pause*) I would like to do just one more piece, one more little bit. I get another image, which is scary, but I think if I get one more image, maybe I'll have that with my eyes open.

Richard: What have you had up till now?

Sarah: Just images of my father; I won't really see him.

Rebecca: What do you see?

Sarah: A hand. Coming toward me, and reaching to me . . . And his face . . . (*her voice becomes so soft that the words are unintelligible*)

This new beginning really is different! Sarah's whole presentation has changed. Her voice is sad, almost tender. How does this fit with the terror and anger that she so recently experienced? How does it fit with the hypothesis that she is dealing with the trauma of sexual abuse? The therapists patiently follow her lead.

Rebecca: Look at the eyes; go back to the picture; look at the eyes in his face . . . Now let yourself know what his intention is. Look at that face, and let yourself know what his intention is. He's reaching out to you . . . He reaches out his hands to you . . .

Sarah: I still can't see it clearly. I know that at night he slept in the same room. For a year, almost a year. (*she sighs sadly*)

Rebecca: As a baby, you mean?

Sarah: No. When I was four. When my sister was . . . when she was sickly. So she stayed in the room with me, and he came and slept in the room with me.

Rebecca: And he'd come to your bed, and what?

Sarah: (*twisting her hands together*) I, I don't know.

Rebecca: Watch those hands.

Sarah: I think he was lonely. Wanted comforting.

Rebecca: What happened?

Sarah: I think he just wanted comforting. I think he wanted me to take him . . . (*begins to cry*)

Rebecca: Let it come, Sarah.

Sarah: (*crying*) I don't know why I'm so afraid. I'm just so afraid of my mother's anger.

A brand-new piece of information—suddenly, Mother is back in the picture. Rather than a feared father, is Sarah dealing with a desired father and a feared mother? Does "the hand" represent both, the tenderness of Father and the punishment of Mother? The sexual abuse hypothesis may be in the process of being disconfirmed; the therapists continue to follow Sarah's lead.

Richard: Say that again.

Sarah: I was afraid of my mother's anger. She, she, she (*stuttering*) . . . abandoned me.

Richard: Let yourself know what Mom will do if you get close to Dad.

The most cruel and terrifying threat to a small child is the threat of abandonment.

Sarah: (*still crying*) She did. She kept saying I was his daughter; I wasn't her daughter.

Richard: And what happens if you get close to Dad's touch? And if his hands are tender? And his voice is tender? And his relationship with you is loving?

Sarah: (*sobbing*) I lose me. I, I just live for him.

Richard: What happens between you and Mama?

Sarah: I become him, and I have no mother. It's like I feel everything he feels, and I don't feel anything I feel.

As Sarah experiences being cut off from Mother, she compensates by moving closer to Father. And she goes too far—like a child going closer and closer to the edge of a pool, and finally falling in, Sarah "loses herself" in Father. She no longer experiences her own boundaries; her desperate search for connectedness has led her to the kind of contact distortion called confluence, in which contact is not truly experienced because there are no longer two distinct individuals to make that contact. Or is this shift in Sarah's responses a defensive maneuver, to take the therapists' attention away from Father's abuse? At this point, the therapists hold several alternative hypotheses simultaneously. They choose interventions that will continue to provide data, so that all three participants—client and both therapists—can gradually eliminate that which is not useful and can focus on the areas in which healing is most needed.

Richard: And if you push him away—

Sarah: Like I know when he hurts, and when he feels depressed, and when he wants to kill himself. I have no me, and—

Richard: What happens between you and Mama if you feel his tenderness? That's how you lose the sense of you, by not focusing on your relationship with Mama.

On the basis of the last few minutes of work, Richard begins to suspect that Sarah's relationship problem with Father grows out of her loss of contact with Mother. This series of interventions is designed to test such a hypothesis.

Sarah: But she's not there for me.

Richard: What happens between you and Mama if he gets close to you?

This is the fifth time that Richard has asked this question. The Adult Sarah can understand the sequence of Dad's tenderness—Mom's angry rejection—child's fear, loneliness, overattachment to Dad; but her emotionally debilitated and overwhelmed Child ego state also needs to understand. Her unwillingness to state the relationship clearly may indicate that, emotionally, she hasn't gotten the message yet.

Sarah: She gets angry.

Richard: Yeah. Just feel that. What happens to a four-year-old girl when Mama's angry with her?

Sarah: I tried to run away.

Richard: What happens deep inside? To a four-year-old girl whose mother's angry because she's close to her daddy?

Sarah: Ahh, I get so confused and I just don't get close to anybody. I just—

A major part of the script decision, in Sarah's own words. Richard interrupts, to keep her from moving away from this point, and probes for the feelings that accompany the activation of this aspect of script belief.

Richard: That's how you solved it. What happens when you feel Daddy's tenderness? What happens when Mama sees him tender with you? And sees you loving him?

Sarah: She, she gets hurt.

Richard: What does she do then?

Sarah: She gets real hurt. She cries, and she gets depressed.

Richard: And what happens between you and Mama when Mama's depressed?

Sarah: Ohhh, I have to take care of her too.

Richard: And then what happens to you, inside?

Sarah: I hurt. I hurt all the time.

Rebecca: You hurt for Mama and you hurt for Daddy.

Sarah: I, I, I just keep it all in to myself.

Richard: Well, this time you put your mama right out there. And just begin with these words: "I want my daddy."

The hypothesis of sexual abuse appears to have less support; it is more likely that the therapists are dealing with a child who was forced to choose between Mother and Father. In order to keep Mother there for her, she had to give up—actually resist—closeness with Father. Yet, at the same time, her need for contact drew her into a confluent loss of boundaries with that same father. She needs to reexperience these relationships in a different way, demanding from the external world that which she needs, rather than burying those needs deep inside and covering them over with pain and depression, and losing her own sense of self in the process.

Sarah: (*sobs loudly*)

Richard: "I want my daddy, Mama."

Sarah: (*very softly*) I want my daddy, Mama.

Richard: Again—and tell her how you want her to react, emotionally.

Sarah: I want my daddy.

Richard: "And I want you to . . ."

Sarah: And I want you to be pleased that he's there for me.

Richard: Oh, good for you, Sarah. Say it again.

This is very much forbidden ground for Sarah; this was the need that she was not allowed to express. Richard quickly reinforces the request, to forestall any automatic self-punishment that Sarah may administer, and then invites her to repeat and strengthen the new response pattern.

Sarah: (*still in a soft, gasping tone; her hands are laced in front of her*) I want you to feel pleased about the fact that he's there for me.

Richard: Now, let your hands know what they're doing. Look at that gesture. Instead of praying for it, demand it. Instead of pleading for it, demand it. (*in a strong voice*) I want my daddy, and I don't want you to get angry. I want my daddy, and I don't want you to be depressed.

Sarah: I want you BOTH to be adults, damn it!

Rebecca: Um-hm. Right!

Richard: "And I want my daddy's tenderness . . ."

Sarah: Ahh, I want his tenderness.

Richard: (*helping her to strike with her hands against a pillow*) Do it with these hands harder, now. "I want his tenderness . . ."

Sarah has consistently kept her feelings dammed up by physically holding herself in. As she learns to move freely, in a manner congruent with her emotional response, she will be able to access those emotions more and more fully.

Sarah: I want his tenderness. I want his tenderness. And I don't want to feel I'm going to be punished if I get it.

Richard: Say it again: "I want his tenderness, and I don't want you to punish me, Mom."

Sarah: I want his tenderness, and I don't want you to punish me, Mom. (*she is crying*)

Rebecca: There you go, Sarah. Keep going—"I want . . ."

Sarah: (*sobs*) I want to be able to say what I want! I want to be able to feel!

Richard: "And I don't want you, Mom, to . . ."

Sarah: (*sobbing*) I don't want you, Mom, to punish me.

Rebecca: Right.

Sarah: (*sobbing even more loudly*) I don't want you to be angry at me.

Sarah's responses have a new quality here: She is dealing with her needs and wants in a genuine way, with body language and voice tone that match the content of her demands.

Richard: Again, harder, with those hands: "Don't punish me!"

Sarah: Don't punish me!

Richard: Harder.

Rebecca: Keep going, Sarah. Like this (*guiding her hands to pound the pillow*).

Sarah: DON'T PUNISH ME!

Richard: "I want my daddy!"

Sarah: (*the words are forced through her tears, as she energetically hits the pillow*) I want my daddy! I want my daddy! And I want him to want ME! And to feel he can have me!

Rebecca: Right!

Richard: "And don't punish him, either!"

Sarah: Don't punish him!

Rebecca: "I want a mommy and I want a daddy."

Sarah: I want a mommy and a daddy! Ohhh . . .

This is the core of Sarah's unmet need: both *Mommy and Daddy, rather than having to choose either one or the other. Again, her clear expression of it is supported, strengthened, approved of. She gains from the therapists the permission she needed, and was not given, as a child.*

Rebecca: That's what every child needs. A mommy and a daddy. A mommy and a daddy who love each other and can both give that little girl what she needs.

Sarah: (*pause; she begins to make a curious, reaching gesture toward Richard but cuts it off and returns her hands to her lap*)

Richard: You're holding something back right now . . . Say that, that the hand was holding back. First thought that came into your mind.

Sarah: (*pause, then very softly*) I want to come over to you, Richard.

As the permission is taken in, and Sarah's Child ego state begins to experience her new freedom to express herself, she takes the first, tentative step to act as she wants to, rather than in accordance with her old restrictions. This is a clear sign that script change is taking place: new behavior patterns replacing old ones. Note that it is Rebecca, still in the role of "good mother," who quickly supports Sarah's request for closeness with Daddy/Richard.

Rebecca: Go on over.

Sarah: (*whispering*) It's scary.

Rebecca: I'm right here with you.

Richard: What are you anticipating Mom will do right now? What's the punishment for your reaching out to me?

Sarah: The punishment is for me to, if I reached out to him, he withdrew.

Richard: That's secondary.

Sarah: But that's what I saw.

Richard: OK, you just said it in here, why he withdrew. She also punished him for being close with you.

Sarah: But I think I felt more his withdrawal. Cause I wanted . . .

Richard: Well, if he got you, he probably lost his wife.

The therapy is in danger of sliding off into a cognitive discussion, before Sarah has had the opportunity really to cement her script change by acting on the new permission. Rebecca brings it back by assuming again the role of the "good mother."

Rebecca: So look at my face . . . What do you see in my face?

Sarah: (*pause*) It's all right.

Rebecca: (*shifting her position so that she is beside Sarah, and there is an unobstructed path from Sarah across to Richard*) Now, go ahead and reach out.

Sarah: (*begins to sob frightenedly*)

Rebecca: Sarah, look at me.

Richard: Let her get her needs met, Mom. Mom, don't you *dare* get angry at her! For what she wants. You *stop* it, Mother!

Both therapists are now overtly supporting Sarah's new behavior: Richard is lending his own energy to Sarah's demands, acting as the strong, able-to-take-care-of-himself father who will protect Sarah from Mother's punishment, while Rebecca is providing a new and positive "mother" for Sarah to experience.

Rebecca: Now look at my face.

Richard: You respect her wants, Mother. And don't punish her. (*Sarah suddenly moves into Richard's arms and there are delighted chuckles from the group; Richard holds Sarah, while continuing to address the fantasied mother*) Don't you ever get angry at this girl because she wants to love.

Sarah: Tell her not to get angry at you, Richard.

Richard: And no getting angry at me! I am going to do what's good for her.

Sarah: (*begins to cry and tremble*)

Richard: Stop it, Mother! Just knock it off! This little girl is just fine. (*Sarah grows quiet and begins to relax in his arms*) And there's room for you to get affection too, Mother. There's room for you to get affection; there's enough affection for everybody. You don't have to be jealous of your little girl. I know you're tired, you need more affection—we all do. And there's enough to go around.

Sarah: (*snuggling into Richard's arms*) Ahhhhh . . . I know that's a big lie. But it feels so good!

Richard: There's enough. There really is.

Rebecca: It was a lie back there, maybe. They didn't know how to make it work. There was enough, but they didn't know how. But look at what's true here. Look at . . . With all these people here, there's enough!

With this final statement, Rebecca sums up the essence of script change: that which may have been needed for survival when the client was young is no longer needed in the present. Sarah's old decision, that she had to repress her needs in order to protect herself (by protecting Father from Mother's rage, and herself from abandonment by both parents) is no longer necessary. Even though the significant people in her early life didn't know how to share affection, the significant people in her life now can do so, and Sarah's expression of needs will no longer destroy contact with those significant people.

This piece of work illustrates a number of central aspects of integrative psychotherapy. It shows graphically the importance of allowing a hypothesis to be tested, and kept or discarded, on the basis of the emerging therapeutic process rather than programming in the responses and directions that the therapist expects. Had the therapists not been careful to allow Sarah to explore her feelings about Father on her own terms, they might well have ended up working with a nonproblem, trying to change a script pattern that never existed. This could have resulted in a new, and similarly destructive, script overlay ("My father really was abusive and not to be trusted," or "Nobody, even therapists, can understand me," or "There really is something wrong with the way I feel"), with a further defensive closing down and strengthening of the old, retroflective pattern.

Another feature of this work is the therapists' sensitivity to closure—or its absence. We saw in Chris's work, in Chapter 3, the importance of stopping the work at the point at which the client has had enough. In the work with Ben (Chapter 4), the piece was ended even though Ben himself was willing to go on; to do so would have weakened the impact of what had been accomplished. In Sarah's work, it was desirable to find a point of resolution, a way in which Sarah could enact the new decision behaviorally. Had this not been done, her powerful and punishing Parent ego state might well have undermined the affective and cognitive changes she had made. To be sure, Rebecca did suggest at one point midway in the work that Sarah might be ready to stop; but this would have been a second-choice solution to her temporary "stuckness." Until she moved into

Richard's arms, Sarah's body language continued to signal her fear, the ongoing influence of the introjected destructive messages. Only as she allowed herself actually to receive that which she so deeply needed—the safe affection and protection of a strong father—did her cognition, affect, behavior, and physiological responses come together into a total experience that could be carried out of the therapy situation into her ongoing social interactions.

9

BILL
Replacing a Destructive Introject

As we have pointed out in many of the preceding chapters, script is formed through defensive decisions made by the Child, or through introjects stored in the Parent ego state; most often, a given script belief or feeling involves elements of both Parent introject and Child decision. If a strongly held script belief is to be changed, the Parental aspects must be defused or decommissioned, and the Child decision must be given up or changed. Sometimes these two processes will take place in tandem; in other pieces of work, either the Child or the Parent aspect will be treated first, with a follow-up needed to deal with the other.

Identification and internalization are natural developmental processes that help a child assimilate and learn about the environment—they facilitate contact. Introjection, on the other hand, is a defense mechanism, an avoidance of contact. The young person introjects parental figures because there is no real contact with them. He or she may also use introjection to avoid conflict too intense to handle, because internal and external supports are not yet fully developed. Through introjection, the conflict is internalized, giving the child the illusion of being in control.

When a client has introjected a particularly destructive set of messages from parents, addressing those messages is often the first task in therapy. Until the punitive parental introject has been removed or at least weakened, the Child cannot make a new decision—to do so would not be safe. The original decision was made out of the need to survive in the face of destructive parental behavior, and until that threat of punishment is changed, the decision must be maintained. A punitive, harsh, critical Parent ego state must be decommissioned (as we have seen in the Parent interview work in previous chapters), cutting off the internal influence. When this cannot be accomplished, the therapist may develop a close, protective relationship with the client and intervene in such a way that he or she forms an interposition—like a wedge—between the influencing Parent ego state and the frightened or adapted Child ego state. In other situations, where the Parent ego state is particularly rigid or the client does not have a sense of self in the face of the influencing Parent, the client may need to internalize the thoughts, feelings, and behaviors of a new parental figure: the person of the therapist and the therapeutic environment provide a temporary relief from the harsh and punitive Parent ego state. The therapist interposes him- or herself between the punitive Parent ego state and the Child, allowing the client to work on early experiences that may otherwise remain repressed. The therapist provides a caring and safe environment, free from Parental abuse, in which the Child ego state can confront parental figures or experiment with prohibited behaviors. After the client has internalized an increased sense of support, has dropped some defenses or made redecisions, then the treatment plan may call for actually defusing the Parent ego state and integrating the entire experience of childhood (seen now from an expanded perspective) into the Adult ego state.

Bill, whom you will meet in this chapter, exemplifies the client suffering from severely destructive introjects. Bill is a young psychiatrist who has finished his residency and is frightened about going on with his career. He acts unsure of himself, and holds himself back in social situations, particularly with women. Bill's mother was physically and psychologically abusive, and Bill's Child ego state is virtually immobilized in the face of her attacks. His terror is so great that he retreats to the same archaic defense mechanism that we saw in Sarah's work in Chapter 8: dissociation, simply leaving the psychological field. As the work progresses, Richard becomes the good parent, who offers his own protection to Bill; later, Rebecca serves as a stand-in for the bad mother. In this new setting, Bill is able to take the first tentative steps toward script change.

During another participant's work, the therapists have noticed that Bill seemed engrossed in the process. His interest was more than cognitive; he was emotionally caught up in the work and his face reflected a kind of wistful longing. Richard decides to capitalize on Bill's identification with the other participant as a way of bringing him into his own work.

Richard: Bill, you looked so keenly interested in Tanya's work—what's happening with you?

Bill: I was more interested in the way you were talking to Tanya, than in her actual story.

Richard: How would you like to be talked to?

Having formed, from Bill's initial check-in and from his behavior during the first days of the workshop, a hypothesis about his Child fearfulness and need for support, Richard is quick to recognize what Bill is responding to. The work with Tanya had involved listening carefully and respectfully to her ideas, reinforcing her ability to think for herself, helping her to decide that she is of worth in and of herself. It is not the ideas—not the content—however, that have fascinated Bill. It is Richard's consistent and caring interest. Richard's question recognizes the appropriateness of Bill's focus, and encourages him to explore it further.

Bill: (*laughing softly*) The same way.

Richard: How is that, Bill?

Bill: Um . . . gently.

Richard: Well, come and sit over here, and let's talk gently to each other.

"Come and sit over here" invites Bill out onto the mat, where therapy is done with those who request time in the group. As Bill accepts the invitation, he tacitly agrees to work, and provides himself with a set of visual and kinesthetic anchors that will further strengthen his experiencing himself as a person who is actively involved in the therapeutic process. Even more important, though, he moves close to Richard, into touching distance—within the boundary that often defines how far support and reassurance can travel between child and adult.

Richard: (*continuing*) You want to include Rebecca in this? Or would you rather leave her out?

It is not clear whether Richard is responding here to some earlier communication with Bill, which led him to suspect that Rebecca might usefully play the role of the bad parent, or whether he is still searching for the best way to build on Bill's response to his gentleness. In either case, Bill's answer is revealing:

Bill: (*pause*) I'd like to turn my back on her.

Richard: All right. You want to do it even more overtly? (*Bill and Richard shift so that Bill's back is toward Rebecca*) Now what does that symbolize?

Bill: That my mother used me to fight against my father.

Richard: She used you as a weapon against him?

Bill: Um-hm.

Richard: How?

Bill: (*pause*) She needed an ally. She came to a place with him where she felt all alone, and she needed somebody to fight for her.

Bill's voice has gotten softer and breathier. He is staring at the floor, rather than looking at Richard. His whole posture is one of cowering, as if he expected to be punished for what he is saying. This quality, as well as the way in which he has shifted to offering excuses for his mother's behavior, signals Richard to attend to Bill's present emotional experience.

Richard: How are you feeling, as you tell me this?

Bill: (*pause*) Sort of . . . frightened.

Richard: Did your dad talk to you gently?

We know that Bill was not treated gently by his mother—did he get good, positive parenting from his father? If so, he can be helped to access his experiences with Dad as a resource in dealing with Mom.

Bill: No.

Richard: How did he talk to you?

Bill: We would fight a lot.

Richard: Was he an alcoholic? (*Bill shakes his head "no"*) Well, why would he fight with a little boy? Instead of talk to him gently?

Notice the repeated use of the word gently. *Richard doesn't know specifically what this word means to Bill, or why it is important—but it was "gentleness" that caught and held Bill's attention. As he explores Bill's interactions with both parents, Richard both speaks gently and kindly, and repeats the words* gently *and* gentle *as a way of continually reminding Bill of this focus.*

Bill: I don't know, he wanted to be gentle, but didn't know how.

Richard: So what's it feel like to sit here and listen to me be gentle?

Bill: Feels like you can be the way that he wanted to be.

Richard: Do you like that?

Bill: Um-hm. I do.

Richard: What do you like about it?

Bill: Well, I wanted to spend more time with my father . . . but I couldn't, because we were always fighting.

The transference is overtly acknowledged: It feels good to be here with you, the way I would have liked to have been with my father. And, slowly, the energy and attention begin to have an effect on Bill. While his voice is still soft, and his manner hesitant, he is gradually gaining assurance. Richard continues to "transfuse" him with good parental energy, while at the same time giving him time and permission to sort out for himself how he can best use this experience.

Richard: Would you like to spend more time with me?

Bill: Yes, I would.

Richard: What would you like to do with me?

Bill: (*pause*) Maybe go for a drive in the country.

Richard: What'd you like to see in the country? Or to talk about while we are driving?

Bill: Just maybe about everything. So that I could understand it better.

Richard: Everything in nature, the countryside, or . . .

Bill: Well, I'm thinking that one of the things that my dad did do is, he sometimes took me for rides on Sundays.

Unlike many clients, Bill is very clearly aware of the transference feelings—of the way in which he is responding to Richard as if he (Richard) were Father. Bill wants to spend time with Richard just as he did during the rare pleasant interludes with Dad. And, in the interest of strengthening that positive aspect of a parental relationship, Richard offers to extend himself in that role beyond the ordinary boundaries of the therapeutic setting.

Richard: Want to go to the garbage dump with me today?

Bill: (*laughing*) Is that where you're going?

Richard: Uh-huh. Take a ride to the dump?

Bill: Sure.

Richard: Most exciting place in town. There's *treasures* in the garbage dump! . . . You never got to play in the garbage dump?

Bill: No.

Richard: I think that's deprivation. (*chuckles from the group*)

Disguised as mild humor, this comment marks a shift into a new phase of the work. Bill has been deprived of the opportunity to act like a child, to play normally; his soft-spoken, tentative, careful manner is, in part, the legacy of this deprivation. And, again, Bill's readiness to pick up on this theme indicates that he, too, understands what has happened to him as well as (less clearly) what may now be possible to change.

Bill: Got to play in the ditch.

Richard: Did you like playing in the ditch?

Bill: Yes, but I had to be careful not to get dirty.

Richard: Wait a minute. Something's crazy. How can you play in the ditch and not get dirty?

Bill: By walking along the edge, very carefully.

Richard: Then you're not playing.

Bill: Oh, sometimes I went ahead and went in.

Richard: At what price?

Bill: I wasn't supposed to.

Richard's question hits Bill hard; not only does he give a nonanswer, but his face contorts slightly, he moves back into a more hunched, cowering position, and his voice is frightened again. Gently still, Richard repeats the question.

Richard: At what price?

Bill: (*long pause; he is fighting tears*)

Richard: Go ahead, Bill.

Bill: (*almost whispering*) If I got dirty, I got spanked.

"Spanked" is a euphemism; Bill has already described the vicious beatings his mother administered to him whenever he showed signs of breaking out of her control. Bill was not allowed to behave like a little boy, and he needs to have that experience—without threat of retaliation. His manner indicates that he has indeed cathected the Child ego state from which the work needs to be done; he is reacting like a little boy now, rather than like a grown man.

Richard: Would you like it if we could fix it up so you could get dirty with no punishment?

Bill: Um-hm.

Richard: What do you think, Vic? You think he ought to be shown one of your favorite places?

Vic: Sure.

Vic, another participant, has attended several workshops and has dealt with some issues similar to Bill's. The previous summer, Vic had been encouraged to play in a muddy area at the edge of the pond behind the lodge at which the workshops are held; it is this mud hole that Richard is talking about.

Richard: (*continuing*) Vic's got a favorite place around here. It's very mucky.

Bill: (*laughing*) The pond.

Richard: Yeah, he found a favorite spot in the pond, that he likes to muck in. Ever had a mud fight? (*chuckles from the group*) When you played in the ditch? Did you ever throw mud balls at each other?

Bill: Well, I, no, I didn't. I went in the ditch but I didn't play, I fell in.

Richard: Would you like to have played in the ditch? And made mud pies, and mud balls, and throw them at each other?

Bill: Um-hm.

Rather than return to a scene of pain and humiliation, of falling in the ditch and facing Mother's rage, Richard redirects Bill to the positive fantasy, and the possibility of enacting it here. Bringing in Vic as a helper allows for the expansion of the fantasy to include supportive, caring playmates; the group's obviously genuine enjoyment attests to their willingness to be a further resource in the playing out of what Bill needed, but didn't have, in childhood. With all these resources in place, and the prospect of fun-with-permission in store, plus the benefit of having been "talked to gently" for some time now, Bill may be ready to take another major step: to begin to deal with Mother.

Richard: Without getting spanked . . . Now what do you suppose you'd feel if you turned around and talked to Rebecca?

Bill: (*pause*) I'd feel good.

Richard: You would?

Bill: Um-hm.

Bill's response here is surprising; we might have expected some carryover of his fear of Mother onto the suggested talk with Rebecca, because he certainly seemed to be setting Rebecca up as a mother-substitute early in his work. At this point, it isn't clear whether he is being a "good boy" by going along with what he thinks Richard wants, or has dropped the connection between Rebecca and Mother, or is dealing with some other part of a real or fantasied contact with her. Whatever is going on, though, it will still be important to provide continuing support for Bill, so that he will not collapse back into weakly submitting to Mother's abuse.

Richard: Well, let's try something. You turn around, where I can back you up and be your support. OK? (*Bill turns to face Rebecca; Richard moves in very close behind him so that he can feel Richard's chest against his back*) Feel my support?

Bill: Um-hm.

Richard: Now you just go ahead and tell her what you wanted to say.

Bill: (*long pause*) I can't say anything.

Richard: Say that again.

Bill: I don't feel like I can say anything.

Richard: Cause you're feeling scared?

Bill: No, cause I'm getting angry.

That Bill would be afraid was a reasonable guess, given what he has already said. His reply is somewhat unexpected, but only because it (and the feelings it describes) comes so soon. Surely that little boy must have been angry about how he was treated; equally surely, to have expressed the anger would have invited swift and severe punishment. The fear that he showed earlier in his work served a defensive function in that it kept him from behaving so as to be punished. That he has been able to go beneath the fear to the angry feelings is a good sign: The work is proceeding well.

Richard: Go ahead and say that: "I'm angry at you."

Bill: I'm angry at you.

Richard: Louder. Cause I'm going to be here so you don't get hit.

Rebecca: I'll listen; keep going.

The reenactment is now explicit. Richard will protect Bill from being punished for his anger; Rebecca will serve as a screen, a symbol of the mother who was the appropriate target for that anger.

Bill: (*pause, then softly*) I'm angry at you.

Richard: Just begin to squint your eyes, so you don't quite see Rebecca. She's just an image out there . . .

Bill, while needing an external object on which to focus his anger, has difficulty using Rebecca in this way. He likes and trusts her, and his positive feelings for her may be interfering with his keeping her in the role of the bad mother. Richard provides a strategy for dealing with this problem, and then invites Bill back into the fantasy.

Richard: (*continuing*) Say "I'm angry." (*pause*) "Angry at you."

Bill: I can't say I'm angry.

Richard: (*holding Bill's hand firmly*) Well, just feel my hand here . . . feel it right into this hand.

Bill: I feel really bad if I say that.

Rebecca: That's something you're not supposed to say to me.

Bill: I'm angry at you. (*long pause*) Cause you kept using me to fight against my father.

By speaking up again as Mother, Rebecca helps Bill to use her in that role. Saying the forbidden words frightens him badly; he is pale and shaking, his face is contorted, and he is breathing rapidly.

Richard: Just take a deep breath—see her, Bill. (*pause*) You're scared, aren't you? Can you feel my touch?

Bill: Yes.

Richard: That touch will protect you. You won't be punished for telling her what you know and what you feel.

Bill continues to breathe very rapidly. He has lost eye contact with Rebecca, and is clutching at the mat with both hands. As his hyperventilation accelerates, he begins to lose sensory contact with his environment. In ego state terms, his Adult is no longer available to help in the therapeutic process; he looks, feels, and breathes like a terrified child. In order for him to have a new, healing experience, rather than reinforce his old script beliefs, Bill must have access to some new source of energy and protection; he must maintain contact with the supportive therapist. Both therapists tacitly agree to take time out from the regression experience in order to bring Bill back into contact with them; they will provide the support that is not, at this time, available to him within his own neopsychic functioning.

Rebecca: Slow your breathing down.

Bill: (*barely able to force out the words*) I can't hear you. I'm tingling all over.

Rebecca: Slow your breathing down. The tingling will go away. Bill, just take a breath in and hold it.

Richard: (*as Bill manages to inhale deeply and then exhale*) All the way out, Bill, push it out. Now all the way in, take it in, hold it—now let it out. All the way in . . . and all the way out.

This is a nice example of the way a very brief grounding can bring a dissociating client back into contact. Slowing his breathing breaks the hyperventilation cycle; it also provides a new rhythm that can help Bill to slow his racing thoughts. As this is accomplished, he is ready to refocus on his affect.

Rebecca: And feel what you're feeling, Bill.

Richard: Lots of feelings there. Angry, and scared. Squeeze my hand, so you feel me . . . What would it have been like if you'd had somebody there as your protector, who you could squeeze onto?

Bill: (*his breathing is quieting*) Been good.

Richard: Um-hm. What does it feel like right now, that I'm here for you?

Bill: Tingling again, all over.

Richard: In a good way? (*Bill's breathing begins to accelerate again*) Breathe slow.

Why is Richard's invitation to think about and feel the support so frightening to Bill? It would be useful to explore this, but it is a side issue in terms of what has already been begun. The therapists choose to go back to the anger with Mother, rather than switching to another avenue of exploration.

Rebecca: Bill, let yourself really feel what you're feeling emotionally. Even though it's scary. Start telling me about being mad at me, for how I used you. You need to feel it.

Bill: Can't.

Rebecca: You need to. Come back to that: "I'm mad at you for using me."

Richard: (*pause; then whispers something unintelligible to Bill*)

Rebecca: Ready to come back to it?

Bill: No, I don't want to be angry with . . . Want to be by myself.

Richard: Feel me. Instead of being by yourself, feel me. (*pause; Bill is hyperventilating again*) Just grab onto me, Bill. Just notice. It's you and me here. Stead of being all alone, you got an ally. Just feel this! Feel how solid my arm is. I can push her away. Would you have liked that, as a little kid?

Bill's "want to be by myself" is a direct return to script. The survival choice he made was to cut himself off and be alone rather than open up to an unreliable father or an abusive mother. Richard makes no attempt to deal with this cognitively—Bill, experiencing the world like a scared little boy, wouldn't be able to hear. Instead, he moves in physically, choosing the primitive modality that even a frightened child can attend to. And the strategy is effective: Bill begins to put into words the core of the struggle with Mother.

Bill: You wouldn't let me be a boy. You wanted me to be a girl.

Rebecca: Mom or Dad?

Bill: Mom. She wanted a girl.

Richard: You tell her what that's like for you.

Bill: I think they wouldn't let me be a girl either.

Richard: Yeah. Confusing, huh? Why didn't she like the little boy in you?

Bill: Because he was, kept getting into trouble.

Richard: Well, I *like* troublesome little boys. You know why? Cause they're spunky. And they grow up to be exciting men . . . Feel me? (*Bill is holding tightly to Richard's arm, and begins to sob*) Just let that come. Let that come. You needed a protector . . . Let it come. (*Bill sobs hard for a few seconds, then grows quiet*)

To reinforce Bill's finally voicing the forbidden idea, and to prevent him from punishing himself internally, Richard moved in quickly with support and warmth. This is almost pure reparenting: giving the Child Bill the kind of approval and healthy modeling that he needed. Bill is literally being taught how to be a male. That the intervention is potent can be inferred from Bill's sobs—a mixture of deep sorrow over what he never had, and the joy of experiencing it now. But his anger with Mother remains unfinished. It is time to go on.

Rebecca: Come on back, Bill.

Richard: Face her now, Bill, as you're holding on to me.

Rebecca: Talk about being mad. (*long pause*) Those feelings that have been buried.

Bill: Um . . . I think I have to be mad for a while.

Rebecca: For a while?

Bill: Um-hm.

Rebecca: Tell me about that.

Bill: I think that's how she got me to give up being mad. She'd spank me until I couldn't be mad any more.

Richard: A terrible thing to do.

Richard is still sitting behind Bill, holding him tightly, and Bill is clutching him in return. Again, the division of roles is clear: Rebecca, as Mother, confronts and invites Bill to deal with his anger and his scare, while Richard serves as supporter and protector.

Bill: Until I couldn't be me any more.

Richard: Couldn't be you any more?

Bill: (*nods*) Till I didn't know who I was.

Richard: Part of the way you're going to find out who you are now is to feel this protection. Feel the strength in my arm? Just feel that muscle there. Feel me wrapped around you. (*Richard is still sitting behind Bill, with his arms around him*) Feel this guy that's inside of my arm?

Bill: Um-hm.

Richard: So your body gets to feel protection instead of hits. Gets to feel affection instead of neglect.

The relationship continues, and Richard clearly states his intention. Bill gets the protection, and the strong male model, that he needed; moreover, he gets it in the context of a confrontation with his punitive mother. To reestablish this latter theme, Rebecca intervenes:

Rebecca: (*pause*) Ready to tell me more about that?

Bill: Hm-um. (*shaking his head*) If I'm starting to feel like a boy, I'll get into trouble.

Rebecca: How do you solve that dilemma? Of being a boy, and you're not supposed to be a boy?

Bill: Kept getting into trouble anyway. For a while. And then I started being good.

Rebecca: What did "good" mean? "Being good" mean?

Bill: Good meant going away and being by myself.

Here is another part of Bill's pattern of withdrawal. Whenever he begins to feel comfortable, so that he might begin to loosen up and join in a conversation or activity, he reminds himself that he must not get into trouble—he must "be good." And to "be good" means to be isolated. He works within a feedback system in which moving out of the old behavior pattern (withdrawal and isolation) automatically sets off a warning signal ("you aren't being good"); the signal, in turn, arouses old feelings of fear and rage, which can only be dealt with by returning to the withdrawn and isolating behaviors.

Rebecca: How do you feel when you think about doing that?

Bill: (*very softly*) I just don't want to do it anymore.

Rebecca: Yeah.

Richard: Hold on to this hand.

Bill: (*a little more firmly*) I don't want to do it anymore.

Richard: Hold tighter, and shout it.

Bill: (*breathlessly*) I don't want to be by myself, anymore.

Holding, and being held by, Richard—the surrogate father—allows Bill to gain energy and courage. He has practiced saying what he really wants, with Richard's support. Now he will be brought back to the original script-forming situation, still with the physical and emotional support of a therapist.

Richard: Just shout it at her, in a nasty way.

Bill: (*breathing harder again, and trembling with his held-in intensity*)

Rebecca: Let yourself feel that, Bill.

Richard: (*coaching*) I—Don't—Want.

Bill: I don't want to be good any more.

Richard: Tell her some more of the "don't wants."

Bill: I want to be . . . I want to be a little boy. I don't want to be a little girl.

Notice how easily and naturally Bill expresses himself in Child language. This kind of smooth transitioning indicates that Bill is still ready to work, and also that Richard has prepared him well to access his early experiences.

Rebecca: Keep going. I want, and I don't want. Just let them come.

Richard: (*simultaneously*) I gotcha, Bill. Come on! That's my guy . . .

Bill: I want you to like me as a little boy.

Richard: Atta boy! Let's go! Keep going!

Bill: (*pause*) I don't know. I don't feel like shouting.

Rebecca: Do it your way. "I want," or "I don't want."

By energetically encouraging Bill, Richard hopes to help him tap into his positive emotional energy, to avoid cutting off his feelings and dealing with this issue at a purely cognitive level. There is always a danger, with this kind of forceful leading, that the client may adapt: may go along with suggestions simply to please the therapist or to avoid a fight, even though his own sense is that he needs to do something else. Rebecca's intervention here is designed to counter this possibility, to give Bill permission (again, a permission he didn't have as a child) to know what he needs and to act on it, even if others think he should be doing something else.

Bill: (*long pause*) I'm gonna stay being a little boy. I'm not gonna be a little girl, and I won't go away, I won't (*his voice dies off to an unintelligible mutter*).

Richard: Cause tell her what being a girl means to you. What you have to lose inside of you, to be girlish.

Bill: I have to be a girl all the time. Sit down, and behave.

Richard: That the difference? Girls are good and behave, and boys are bad?

Bill: No, girls have all the power, too.

Bill has clearly indicated that he's not ready to confront Mother with energy, even with the backing of Richard. It's too dangerous, he has too much to lose, and he's just not strong enough yet. Richard accepts this and moves back into a more supportive role. Providing Bill with good fathering, in terms of both feelings and information, will give him new and positive experiences to integrate in the days to come; as that integration becomes firmer, he may be ready for another step. For now, though, Bill has set the limits of what he is willing to accept and work with.

Richard: Boy, somebody lied to you, Bill.

Bill: That's the way it was in my family.

Richard: Well, they lied to you.

Bill: They got to do whatever they wanted to do.

Richard: Girls? (*Bill nods*) Well, then I would think you might get all confused, and think sometimes you wanted to be a girl and sometimes you wanted to be the young man that you were. Been confused a lot about what sex you were?

Bill: Um-hm. My mother didn't really want me to be a girl, but she didn't want me to have any power, either.

Richard: So what do you do with that little thing hanging between your legs, if she wants you to be a girl?

Bill: Forget about it.

Richard: It's too enjoyable to forget about . . . How did you forget about it?

In this and the next sequence of responses, Richard continues to draw out the little boy's experience of growing up and forming a sense of who and what he was. The questions and comments combine interest, support, and permission-giving with positive male modeling: the essence of the relationship that Bill needs.

Bill: I didn't grow up. I just stayed a little boy.

Richard: Hm. Well, there's certainly more pleasure in a man's organ than in a little boy's organ, isn't there?

Bill: Well, little boys can have fun too.

Rebecca: Is that what you did?

Richard: How do you have your fun?

Bill and Richard have closed Rebecca out at this point, and both ignore her question. This is "man-talk," the kind of father-son exclusiveness that can only happen when Dad is both open to talk about male issues and powerful enough to keep Mom out—exactly the kind of parenting that Bill was denied.

Bill: How did I have my fun?

Richard: Uh-huh.

Bill: (*chuckling*) Off by myself.

Richard: Did you play with that little wing-ding off by yourself?

Bill: Um-hm.

Richard: Is that how you knew you were a boy? Did you go and masturbate?

Bill: Um-hm. I started really young.

Richard: Did you masturbate a lot?

Bill: Um-hm.

Richard: And she never caught you?

Bill: Yes, she did.

Richard: What did she do when she caught you?

Bill: It was already too late.

Richard: What do you mean? You'd already popped?

The casualness of this question contains acceptance of Bill's behavior, as well as information about the naturalness of his physical responses. Again, it is man-talk, "this is the way we guys are."

Bill: No, I was already having too much fun.

Richard: Then what did she do when she caught you?

Bill: I don't know.

This is almost certainly a defensive retreat. Bill's Child ego state does not want to deal with Mother, with her punishment, her disapproval, her power. Rather than recall what happened, and risk reexperiencing that pain, he begins to withdraw again. Richard draws him back into contact, turning to a new idea rather than challenging the "I don't know."

Richard: Thank God for masturbation . . . What do you suppose life would be like if you hadn't found out about it?

Bill: (*pause*) Hm. I don't know, I wouldn't have had anybody.

Richard: You mean, playing with yourself was like having a friend?

Bill: I had myself.

Rebecca: It's still awfully lonely. Maybe feel good for a while, but you're still alone . . . What are you feeling now, Bill?

By her tone of voice and a shift in body position, as well as by her words, Rebecca signals that she has left the role of mother and has returned to being simply the cotherapist in this piece of work. She is, nevertheless, still a woman; her implicit support of Bill's masturbation, and her concern about his loneliness, may help to counter the old ideas that women/mothers disapprove of masculinity and want boys to be girlish/good/alone.

Bill: Much better. (*laughs*)

Rebecca: But still lonely.

Bill: Um-hm.

Richard: What else do you want to tell us, Bill?

Is Bill really satisfied with support and permission around being and acting like a boy, or does he have some other issue he wants to raise? If there is no new piece, the work can move to a conclusion that will cement the relationship, will provide further cognitive and experiential raw materials that Bill can use to enhance and expand his masculine identity. But Richard wants to be sure that the shy, frightened Child has indeed told as much as he wants to tell, for now.

Bill: (*pause*) I can't think of anything else.

Rebecca: Is there anything else you *want* right now?

Richard: (*pause*) Tell us what you *don't* want.

Bill: I don't want to stop being a boy . . . but I don't want to be depressed.

Richard: Well, OK. We'll set up a program. Take you to the garbage dump. And maybe Vic will show you where he keeps his dirtiest mud. Blackest mud you've ever seen. (*chuckles from the group*) And it even smells dirty. And maybe you could even throw it. And maybe you could get your clothes dirty. And then you know what we would have to do? We'd have to put them in the washing machine.

Rebecca: Look at Frankie!

Frankie is the young man whom we met in Chapter 5. He is now grinning delightedly at the program Richard is describing for Bill.

Richard: Frankie may not be brave enough to do that. You see, he was raised as a sissy too. (*laughter from the group*)

Issues of sexual identity usually involve shame; the boy who feels or acts like a girl, or the girl who labels herself too masculine, is encouraged by adults and peers alike to believe that these experiences are wrong and bad. That Richard can refer to being "raised as a sissy" in such a matter-of-fact way defuses the shame, makes what has been unmentionable suddenly ordinary. Other members of the group had been touched by that sense of shame, the conspiracy of silence that so often surrounds sexual issues (which has already been pointed out in Robert's work, in Chapter 6); their laughter signals release of tension.

Richard: (*continuing*) Do you think you two could grow up together, with a little encouragement?

Bill: Um-hm.

Richard: What do you think I should do with Frankie? He was also beaten for getting dirty. His mother also beat him. "You have to be good!" He didn't even know what she was talking about. What do you think I should do with Frankie, to liberate him?

Bill: Talk to him the way you talked to me.

Richard: I've been doing that, for a couple of years. Sometimes he doesn't believe it, that it's real. Sometimes he does. Does this feel real to you? (*Bill nods*) I'm glad for you. Cause you're sure holding on to me.

Bill: I think it feels real because I, it feels good just to know what to do.

Richard: Well, part of the way you're going to know what to do is, I'm going to listen to you. But you know something? If I'm going to listen, you've got to talk. You gotta tell me, "I like this, and I don't like this." "I want this, and I don't want that." You gotta take the risk of talking.

This is not only another permission for Bill, another piece of the relationship process, but it is also an explicit direction for him as a client in therapy. It is thus a duplex message—a message delivered simultaneously to two ego states. The Child hears "It's OK for you to say what you want," while the Adult hears "This is the way you can make your therapy more effective." And both messages are important for Bill.

Bill: When I'd try to talk with him I'd get into fights with him, and he didn't understand.

Richard: Well, you want to get in a fight with me?

Bill: (*laughing*) Not right now.

Richard: I like to fight . . . But we gotta do it on the mat. And the winner of the fight is the first one who gives the other one a bibble.

Bill: A what?

Richard: A bibble. You don't know what a bibble is? Well, I will have to show you that now.

Richard has moved back from Bill as he talks, and now reaches out and begins to wrestle with him. The "bibble" he is talking about is the flatulent sound made by blowing while one's mouth is pressed against skin—in this case, the skin around the belly button. Before Bill realizes what is happening, Richard has pushed him down on the mat, pulled up his shirt, and given him a resounding "bibble."

Richard: See, it's when two guys—get up on your knees, there. Push against me. Two guys fight, like this, and they push, to see who's stronger, and then suddenly, one of them takes the other guy's shirt and pulls it out and goes like this (*he demonstrates*)—and that's the bibble! (*applause and catcalls from the group*) So I won, I'm the hero.

Rebecca: But you'll have your chance, Bill.

Richard: That's the kind of fighting that you needed. The delightful part of that kind of fighting is that you've got to be loving, to win. Because who wants to bibble somebody they don't love? (*he dives in and bibbles Bill again*) I'm the champ. And no sissy could ever bibble me.

Rebecca: There's your chance, Bill.

Richard: You gotta be manly. To get the champ.

Female group member: Sometimes it takes a bunch of kids, together, to bibble their daddy.

> *This remark releases both Frankie and Vic, who leap onto the mat and, with Bill, attempt to wrestle Richard onto his back. A free-for-all develops, and after much struggling and thrashing about, Frankie and Vic manage to pin Richard so that Bill can administer a triumphant bibble. The session ends to the cheers of the group.*

The debate over whether homosexuality is "aberration" or "normal" has raged for decades among mental health specialists; there is no reason to believe that the conflict has ended or that the last word has been heard. In Chapter 6, we examined a therapeutic session with a young man whose sexual identity had been clearly formed and whose homosexuality was Adult ego-syntonic; his goal was to rid himself of an old, introjected criticism of that identity, which was in conflict with his Adult ego state choice of life-style. Bill's situation is quite different; he has made an Adult ego state choice in favor of heterosexuality, but at a Child ego state level is still experiencing confusion about that choice. The absence of adequate male models during his early years, together with the influence of a harshly punitive mother, led him to form decisions and beliefs about himself that were incompatible with a comfortably masculine self-concept. In order for him to be able to function as a healthy adult male, his Child ego state needs new experiences—a chance to act out what has been inhibited and fixated. The old, faulty reactions need to change so that he can reexamine his archaic decisions and beliefs and replace whatever parts are interfering with his ability to be flexible, creative, and intimate in his relationships with others.

The relationship with Richard is only the first step in Bill's therapy. As the old, limiting Parent ego state is decommissioned, Bill will need to do further redecision work. Both Parent and Child ego state material will then need to be integrated into his overall personality functioning. The first order of business, though, is to deal with the Parent ego state; as long as that Parent continues to intimidate him, he will not be able to summon the resources that he needs in order to change—or even to make a free choice to remain the same.

The relationship with the therapist provides the Child ego state with a new parental model. And, for the therapy to be successful, information needs to be taken in through all channels: cognitive, emotional, behavioral, and physical. In the segment presented in this chapter, Bill takes in information from both therapists; he is also invited to make emotional contact with both. Behaviorally, he is invited to confront a symbolic Mother in a new way, with new and positive support. And the wrestling match, as well as the proposed mud play and the trip to the dump (both of which did occur later in the workshop), invite behavioral and physical experiences quite alien to the actual course of his childhood development.

Because the therapists had not known Bill before this workshop, they had not had an opportunity to assess the degree to which his early experiences had created a damaging script pattern. They did not know, before this piece of work, how thoroughly the combination of punitive Mother and withdrawn, disapproving Father had succeeded in discouraging and confusing the Child Bill. Had the damage been less pervasive, Bill might well have been able to follow Richard's lead in energetically confronting Mother and moving to a new decision about himself and his masculinity. As it became apparent that Bill felt too powerless and frightened to do this, the goal of the session shifted: Rather than push for a redecision, with the possibility of failure and an actual strengthening of Bill's sense of inadequacy, the therapists focused almost exclusively on the relationshp between a father and son. With this new framework, Bill could take the risk of opening himself emotionally to healthy parenting, could allow his Child to try previously forbidden behaviors, and could experience "success" as a client. All three of these outcomes pave the way for further therapeutic growth.

Bill has much more work to do, before he will be ready to face the world with a comfortable sense of his own neopsychic potency. But his work is well begun. The seeds of growth have been planted; his Child ego state has had a small but heady taste of the kind of parenting all children need and deserve. Whether he chooses to follow up this work with further formal therapy, or to integrate and work through the experience on his own (or both), he leaves the workshop in a significantly different world from that which he knew when he arrived.

10

GLENDA
The Empty House

Integrative psychotherapy emphasizes the importance of our fantasy activities. In our day- and night-dreams, our images, and our creative productions, we express the varied aspects of ourselves. Each fragment of these fantasies—each object, each person, each house or hill or ocean beach—is also a fragment of self, expressed in symbolic fashion. As we saw in Emily's work in Chapter 7, clients can be led to "decode" this symbolic language. Dreams and fantasies can be a means of discovering oneself, one's thoughts and feelings and desires that may be tucked away out of conscious awareness: once these aspects of self have been brought into awareness, they are available for psychotherapeutic work.

In the session presented in this chapter, therapists and client work not with a dream, but with a consciously created fantasy. The fantasy is built on a memory: the recollection of the house that the client lived in during childhood. This recollection is highly emotionally charged, as the client's previous work has revealed. On the surface, the emotional meaning of the house has to do with a traumatic event that occurred there: The client's father, enraged at her mother (from whom he was estranged), arranged for movers to come in and take away all the furnishings in the home. The client and her mother returned from an all-day shopping expedition to find their home stripped bare. As we shall see in the work, however, the emotional meaning of this house goes far beyond its role as the site of a painful memory. The house is a metaphor for the self, and each room and object and characteristic of the house is a symbolic representation of the client's personal experience.

Glenda, the client, became mute as a small child and remained without speech for more than a year. Even now, when under stress, she frequently experiences difficulty in speaking. Her gestures, with hands and face and her whole body, are fluid and eloquent. Where possible, in the work, we will describe these gestures. The reader should be aware, however, that a significant portion of Glenda's communication is lost in relying on the printed word.

In a previous piece of work, Glenda began exploring the image of her house and its meanings: the impact of this work was sufficiently intense that she very quickly began to "talk" in gestures rather than words, and eventually closed down altogether. She sat huddled on the mat, clearly involved in her experience, but unable/unwilling to communicate what was going on for her internally. She began the present session with a request to use the image of the house again, to take yet another step toward bringing her old, terrifying experiences into full awareness while at the same time utilizing the contact and support of the therapists.

The work moves immediately into a guided fantasy in which Glenda, eyes closed to facilitate the visualization process, goes through the rooms of the house, describing each one as if she herself were that room: "I am an empty living room, and I have three large windows . . ." Working slowly and patiently, the therapists help Glenda to explore each room, and the feelings associated with each. We pick up the work as Glenda prepares to "be" her own bedroom.

Glenda: . . . So I'm out in the foyer, and I go to my room. And I have a crib in the bedroom . . . I am the room . . . They're taking my bed, and my bureau, and my chair, it's like they just tore through the whole house. Swept it. And they didn't care, they just did it, as I'm watching them, they didn't care, it was just their job. Just take it.

By this point in the work, Glenda has learned to step into the role of the room, to "be the room," and does so with little or no coaching. The sense of being violated, invaded by some mechanical, uncaring, unfeeling force is strong here, as she deals with the event of the movers coming in and stripping the house. The therapists are looking further, however, for some more deeply personal meaning in the "my room" symbol.

Rebecca: They don't know that you're a special room, do they? Describe your specialness, room.

Glenda: That's interesting, cause that room I see as dark.

Rebecca has no idea as to the significance of "darkness" here. But it is significant, as shown by Glenda's own surprise at the discovery, as well as her breaking out of role and back into commenting from her own person. To probe further, without suggesting or programming an interpretation, Rebecca simply rephrases Glenda's description as a self-referent of the room.

Rebecca: I'm dark . . .

Glenda: I don't see that room as a happy room.

Rebecca: Well, tell us about that, room. How come you're not a happy room.

Glenda: Cause I'm always in the dark there. And I have a window. Somehow the light doesn't get in. In my room.

Rebecca: And what happens inside of you, room?

Glenda has not responded to two invitations to go back to her "be the room" mode: Rebecca simply goes on as if she had, addressing her each time as "room." This time, Glenda makes the transition.

Glenda: What happens inside me? I don't know, but I'm not a happy room . . . There's a little girl that stays inside me.

Rebecca: Um-hm. Tell me about that little girl. The little girl in you, room.

Glenda: I'm trying to stay connected.

It isn't clear whether Glenda is referring here to trying to stay in role as "the room," or whether she is struggling not to shut down and disconnect from the therapists altogether. This latter possibility suggests another advantage of maintaining the frame of reference of "the room": It allows Glenda to stay partially detached from the pain and terror that she felt as a child. Looking at herself, from the perspective of "the room," will allow her to explore the early experiences without being overwhelmed by them. Rebecca, still addressing "the room" (which can look at the little girl inside of itself), uses the idea of being connected in terms of the little girl's hiding or disconnecting from that room—a metaphor for Glenda's internal fragmentation and dissociation of the various parts of herself.

Rebecca: Does she not show you much of herself?

Glenda: (*long pause*) I can't connect to her. She's just there. She's there because she's there. That's my sense. She's there because she knows that's her room. I don't know if she likes it or not; she's there.

Rebecca: What's she like when she's in you?

Glenda: Well, my thought that comes to me, I don't know if I'm right, I see her being, you know, kind of like, I see her trying on a dress, pink dress, that she had when she was, as an infant. And I see her watching her brother have a temper tantrum. I thought he was going to hit his head for sure. And cut it. She got scared. He really screamed and jumped. I don't remember if my mother came in or not. I think she did later, but she didn't when he did it. I was really scared, but I don't, I don't know what kind of girl she is. She's quiet. She's quiet, she's not going to do what her brother does. And sad. I don't know why, I'm just saying that. She's sad.

Glenda's fragmentation shows even more clearly here, as she switches roles from self-as-child to "room," and from past-tense remembering to present-tense experiencing.

Rebecca: You know what she's sad about, room?

Glenda: Yeah. She doesn't like that her parents argue.

Richard: Is that when she was quiet?

Glenda: She doesn't remember.

Richard: Is that when she goes quiet, room? Is that when you hear her get quiet and not talk?

The assumption is that "the room" knows everything it wants to know; "I don't remember" is not accepted. By repeating the question, Richard encourages Glenda to continue the process of half-remembering, half-constructing her fantasy.

Glenda: (*whispering*) When do I hear her get quiet and not talk?

Richard: When her parents argue? When she goes mute?

Glenda: She was always in the middle, between them. I don't know, all I know is she's quiet. She's quiet . . . My thought is, she wishes she weren't there. But there she is; she's stuck in my room. There she is. She's there. She wishes she weren't. She feels responsible. Very responsible. She felt responsible for her brother and the temper tantrum.

Rebecca: Is there a room that she does feel happy in?

Glenda: In the living room. Yep, that's her happiest room.

Rebecca: Um-hm. With the golden swan.

Glenda: Um. And the bright light. It was a happy room.

Rebecca is referring to an ornament that Glenda has described earlier, a ceramic swan that she loved to look at. Taking her back for a moment to her "happiest room" gives her a brief time out, a rest; the therapists must be careful to avoid pushing Glenda so fast that she will again disconnect from the process and go mute. She seems to be reenergized by accessing the "happy room" and so Rebecca goes back to the exploration of the rest of the house.

Rebecca: Anything else you want to say about yourself, bedroom?

Glenda: (*pause*) I feel closed in . . . smothered . . . I would want that room to breathe. And be liked. I want my room to breathe and be liked, and I would like to be in that room. I don't like that room. I have to . . . my room, my room . . . I want my room to be liked. I don't like the dark.

Rebecca: Let's move on and be the parents' room.

Glenda: I have one more room before we get there. That's the spare room. And the spare room is a bunch of clutter. And I don't know any more than that about that room.

Rebecca: I'm a bunch of clutter.

Glenda: I'm a bunch of clutter. That's not a very bright room, either; it's a little bit brighter, though. A little brighter than my other room. My parents' bedroom—

Rebecca: Wait, you don't have to move so fast. How do you feel, room with all your clutter?

Having spontaneously mentioned the cluttered room, Glenda quickly moves away from it. Given that Glenda brought it up herself, Rebecca assumes that it is important, and blocks Glenda's resistance to further exploration there.

Glenda: I feel . . . frenzied. But now I'm empty. They even took my clutter. They took everything; they even took that. Even though it was not even worth anything to them . . .

Rebecca: Ouch.

Glenda: Wasn't worth it. And they still took it. Doesn't make sense. (*pause*) That room's a very righteous room. That room is saying, "What are you doing? Taking my clutter?" (*pause*) "Where are you going to put it? You don't need it." They're not listening . . . They're not listening because they're just too busy doing their job. I guess that's the ridiculous . . . I guess my spare room sees how ridiculous this is. Taking the furniture; taking my clutter to top it off.

Rebecca: You're an important part of this whole house.

Glenda: What is?

Rebecca: You, room. Are an important part of this whole house. You collected the clutter.

Rebecca's comment here is based partly on the spontaneous mention of the room, partly on the increase in Glenda's energy during her last comments, and partly on the idea that Glenda, experiencing her fragmentation, may be able to relate more closely to the "clutter" of this room than to the orderliness or the barrenness of the others. Glenda's response validates these hunches; it is a clear description of her script belief about herself.

Glenda: I don't know if I'm that important. I'm just, I'm a place where people stick things that they have no other place to put.

Rebecca: That's important. What would the world be like if we didn't have junk piles? And you're able to see the ridiculousness of things. Cause you're both important and nonimportant at the same time. A very, very perceptive part of this house.

Glenda: The clutter room?

Rebecca: Sure. Clutter room is always important.

Glenda: Well, I didn't feel that way. No one really stayed in my room very long. But I was kinda glad anyway; rather be by myself. Don't like to get involved.

Glenda may be making another veiled reference here to her becoming mute and thus isolating herself. Rebecca finds a positive connotation for the isolation: It helps Glenda see things clearly, and it also provides a different perspective from which she can experience her own reactions, both past and present.

Rebecca: Helps you to see things clearly, too. See ridiculousness. (*pause*) Anything else you want to say, room?

Glenda: Um . . . I still feel smothered, just like the other room. My room . . . that spare room, I'm . . . that room is probably the bravest room, the gets-angry room. Trying to save everyone else. (*pause*) But it doesn't work, anyway. The hopelessness seeps through my walls. (*shakes her head*)

Richard: Do that gesture with your head . . . more . . . see how you feel with that gesture. (*Glenda continues to exaggerate her head shaking*) Give that gesture a voice.

Because Glenda has a tendency to stop talking, the therapists are particularly attentive to nonverbal communications. Here Richard makes an explicit request that she translate the gesture into words, to assist Glenda in maintaining contact with them.

Glenda: (*pause*) Actually . . . I think I stimulated, this movement was just like, it'll shut me down. And it's like, if I move my body, I can . . . stimulates me to just shut down. I mean, I can phase out with it.

The request has helped Glenda to notice and take responsibility for her choice to close down, rather than to stay with the process at hand. As she owns her own power, her own choosing, she is better able to make that choice a conscious one—she can decide, with awareness, whether to continue the therapeutic process. Richard's next comment ties together Glenda's physical response with her emotional experience, using the metaphoric device that has been used throughout the work.

Richard: But that gesture of yours sort of comes through the walls.

Glenda: Yes.

Rebecca: Now feel the desire to shut down. When that hopelessness comes through the walls. (*long pause*) Are you shutting us out now? (*pause*) It's when you go inside yourself, cause when you feel that hopelessness in your house, and every room closes in, dark, and it's getting suffocating, and it comes through the walls.

(*pause*) I think it's time for us to go into that parents' room. Is that where the hopelessness stems from?

Glenda: (*nods; she is physically slumping down into herself—she looks very young and defenseless as she curls over and hangs her head*)

Rebecca: (*continuing*) Just be the parents' bedroom now . . . Describe yourself, room. (*Glenda continues to gesture, patting and pressing the space around her in small, graceful, pleading motions*) So much that can't come out. Seeps through the walls. There's so much to say, and things you can't say.

Throughout this and the following speech, Glenda continues to gesture mutely. Rebecca's comments are partially in response to those gestures, and partly a leading on from the nonverbal messages.

Rebecca: Almost like you didn't exist. Your existence wasn't as important as what was going on in there. The existence of the bedroom was not so important . . . I wonder if that stuff inside the bedroom needed to come out . . . That was the furniture that needed, I bet, to be moved out of the house. And all the other furniture kept. Including the spare room. All the clutter needed to be kept. (*Glenda shakes her head "no"*) Not all? It was parents' furniture that needed to go. (*Glenda again indicates "no"*) Needed to stay. And something else needed to happen . . . And it could have happened, bedroom . . .

Glenda: (*almost unintelligible*) . . . want to go there . . .

Rebecca: Want to go where?

Glenda: I don't, a bedroom . . .

Rebecca: (*pause*) Bedroom's off limits.

Glenda: I, I know I said that but I don't know why I said that.

Rebecca's nonjudgmental patience has signaled her willingness to deal with Glenda at whatever language level she chooses. In response, Glenda emerges from her short period of mutism; Rebecca quickly takes advantage of Glenda's shift and returns to the exploration at hand.

Rebecca: I'm a bedroom . . .

Glenda: I'm a bedroom . . . I feel more like I'm outside.

Rebecca: Tell me more about that, bedroom.

Glenda: It's like I should be outside right now . . . I don't know why, in that bedroom I feel outside . . .

Richard: Tell me more about you, bedroom.

Again, Glenda is shifting between answering as the bedroom and answering as herself. By asking her to tell about herself, "bedroom," Richard attempts to solidify the role. As we shall see, the attempt eventually succeeds, but only after several more exchanges.

Glenda: (*pause*) I don't know, except I'm empty. They took all the furniture out of that bedroom too. I don't have any feeling for that bedroom. It has no feeling.

Rebecca: The room does have feelings.

Glenda: Hm-um. That room's empty.

Richard: Umm. Consider that a feeling. Call it a mood.

Glenda: I'm not able to feel connected to that room.

Richard: Then say the opposite of connected.

Glenda: Disconnected. I'm disconnected from the rest of the house. I'm all disconnected.

Rebecca: How come, room? How come you're disconnected?

Glenda: Can't come together with the rest of the house.

Rebecca: What happened inside of you, room? What keeps you so separate?

Glenda: I don't know. I just cannot move with the rest of the house. I would like to but I can't. Cause the people that are inside me, they're not, they're not happy . . . they fight . . . wish they'd stop.

We are back with the pain that existed between Glenda's parents. Somehow, it is related to her sense of isolation, of being disconnected: The two themes, fighting and disconnection, weave themselves together in an almost organic way as the work continues.

Rebecca: So you could be more connected?

Glenda: Yeah. Their connection is, uh, the fighting. They're too young . . . There's another room . . . Guess that little girl in that other room feels responsible . . .

Rebecca: Does the hopelessness come from you, bedroom, or does it come from her bedroom?

Glenda: (*pause*) I don't know.

Rebecca: The hopelessness that seeps through the walls.

Glenda: I don't know; I think it's a mixture.

Rebecca: Yet you described yourself as being a powerful room. Is that because you are disconnected? There's power in being disconnected.

It is unclear where the reference to a "powerful room" comes from. It may have emerged in a previous piece of work, or Rebecca may simply have become confused between Glenda's description of the parents' bedroom and her earlier statement that the store room was "the bravest room." If the reference is a mistake, it doesn't seem to have done a great deal of damage to the process.

Glenda: Um-hm.

Rebecca: Or in being able to take it all?

Glenda: At least there's a strength there.

Rebecca: Sounds like that's important. That there's power in being able to take it all. And power in being disconnected.

Glenda: I'm tired of doing that.

The first breath of hope and energy for change! It's very faint, and is almost immediately submerged again in the heaviness and isolation that has pervaded the work so far, but it is a signal of some kind of therapeutic yeast, working away under the surface.

Rebecca: Um-hm. What would you like to be different, room?

Glenda: I would like . . . the occupants not to fight. (*sighs deeply*)

Rebecca: (*pause*) There's that pain.

Glenda: I know I must feel anger, but when I do it I can't help it. I feel like taking it out on me.

A common way of protecting ourselves from the pain of old traumas is to "go cognitive," to remove ourselves from actually experiencing what is happening and to begin to think about, to analyze, the experience instead. Glenda does this here: Her response is one of thinking about her feelings, rather than feeling them. Rebecca's response is designed to refocus her on the feelings themselves, rather than what she thinks ought to be there.

Rebecca: You don't have to take it all. You don't have to stay disconnected . . . A room shouldn't be treated that way . . . Neither should a child.

Glenda: I'm stuck. I can't . . . I feel very self-destructive.

Rebecca: Well, I think you gotta be willing to be angry outside.

This is an interpretation, based partly on previous work and partly on Glenda's comment that she feels like "taking it out on me." Children who have no permission to express (or even experience) anger toward things and people in their environments often turn that anger inward. Because Glenda continues to internalize her angry feelings, keeping them inside rather than expressing them and moving through them, she stays stuck. This pattern is so old, so ingrained and well-established, that she is no longer experientially aware of it; she knows enough at a theoretical level to say that she "must feel" anger, but this is an intellectual hypothesis rather than a true knowing from experience.

Glenda: I can't connect; it's difficult for me to see a connection.

Rebecca: Take the risk. Stand and look at that empty house.

Glenda: I don't want to do that yet. I want to be the whole house.

Rebecca: OK.

Glenda: I'm the whole house. I'm not connected at all . . . I'm like, I'll lose if I think I'm connected . . . and if I'm not connected, I'm stuck. I'm too involved.

Glenda's request to be the whole house seems to come from a deep sense of needing to complete a process, needing to deal with the symbolism of her journey through the rooms in a way that will bring the parts together. She is trying to report on a complex set of thoughts and feelings, and her experience is racing faster than her words can keep up. The resulting statement is confused and confusing, both to the therapists and to her. Richard suggests a way to get some clarity:

Richard: Be Glenda, and talk to that house. Look at the house and talk to it.

Glenda: (*pause*) You were a good house . . . You tried to keep everyone protected . . . from all the elements outside. And you did it, too. You did your job.

Remember that each part of the fantasy production is an element of the self. For the first time, Glenda is appreciating her self-protection.

Richard: Tell that house what's happened to it. What those movers did to it.

Glenda: They made you empty. (*pause, then whispering*) It wasn't the house's fault.

Rebecca: Tell that to the house. It wasn't your fault.

It is a reasonable assumption that any young child whose parents quarrel or separate carries a sense of guilt or responsibility. Children, being developmentally egocentric, experience everything that happens in their environment as connected to themselves; if parents don't get along, it must be the child's fault. In this segment of the work, Glenda is dealing symbolically with her archaic sense of guilt, a feeling that she has referred to before in connection with her brother's behavior but not directly with reference to her parents.

Glenda: It wasn't your fault.

Richard: Now say that in the first person.

Glenda: It . . . wasn't the house's fault. It wasn't; the house is a house. It's not a person.

Richard: Say it in the first person.

Glenda: It wasn't my fault.

Richard: Say both parts to the house. It wasn't your fault, house . . .

Glenda: It wasn't your fault, house.

Richard: And the other part? (*long pause*) Someone just told that little girl it's her fault.

Glenda: It was never her fault.

Rebecca: How about being that house, and talk to the little girl. Bet the house knew that little girl in there . . . That empty house that sees a very bewildered little girl.

The old sense of confusion and isolation is so strong for Glenda that when she tries to deal with it directly she feels overwhelmed. By "being" the house, she can experience a feeling of groundedness, of solidity, as she reexplores the old issues: She can know, experientially, what was happening for the little girl, but not get enmeshed in that child's feelings. Again, the technique provides a way to feel, yet not be overwhelmed by the feelings.

Glenda: I can empathize a little better when I'm the house . . . than when I'm her.

Rebecca: Um-hm. Then be the house. House, you talk to that little girl. She's very bewildered about your being so empty. She even blames herself—she doesn't know what to feel, it's so overwhelming.

Glenda: (*whispering*) She feels really bad.

Rebecca: Tell her, house. Tell her what you know about her. What you see in her.

Glenda: (*still whispering*) I don't know what to say.

Richard: House, is she very sad? To compensate for not being angry?

Glenda: (*beginning to cry*) No, she's just sad.

Richard: That's even more important than the anger, huh?

The interpretation that Glenda was angry doesn't fit for her right now; she is not ready to deal with any anger or outrage at what was done to her and her mother. Notice how Richard responds to her correction, without forcing the issue of anger, yet reserves that avenue for later work.

Richard: (*continuing*) It's like someone took all of her insides out, too . . . Keep talking to her, house. She listens to you.

Glenda: Seems kind of dumb for a house to talk to a little girl.

Rebecca: I think it's very smart, for a house to talk to a little girl. Houses are big, and they hear all kinds of things, and they watch all kinds of things.

Glenda: I think she knows that.

Glenda may be signaling her openness to accept the house as a symbol of internal nurturing. Certainly the work moves to its conclusion in a way that would support such a hypothesis.

Rebecca: Um-hm. And she needs something from you, house. You know what you need to give her, what she needs from you.

Glenda: (*crying*) She's so confused.

Richard: Something she's waiting to hear from you, house. So she doesn't have to be so confused. Something you can tell her, to make sense out of the whole process.

Glenda: She thinks it's her fault.

A major step from her earlier statement, "It was never her fault." Glenda is now aware of the experience of guilt, rather than keeping it out of conscious awareness.

Richard: Talk to her about that, house.

Glenda: It won't make any difference.

Richard: Talk to her about it anyway, just in case.

Glenda: The house isn't even here.

Rebecca: You don't have to be here, house. Just talk to her . . . You've watched this little girl for a long time. You've seen her loneliness. You've seen her feel the hopelessness from the walls . . . You've seen her listen to her silence. That silence has communicated a lot. Talk to her about it . . . Cause if she knows that you know too, she won't be so confused.

Glenda: (*whispering; her first words are unintelligible*) . . . you can touch me with your hands; I can't touch you.

Richard: But you can touch her with your wisdom.

Glenda: I don't know if she'll believe me. (*Cries*) I want her to, but I don't know if she believes me.

Rebecca: But she hears you, and that's what counts. She'll think about it for a while. Is there anything else that you can tell her?

Glenda's "I don't know if she believes me" strongly implies that she has already constructed the message that the "house" needs to give the little girl. Her tears are evidence that the message has been received, that she is, in fact, responding emotionally to some internal self-nurturing. Rather than insist that she share this process externally, Rebecca chooses to acknowledge what has occurred, and move on toward closure.

Glenda: It's like something's really there.

Rebecca: Um-hm; she can feel you. She sure knows your protection.

Glenda: It was a good house.

Rebecca: I wonder if it would be good to know something about, that other people are going to come in and fill your space, fill it with love and laughter, with meals again, with living and sleeping, and all kinds of feelings, and that you're going to be full once more. And so can she.

Glenda: But the little girl won't be there.

Rebecca: She can take other people in, too . . . Maybe that comes later. Anything else you want to say to her now, house?

Glenda: Yeah. I don't want to say good-bye.

Rebecca: Is there some symbolic way that you need to stay with her? Maybe she needs to find a little house, in a picture or something. As a way of having you for a while.

Glenda: I don't know.

Rebecca may have moved too quickly here, trying to set up a way for Glenda to continue the nurturing process on her own. Glenda isn't ready to let go yet; sensing this in the quality of her "I don't know," Rebecca backtracks.

Rebecca: Want to go back to saying, "I don't want to say good-bye yet"?

Glenda: I don't want to say good-bye, but I can't hold on . . . Guess I feel like I want to say good-bye, but I have no feelings. Just blank, closing down.

Rebecca: That's a feeling.

Glenda: I know. It's the old feeling.

Rebecca: Then I don't think you should do it.

Glenda: Why do I have to say good-bye, anyway? Why do I have to say good-bye? I don't have to say good-bye to you. I don't want to!

Rebecca: That little girl was feeling a whole lot.

Glenda: It's hard to let go.

Rebecca: In her mind she's holding on. In her heart she's holding on.

Glenda: She can hold on hard.

Rebecca: You two are a lot alike. (*pause*) You need to come back . . . Open your eyes when you're ready.

With this intervention, Rebecca puts a final bit of glue on the growing interaction between the nurturing part of Glenda (the "house") and the confused Child part. She then, quite matter-of-factly, indicates that it is time to end the piece of work.

Clients who "close down," who carry on significant parts of their work internally, present a kind of therapeutic dilemma. If the therapist insists that they communicate their experience aloud, they may shut down altogether, or may get into a struggle around the issue of whether or not to obey or adapt to the therapist's directions. On the other hand, trying to follow along with that internal process forces the therapist to guess about what the client is thinking and feeling, and thus risk missing important pieces or even straying far away from the client's actual work. By constructing and staying with a metaphor or symbol, the therapists steered a middle course in Glenda's work: They have been able to make interventions that are ambiguous, and Glenda was free to understand whatever part of the intervention actually fit for her.

As we have pointed out, the metaphoric approach also serves as an emotional safety valve, a way to "bleed off" affect that may be too overwhelming to be experienced directly. Later in treatment, when Glenda has learned to accept and use the therapists' protection more effectively, and when her Child ego state feels less vulnerable and defenseless, she will be ready to deal with these painful issues head on—to confront the quarreling parents, decommission any possible introjected punitive Parent ego state material, and help her Child ego state to find a better solution than going mute, withdrawing, and isolating herself from the contact that she needs in order to be fully alive.

11

CHARLES
A Study in Contact

The heart of psychotherapy is contact. Contact between the self and the external world, and contact and integration within the self, defines psychological health. Contact between therapist and client encourages, fosters, supports, and invites other contact experiences.

While integrative psychotherapy makes use of a broad range of concepts, the notion of contact remains basic. As we have seen in previous chapters, contact pervades and undergirds all of our work. Often, the importance of the contact itself is overshadowed by the drama of other aspects of the therapy—an important redecision, an intervention with a Parent ego state, the reworking of a dream or fantasy. The piece of work presented in this chapter has none of these; it is a nearly pure example of contact.

As you read through the transcript, notice the ways in which the therapist consistently maintains and invites contact. Every comment, question, paraphrase, or interpretation has two primary goals: furthering a sense of contact between therapist and client, and enhancing the client's awareness of internal sensations, experience, and memory. Any other benefits are of secondary importance.

The client, Charles, brings to the work a host of defensive behaviors. He has used these defenses for many years, and is for the most part quite unaware of them. They feel necessary, a part of his basic self, the only way for him to be. Yet the defenses serve to interrupt contact and keep him locked into his script: He retroflects (that is, he talks to himself rather than interacting in a genuine way with others); he is highly sensitive to criticism; he wants a great deal of attention and feels resentful and disappointed when he cannot get it. By countering each of these script behaviors, over and over again, with a patient and consistent offer of contact, the therapist provides Charles with a new experience of being-in-the-world, an experience in direct contradiction to the expectations he has built up over the years. Charles, a man in his late fifties, has a dry, pedantic manner. As he begins his work, his expression is remote, his gestures stilted, and his voice overprecise, as if he is telling a well-rehearsed story. This "rehearsedness" is another aspect of his retroflection: He often appears to be more involved in listening to himself than in reaching out to someone else. Richard and Rebecca have had ample opportunity to observe this behavior through the early days of the workshop, and have decided that establishing genuine contact with Charles will not only be therapeutic, but also a necessary precursor to any other work that might be accomplished.

On the previous day, Charles had wanted to work in the group but had turned down a chance to use an open half-hour before the luncheon break. He now moves onto the mat in the middle of the morning session, and begins to explain why he chose to wait:

Charles: I didn't want to work yesterday, when we had only half an hour. I felt I'd be adding more anxiety and more distress than I already have now. I've been wanting to work with you, Richard, and I wanted Rebecca to be present while I worked . . . I've connected with the work of Chris and Jerry, and Robert. And . . . (*pause*) My mother was, uh, I never really felt my mother was very much of a mother to me. She was, of course, but from an emotional point of view I never felt I had a mother.

Richard: What does that feel like for you?

Charles: At the moment I don't feel anything.

Richard: I think that's a feeling.

Charles: When I remember my mother, with one or two exceptions, I can count them on the fingers of one hand, um, what I remember is her needs, and me looking after her. And this was from quite an early age. Prior to that, I could remember sleeping in my mother's bed, as happened in the case of Chris; I never ever remember my mother and father sleeping in the same room let alone the same bed. I never remember that. My mother used to sleep in her bedroom, and my father used to sleep in the cold room at the other end of the house. And in the early years I do remember sleeping with my mother. When I thought about it later on, I used to think that there was a reason, or several reasons for that, and one of the reasons was that my mother didn't want my father in her bed. And she kept me there to protect her. I also remember wanting to cuddle up to my mother . . .

Charles's tone has become almost singsong; it sounds like a well-rehearsed monologue, one so familiar to him that he hardly needs to think about it as he tells his story. There is little feeling, and virtually no contact with the therapists. This pattern must be interrupted, but in a way that will not drive Charles even further into his defensive posture. Richard accomplishes this by framing the interruption as a means of enhancing his understanding (Charles isn't doing it wrong; it's just that Richard needs help); he further predicts and thus defuses Charles's irritation over being interrupted.

Richard: Are you willing to go a little slower, so that we can make this more than just a recounting? So that, as you tell the story of your life, we can make it more therapeutic? To do that, I'm going to ask you some questions along the way, that may feel slightly irritating, and yet if you go with them, they are going to make the recounting of this experience more therapeutic.

Charles: I've recounted—sometimes I feel—I want to do this, but sometimes I get messages that are telling me, "But Charles, you've said this many times in groups." Which I have.

Richard: Oh, Charles, you've probably said it time and time again. Cause you're struggling for resolution.

Charles: That is true.

Richard: And that is one of the reasons why I'm going to take the time with you, to slow down the process, so you account for your feelings at each step along the way. And as we've gone on here, now, I've watched you start speeding up. And that tells me you're trying to get past the feelings.

Charles: Well, it's not something that I'm aware of. Maybe it's because I want to mention an experience with my father, which I think very much influenced . . . well, I made a decision as a result of that experience which very much influenced my relationship with my mother.

Richard: I'll patiently listen. And will provide the time; this is going to take a long time. You said that clearly yesterday. Now, what did you feel when you were used as a buffer between Mom and Dad?

Charles: What did I feel then, or what do I feel now? I'm not sure what your question is.

Richard: I want to know what you feel. And I left it ambiguous. Cause one of the things I'm going to look for is how you switch back and forth between now and then.

Rebecca: I think, Charles, also another thing that's important is that there's no "right" answer. The right answer is the one that comes to your mind first. There's no need to figure out which one he's looking for. It's your answer, not his question.

We have two interventions here, one from each therapist. Richard gives information about his intentions, which helps Charles to feel more in control of the process, less manipulated. Rebecca's comment is also aimed at the control issue, explicitly giving permission for Charles to decide what he wants to deal with. Charles responds by describing both his response then, to his parents, as well as his here-and-now (almost) feelings in the workshop.

Charles: My answer is, I feel, I was going to say irritated, when I as a little boy am used as a pawn in the struggle between two adults. And these are two adults who supposedly love me. And I was very touched by what you said to Helen, that one of the responsibilities of a parent is to protect that child, even at the cost of their life. I was very touched by that.

Richard: Will you describe that inner touching?

Charles: Because that's what I would do for my children. I wouldn't hesitate.

Richard: You really needed that.

Charles: Yes.

Richard: You needed them to do something for your welfare. What was that something you needed them to do?

Charles: I needed them to show me that they loved me, and cared for me. I was going to add, that they were willing to protect me. My father would have protected me. My mother, she wouldn't, she couldn't protect me. Because my mother was smaller than I was. At that age. She was emotionally younger than I was. And all her life, her relationship to me was more like I was her father and she was my daughter.

Richard: What's that like, to have a mama who's your daughter?

Charles: I feel very sad. I feel like I didn't have a mother. And sometimes I catch myself being irritated when I see women crying, and I know on one level that they have needs, and I can appreciate those needs, but at the same time I'm saying "Maybe I should cry, to let you know that I also have needs." Just because I don't cry—

Richard: To let who know?

Charles: To let *you* know. To let you know that I also have needs. But their needs always come first, because they are crying, and because they show outwardly that they are in pain, that they have problems . . .

Throughout the workshop, as people deal with intensely emotional issues, there is a great deal of crying. By this time, late in the week, several people are moving spontaneously into their own personal therapeutic process as they observe other participants work. One of the women in the group has done this now, and is sobbing quietly in a corner of the room. Charles's comment about people crying is almost certainly in response to this—he is distracted and annoyed, and expresses it in a veiled way. More than simple distraction, though, his annoyance is a sign of his own internal neediness: His early experience was that others' needs always took precedence over his, that there was not enough nurturing to go around and he was the one to be shortchanged. Because of this, he is hypersensitive to any threat that some of the attention that he wants may be given to someone else.

Richard: Is that what you learned to do? Rate her needs over yours?

Charles: I think without question, her needs were always the highest priority in our home. And she was the sick one, she was the one that was going crazy, and she did, and many times she had severe depressions, and . . .

Richard: And you were supposed to fix it?

Charles: And I did. I did. With time. Because I remember one specific instance where my mother had broken down, and we had called the doctor, I remember his name, Dr. Vance. And he used to come. And in those days he would give a tonic. And he was running out of tonic. And he suggested that the best thing to do under the circumstances was to commit her to the, we used to call it the insane asylum. And my father and older sister, who was also more like a mother to me, they were prepared to commit my mother to the insane asylum.

Richard: And what did you feel at that time?

Charles: And I didn't want her to go.

Richard: What did you feel?

Charles: I felt that was wrong. That we could—

Richard: That's still a thought. What did you feel emotionally when you thought it was wrong to commit her?

Richard insists, in this series of interventions, that Charles interrupt the monologue and attend to his question. The tactic will serve one of two purposes: Either Charles will, in fact, move out of retroflection and into contact, or he will provide further diagnostic information about the nature and strength of his defenses. And, as his response shows, the latter does occur. He outwardly complies with Richard's demand that he talk about his feelings, but within a few seconds he returns to his well-rehearsed story. He has defended against his emerging pain (and against the possibility of loss of control), but at the expense of the genuine contact that he so desperately needs.

Charles: Very sad, and very scared. I was scared—I was afraid that if she left, she probably wouldn't come back.

Richard: That must have been a very strong, strong emotional pull in you. And quite probably right in that thought. What does it feel like to know she won't come back?

Charles: (*pause*) That's scary. That's scary.

Richard: I bet that's an understatement. I bet devastatingly scary.

Do you experience it as devastatingly scary?

Charles: At the moment I don't.

Richard: Did you as a little boy?

Charles: I'm not sure. What I was aware of was that I loved her very much, and that I was willing to look after her. And I did. They decided not to send her to the insane asylum. And they kept her home. And, uh, I was in my first year of high school, so I must have been 13.

Richard: You were almost a young man.

Charles: And I would come home, she would lie in bed, and my father was at work, my sisters were at work, and it was winter time. And I used to come home, and I would make the stove. It was cold in the house. And I used to feed her, and I used to comfort her. And tell her that she would get well. And I used to stroke her hair, and her face. (*sobs briefly, then continues*) And she would tell me that she wasn't doing to get well, that she would die.

Richard: (*softly*) And what did that feel like? (*Charles sobs once more*) Must have been so anxious every day coming home. What did that feel like, Charles?

Charles: (*pause*) And yet part of me—

Richard: Charles?

Charles: Yes?

Richard: What did that feel like? I want to know what your feeling is.

There is a pattern, a rhythm, developing in the work: Charles tells his story, Richard interrupts, Charles makes momentary contact both internally and with Richard and then reverts back to retroflection until the next interruption. The very predictability of this pattern makes it less threatening to Charles, and with every repetition he seems able to stay in contact a bit longer.

Charles: I would guess—I don't feel it, but I would guess I was terrified. I was terrified.

Richard: You just told me something very important. The significance of internally discounting the degree of feelings. You see the importance of what you just communicated to me? How significant it was to you to deny your feelings, in order to cope? See, I think in your case, not feeling is a feeling. And it signals to me the high degree of your emotion. Does it signal that to you?

A new element is added to the pattern: Richard defines the absence of feeling as signaling its direct opposite. No feeling means, in fact, very intense feeling. And by agreeing with the new definition, Charles opens the door to further exploration of that intense feeling. Now "I feel nothing" doesn't shut off contact, but instead is a way to talk about emotions too difficult to discuss directly.

Charles: Yes, I'm aware that I have, that I'm very much of a feeling person, that I have intense feelings. I'm aware of that.

Richard: And I think when you *don't* feel, it's a sign that the feelings are so intense, it's like your brains want to short-circuit.

Charles: That's quite possible. I've also, in the years I've been in therapy, as a result of the work that I've done, I also experience feelings at times that overwhelm me. I can't control them.

Richard: And your mother telling you she was never going to get well—is that an overwhelming sensation? If you allowed yourself to believe it?

Charles: That could be.

Rebecca: It could be if you let yourself feel it?

Charles: Yeah, if I let myself feel it. That's right. That's right.

Richard: See, the problem with defense mechanisms is that we're not aware of our feelings, but our body feels it anyway. And then we pay the price many years later.

Charles: I believe that. I believe that. And that's one of the reasons I'm always tense, because I'm repressing my feelings. I think there are many reasons why I'm anxious, and that's certainly one of them.

Richard: The more I understand you, the more I realize how complex your anxiety is. Event after event after event, and you not having the security of somebody to help you as a little boy, become relaxed.

This reference to the "complexity" of Charles's anxiety marks a key point in the work. It matches, in a way that has not previously been accomplished, Charles's experience of himself, and thus establishes that Richard really does understand him. To be understood, to be met on his own terms, is for Charles the essence of contact—the door through which therapy can take place has opened a bit further. We shall see, as the work proceeds, how both Charles and Richard refer back to the notion of complexity.

Charles: I wish I'd heard that many many years ago. About how complex my anxiety is. Because a lot of people that I worked with thought that it was something very simple, like expressing anger.

Richard: Well, I'm sure that they were right about one facet of your anxiety.

Charles: That is true.

Richard: You're like one of those long shaped diamonds, that have facet after facet, and every one of them gives a different sparkle, a different glow, to that diamond . . . So go on with your story, so I can understand you.

Again the gentle, yet insistent request for contact. The storytelling is not framed as a defensive maneuver, but as Charles's attempt to be understood (which, in a very real sense, is true), and the therapist's interruptions are, again, defined as being in the service of that understanding.

Charles: I used to stroke my mother's hair, and stroke her face, and kiss her, and put my face beside hers, and do what I think a mother should do to a son, and keep on encouraging her and saying nice things about how much I loved her; and then she would get well.

Richard: And what was your hope, Charles?

Charles: That she would get well. And maybe someday do that for me. But she never did.

Richard: What's happened to your hope over the years?

Charles: (*pause*) Maybe at one time I, I gave up. I repressed my hope. I repressed my hope of getting back from . . . I was going to say "from a woman." That was only part of it.

Richard: Well, I think we both know about repression. Although we repress it from our awareness, it always leaks out.

Charles: That's true.

Richard: Like anything put in a pressurized container will find the smallest little crack to work through. And how does your hope leak out in day-to-day relationships with people?

Charles: I will use different, I would say "detectors" to indicate to me where I can get some of that from certain women.

Richard: And it's primarily women you—

Charles: At the moment, it is women. At the moment. Cause I have another problem with men. I know very well I want it from men, and that—

While the questions and interruptions are important as a way to maintain and develop contact between therapist and client, Charles is beginning to show signs of irritation and withdrawal. His answers are increasingly pat, intellectualized, as if he is analyzing someone else rather than experiencing and reporting his own feelings. Again, there is no direct confrontation of the defensive behavior—this would drive Charles even further away—but rather an indirect acknowledgment of the therapist's "interference."

Richard: I'll back off from my questions, so you can get on with what you wanted to say.

Charles: OK. I think I still had, um, this occurred actually after I had a certain experience with my father. When I'd given up on my father. And it became . . . it became vital for me to maintain my relationship with my mother, regardless, because I felt, I felt I'd really given up on my father; there was no chance of getting what I wanted from my father. And the reason I gave up on my father, at least the reason, I had made a decision. I was a very energetic, very active young boy, and a leader of the boys on our block. And we were tough boys. I needed a haircut one day, and my father told me that he thought I needed a haircut. And this was during the Depression, and I didn't completely trust my father. And I said to him—

Richard: So already there was—

Charles: There had already been some history here. And I said to my father, I want you to promise me that if I go to the barber with you, that he's going to give me a haircut, and he isn't going to give me a bald head. Because it wasn't, it wouldn't surprise me that in my father's interest to save money during the Depression that my father would tell the barber to shave every hair off my head.

Richard: For the summer.

Charles: And this was summertime. And this would have been very humiliating to me.

Richard: Sure. Did they call them "Baldies" in those days?

Charles: They called them "Baldies" plus some other derogatory terms. And my father promised. He said "I promise you that that won't happen." And I repeated my question again. I said, "I want you to promise that I won't get a bald head." Father says, "You can trust me. I promise you." OK, then we went off to the barber, who had his barbershop around the corner. And no sooner did I sit down in the barber's chair then both the barber and my father physically grabbed hold of me, and while my father held me down, the barber proceeded to cut every hair off my head. He shaved every hair off my head.

Richard: How old were you?

Charles: I must have been about 10 years old. I would say about 10.

Rebecca: That's awful, Charles.

Richard: That's quite a humiliating experience.

Charles: I felt, with one incident, that I lost all my trust in my father. I had been humiliated.

Richard: Tell me more about what you were saying about being in the barber chair. Held down and violated.

Requests for more information are phrased in terms of what Charles had intended to say: Instead of suggesting that he is not telling enough, this technique shifts the therapist's position to one of consistently supporting and assisting Charles's own efforts. Charles remains in control, and doesn't need to defend against any "intrusions" of the therapist.

Charles: I fought, I struggled with every ounce of energy I had. But these were, these were two grown-up men, and they were using all their strength to keep me down.

Richard: Were they laughing too?

Charles: They weren't laughing, because I was fighting. I would have—(*clenches his fists*) When I hear of people—

Charles has become more animated; he has lost some of the monotonous, rehearsed quality and appears to be experiencing some of the feelings of that abused little boy. The self-interrupted sentences are significant, as they are evidence of a deeper, less-available-to-awareness layer of defense. Richard's intervention is an attempt to take advantage of this new level of openness:

Richard: (*interrupting*) You would have what?

Charles: I was wriggling and struggling and fighting, I wouldn't, I wouldn't sit quiet! Under any conditions.

Richard: Finish that sentence, though, that you blocked yourself from.

Charles: What was I saying?

Richard: "I would have . . ." and you did that with your hands. Feel that.

Charles: I would have . . . I would have torn their balls off! I would have hit them at their, anywhere! I would have, I would never remain passive, I would never remain quiet, when I was being violated. But they were, they were imposing their physical strength on me. And I couldn't do anything.

Richard: What did you decide, that day in the barber chair?

Charles: I, before I answer that, I just want to deal with the hurt I had, just for a moment . . .

Charles resists the invitation to explore the barber chair experience more deeply. He has reached the limit of his tolerance of feelings; he needs to retreat into the relative safety of storytelling. Richard doesn't push, but follows patiently. Other opportunities will come; right now Charles needs to control the flow of the work.

Richard: You take it your way; we'll come back to that question.

Charles: I remember after that experience, after having all my hair cut off my head, shaved off my head . . . my going off by myself, like a little dog or cat that's been wounded. And just licking my wounds by myself. And deciding that I'll never ever trust my father again. I'll never ever ask him for something, I'll never ever get close to him, I'll never ever show that I love him. Even though (*sobs*) I cried because I loved him so much. And I still do.

Richard: As though he had died for you that day, emotionally.

Charles: That's right. I'm more aware of my love for my father than I am of my love for my mother.

Richard: Well, it sounds as if he was the more contactful parent. Until he violated you. (*Charles sobs*) See, emotional abuse like that is even more hurtful than physical abuse.

Charles: I believe that, because I think I can take any kind of physical abuse. Because you usually repair after some physical abuse.

Richard: If he had strapped you, at least the bruises from the strap heal. But he also rubbed salt in the wounds. Cause then you had to face your friends. So you got a double humiliation.

Charles: And what I felt was, this is why I struggled so hard with understanding, is that I felt my father just didn't understand me. He just had no idea. To him it was more important to save that 25 cents—true, it was the Depression, and money was hard to come by—but for him the 25 cents was far far more important than how I felt.

Richard: Why the hell didn't he put a bowl on your head and cut it himself?

This intervention is aimed directly at the little boy—Charles's Child ego state. The controlled, analytic, nonfeeling aspect of ego that Charles most often uses would not find it a helpful or even particularly relevant comment. But the Child, feeling alone and betrayed by the person he trusted most, may welcome the support. It is a way of saying to that Child, "I'm on your side." It also begins two important aspects of Charles's work: (a) reversing his defensive decision to isolate himself; and (b) contacting his denied desires for a good father—a father who would acknowledge and respect the needs of the child.

Charles: He could have done that.

Richard: And saved the 25 cents and could have taken you out and bought you an ice cream cone, huh?

Charles: In those days ice cream was two for 5 cents.

Richard: And the two of you could have walked down the street, eating your ice cream cones after he cut your hair, and you would have had 20 cents to spare.

Charles: My father never bought me an ice cream. (*pause*) Yes, I made that decision to turn my back on my father, even though I loved him so much.

Richard: What a hard decision.

Charles: And I still struggle with that, because I feel that is one of the main reasons that I have difficulty in my contact with men. It's as if I'm saying, I'm still waiting for my father to at least either apologize to me for what he did, or at least to say that he understood how I felt. I'm still waiting for him.

Richard: Is he still alive?

Charles: No. My father has been dead for 28 years. Cause that's the age of my son . . . I think that he was the loneliest member in our family. He cared for me, as much as he could show that he cared.

But he couldn't show that very much. When I was little, he showed that more than he did when I was older.

Rebecca: Can you feel that inside, that he cared for you?

Charles: (*pause*) I could remember incidents; I think I mentioned that he taught me the Greek alphabet. I remember sitting on his lap, and he taught me the Greek alphabet. I remember him telling me stories, at that time . . .

Rebecca: (*interrupting*) Can you *feel* that he loved you? That he cared for you?

Charles: I have trouble. I have trouble feeling that.

Richard: Because of your barber chair decision?

Charles: Possibly. Because I'm also making—I was going to say I make myself tense, although I don't feel my body that tense right now, although I still have no feelings. I have no feelings.

There has been a definite, though still slight, change in Charles's presentation. While he is still describing himself as not feeling, he now seems to be puzzled and bothered by this lack. Rebecca neatly connects "no feelings" to "feeling empty" and relates the two "feelings" to the lack of respectful contact from Charles's parents when he was a boy.

Rebecca: So you had two parents who really weren't there, with you.

Charles: That's right.

Rebecca: That's pretty empty.

Charles: That's why it became so important for me to focus on my mother, and to maintain a relationship with my mother—

Richard: But a mother who used you for her needs.

Charles: —with my mother, because there seemed to be the illusion of maybe getting something from my mother. My mother was always saying how much she loved me, and how she wanted me close to her, and to be with her. But it was an illusion. Because when I got close to my mother, for my needs, she was using me for her needs. But I always kept on, I had no alternative. And I would think that if only I got better at what I was doing, if only I became—I felt the fault was mine.

Richard: Keep going.

Charles: The fault was mine.

Richard: If only . . . If only . . .

Charles: If only I could get better and better . . . If only I would be perfect, then I would earn and deserve my mother's love.

Richard: What's the implication there for you?

Charles: I'm not quite clear.

Richard: Because what I hear you saying is that basically you're unlovable as you are.

Charles: That's right. That, I'm lacking something.

Richard identifies, and Charles confirms, a fundamental script belief, one that forms a basis for much (all?) of Charles's defensive system. As long as he believes that there is something intrinsically and unchangeably wrong with him, he will continue to behave in ways that will support that belief—and will invite others to support it, as well. Eventually, Charles will need to deal with this belief at an affective, nonrational level—the level at which it was originally formed. But Charles is not yet ready for this kind of intense emotional work—he is too frightened, too well defended. The process must remain largely cognitive, with Charles in control. The script belief can still be challenged cognitively, in preparation for later affective work.

Richard: What's wrong with you?

Charles: And something is wrong with me. Because I was brought up, I mentioned my older sister. In many ways she was my mother. She was in her twenties when I was born. And I don't trust my feelings—you're quite right about me being kind of complicated.

That Richard understood and validated his complexity is a touchstone, a reassurance for Charles that he has been heard and taken seriously. Reminding himself of this helps him to risk the next tiny step of self-revelation.

Charles: (*continuing*) I don't trust my feelings because when I was little I used to perceive things at home. And I thought I was quite objective in my perception. And I'm sure I was. However, my sister and I felt our house was not a house of love. Our house was a house of anger, and resentment, and a lot of hate between the members of our family. But my sister used to tell me, "Our home is a home of love. We never argue—look at the neighbors. The neighbors are always fighting; we never fight."

Richard: I bet you would have liked it if they would have fought outright, huh? Was it a cold war?

Charles: That's right.

Richard: Good screaming match sometimes clears the air, doesn't it?

Charles: I started to think that my feelings are not right. They're the adults, they're the adults and they know what life is all about. I'm just a little kid. So I'm wrong, and my feelings are wrong. And my thoughts are wrong.

Richard: You just got confused. You needed somebody to help that little kid stay straight.

Charles: And I've been struggling; I'm on the road back.

Richard: What age are you talking about there?

Charles: I'm talking about, I would say seven or eight. Maybe even earlier.

Richard: From the sound of the confusion, I was going to say even four.

Charles: Maybe even earlier.

Richard: Cause I imagine, given your intellectual capacities, that at four you were really more advanced than the other kids around. That's probably why you were the leader of the gang. And I bet your perceptions of things were much sharper than anybody ever gave you credit for. And that you had to deny your perceptions. And that's crazy-making.

Charles: I think that's very true. And today, I keep on, any time I want to deal with something, I have to struggle real hard. I have messages in my head telling me not to do it, regardless of what I want to do or say. Not to do it! And for many different reasons. Sometimes I just have to clear—(*he pauses, shakes his head*) I just have to try and set aside what's going on in my head.

As Charles begins to allow himself to feel, his gestures and body language begin to convey what he is experiencing. Calling his attention to these nonverbal cues may help him to increase his level of awareness, and asking him to talk about them may lead to a greater sense of contact between him and the therapists.

Richard: Now tell me what just happened inside, so I can know. That head shake.

Charles: Sometimes it's a real job to just clear out what's going on in my head.

Richard: Describe that fog.

Charles: It's not a fog. I just have these, messages. Telling me not to do it, and many times . . . I'd like to back up a bit. Not that long ago, before I started back in therapy, those messages used to be so intense it was like a hurricane in my head. I couldn't think.

Richard: Now I see why you said not like a fog.

Charles: It's not like a fog at all.

Richard: Much worse.

Charles: It's like a storm. It's a storm that's raging all the time. And I've got to struggle; I find sometimes when I hear people's names, when people are introduced to me, I have these messages going on like I won't remember their name, don't try to remember their name, you're trying to remember the name because you want to use their name so they'll, you'll get, you want to get them to like you. And I have this with a high degree, with a high level of intensity.

Richard: Is it like your older sister's voice saying you won't remember their name?

Determining the source of the introjected messages, as well as their content, will help in planning future treatment strategies. Later in therapy, "Parent" interviews with sister, father, or mother may be needed in order to counteract the effects of that early scripting process.

Charles: My older sister's voice. Plus my father's voice. I hear both.

Richard: And do you have a remembrance of his ever saying that to you? Or of her ever saying that to you?

Charles: No, they never said that to me. No, I've used that myself. I have made that up myself. I was, like you said, I was a little kid who didn't have, I couldn't check things out with anyone. And I felt I was bad; I felt I was wrong.

Richard: Trying to make sense out of all that confusion, that storm raging in your head . . .

Charles: The other part of it, Richard, is that I took out of my relationship with my mother that she didn't want me to leave her. I think that's part of it. I also wanted something from her. I wanted her love, and to be close to her. But I felt that she didn't want me to leave her. And when I get close to women (*pause*) I still feel that. That if I were to really get women to love me, that my mother would become very angry at me. That she would be left alone. I wouldn't be there for her. Or certainly not there to the degree that she wanted me.

Richard: And then what happens, if she doesn't get what she wants from you? What happens to the little boy?

Charles: Then there's no chance of me getting what I want from her.

Richard: And feel that sense of pain, Charles. That you defend against, by being the caretaker. What you're telling me is a story of neglect. How neglected little Charles is. Oh, what a painful, painful experience, that you probably have to defend against, because it's so painful. Now you're talking about what must be real pain—no longer anxiety.

Charles: I don't feel anything.

As Richard leads him slightly beyond the level of awareness that he allows himself, Charles slides back into total denial of feelings. But this time his report of feeling nothing can be translated: It has been established that "no feeling" really means "intense feeling." Richard reiterates this assumption, suggests a historical basis for it, and then invites him to risk another step forward, another "peek into" what lies below the defensive numbness. As will be evident from his next response, Charles is still not ready to take this further step—but each invitation, given gently and supportively, with no hint of criticism, takes him just a bit closer to opening up.

Richard: Sure. Can you see the importance of what we've already established? That for you, the "I don't feel any pain" is a feeling. It is a statement to us, us being you and me both, of the degree to which the feelings are so intense. (*pause*) Probably just like your mother's tremendous degree of intense pain also, that was defended against and showed up as her craziness. Except fortunately you're a little brighter—maybe a lot brighter—and have found other ways to sublimate it. Through work, through activities, through creativity. But as you get older, it still eats away inside. Can you tell me about, can you peek into that pain in you, so both you and I will know a little bit more about it? Will you let yourself know?

Charles: I want to tell you about another incident . . . probably before my mother had her breakdown, I remember my mother in the kitchen one day. She was serving us lunch. And, um . . . we were all seated around the table, and she was serving us lunch, in the process of serving lunch, and she turned and asked—we had a gas oven. And she turned the gas jet on, and she said she was going to kill herself. And when I saw that my sister got up and turned the gas jet off. But again I think I made a decision then, to always look after my mother. And to—

Richard: How frightening—

Charles: And to make sure that I would do everything to keep her alive.

Richard: How frightening . . . no chance to relax, in your own kitchen. No chance to just be afraid; you always had to be vigilant, with a decision like that.

Charles: And I think that's one of the reasons—one of the reasons—that I'm anxious today. Because I've taken on my mother's anxiety. My mother was that little girl, anytime there was a little breeze, to her it was like a hurricane. To her.

Richard: What's it like to constantly be vigilant for her safety?

Charles: I had to change my personality. I had to change from being a very energetic, active, energetic boy, spontaneous, acting on any stimulus, to being, to becoming very controlled. And very cautious. And to check things out. Any time I was going to do something, check out what could be the possible effect on my mother.

Richard: Yuck.

Charles: And any time I wanted to use my energies, and be myself, I had to restrain myself because I had too much energy for my mother.

Richard: Are you telling me then that you had to develop a false personality?

Here Richard reiterates and specifies what Charles has said about changing his personality. Richard's question serves to underline the importance of what Charles has just revealed. If Charles accepts this designation, it can become another pointer for future work: Richard can help him begin to differentiate between thoughts, feelings, and behaviors that are a function of the "false personality" and those that belong to his "true" self. And it is through the "true" self, of course, that real, healing contact can occur.

Charles: I had to change my personality.

Richard: And what does that mean to you, inside?

Charles: I had to put a straitjacket on myself.

Richard: But what happened to the real self?

Charles: I could not show that.

Richard: What happened to it?

Charles: It's still within. I had to repress it.

Richard: (*at the same time*) Did you destroy it?

Charles: No, I never destroyed that.

Richard: Did you put it in a vault?

Charles: I had to repress it. I had to constrain it, restrict it.

Richard: Do you ever let the real self out?

Charles: My wife says I'm spontaneous sometimes in bed.

Richard: Well, good! I can't think of a better place to let it out! But—is that enough?

Charles: No. No, it's not.

Richard: What do you mean; or what does your wife mean, when she says that you let your real self out in bed?

Charles: What she means is that I am spontaneous, I will, I will be playful, I will be loving, and I just act the way I feel.

Richard: And other times, when you're not in bed, do you have the capacity to be spontaneous? Or playful? Or loving?

Charles: Do I have the capacity?

Richard: Or is that buried?

Charles: I sure have the capacity, but I don't use it.

Richard: OK. (*pause*) Go ahead; you were starting to tell me about your true self. That got locked up.

Charles has accepted the distinction, and the labels "false self" and "true self." Now he can be helped to begin to experience and act out of the "true" rather than from the artificial defenses of the "false" self. The false self is a kind of defensive second skin, which covers and constrains all of Charles's spontaneous, contact-seeking self, and defends his soft inner being.

Charles: I used to act with a lot of feeling, intense feelings; I had feelings about things. Either good or bad; I was happy or angry. And I used to act quickly; and I didn't stop to think what the consequences would be. I was really spontaneous.

Richard: That means that there's some health there that we can build on. See, that's the hopeful part; you said earlier you were despairing. Because that's there, we can really build on that. That's the part that gives me hope, that your anxiety is curable.

Charles: I certainly know that it's improvable. Whether it's curable; I've always hoped that it was. Because I've been improving it over the years, step by step. I would hope that there would be some faster ways. I've experienced one way that I thought was, was fast. In fact, my first big change, and I've mentioned it to you more than once, when I expressed anger. What I considered to be for the first time, in a group. Then my anxiety really dropped. I think of it as a quantum drop.

Richard is moving toward closure; time is getting short, and it is also important to stop on a positive note. Too abrupt a breaking off, however, could push Charles back into his old script system: "I've been abandoned and rejected, there really is something wrong with me, even this therapist can't help . . ." To avoid this, Richard moves to build an explicit bridge from the present work out into the other activities of the workshop, so that Charles can experience his therapy as continuing beyond the point at which the formal work has ended.

Richard: Hey, Charles—think you could go to bed with all of us?

Charles: I sure could!

Richard: (*chuckling*) What would we see? . . . I'm speaking metaphorically, of course. If you bedded down with all of us; decided to use these next couple of days with us, the same way you do with your wife in bed—who is going to emerge? What would we see? What would we hear? What would we experience?

Charles: A person who isn't afraid. Who doesn't have anxiety. Who feels safe. A person who would want to play—a man who'd want to play, and have fun.

Richard: And what would be different on the volleyball court?

The volleyball games, built into each day's schedule during the workshop, provide an excellent opportunity for participants both to observe themselves literally playing out their scripts and to experiment with new, out-of-script behaviors. Because playing volleyball is not a part of the daily routine of most people, behaviors there are not so locked in by habit and practice. Participants can see their old patterns more clearly, and may also be more willing to risk changing those patterns in the context of an activity that is itself new and unfamiliar.

Charles: I know I could be different on the volleyball court. Very different.

Richard: Will you describe that, so I can know it? If you were your true self out there, how would you be?

Charles: If I were my true self and really wanted to, I would play with every ounce of energy I had. I would play to win. I would play to win, so that my team won. Our team won. And I would support everyone. I would be in Ruth's territory, backing her up. I would let her play her part, but I'd be there to support her when she needed it.

Richard: And what's the excuse you use to stop yourself? From being that true self?

Charles: Well, I say, "Don't hog it. Don't try to get too much attention. People aren't going to like you if you stand out." (*pause*) George was saying yesterday that I was not expressing my anger, that he was hearing my words, and I was using a lot of verbiage, and he thought there was anger underneath that that I was not expressing directly. And he's right. And other people have given me similar feedback. And they were right. But what I hear in that, and I want to change that part of me, and I'm very grateful for that feedback; but I hear something else in it.

Richard: Hm. What's that?

Charles: I've been thinking about that. I hear a threat. I hear a threat that if I don't improve, if I don't express my anger, directly, that he's going to reject me.

Richard: Now that's script.

Charles: Yeah. Plus—OK, let me repeat my statement now. What I hear in that is that, regardless of all the qualities I have, and I think I'm a good person, that because of one shortcoming, that George is willing to reject me. If I don't change that shortcoming. And regardless of all the improvements I've made over the years, he's still willing to reject me because of that one shortcoming.

Charles's bid to introduce new material, in order to prolong the work, was predictable for at least two reasons: He has been starved for contact and attention, and wants this to continue; and his old script system demands that he somehow "prove" that there is something wrong with him—how better to do this than to force his therapist to reject him? Richard avoids the trap by pointing out, again, the script connection.

Richard: Now, Charles. That's the lie. That's the lie that the little boy used to make sense out of his confusion. There's the script belief, that "something's wrong with me." And you'll use George as evidence, to maintain that belief, "Something's wrong with me," which is a defense against your feelings of Mother not being there for you. You decided as a little boy, "Something's wrong with me."

Charles: I believe that.

Richard: You decided it defensively. You know why? Cause you got power with that decision. Pseudopower, but at least something you experienced as power. Cause as long as there was something wrong with you, you could get fixed. You could change you; you could use your intellect to figure out how to improve you; you could even go to therapy and have your head shrunk. There's a pseudosense of power in a kid who says "There's something wrong with me." Cause then you don't have to feel your helplessness with an emotionally disturbed mother.

Charles: That sounds possible.

Rebecca: That sounds to me like a good place to stop.

Richard: (*very long pause*) How does it seem to you, Charles?

Charles does not want to end this piece of work; his body language makes that clear. Richard asks him to express this want openly and directly—again, to make a specific, observable change from his old pattern of hiding the reactions of his true self behind an adaptive, false self mask.

Charles: How does what seem to me?

Richard: What Rebecca just said. She said it seemed to her like a good place to stop. How is it for you?

Charles: No.

Richard: Tell Rebecca that. Be true with Rebecca. Tell her your true self right now.

Charles: I would like to resolve my problem.

Richard: Tell her! Charles, look at her!

Charles: (*to Rebecca*) I would like to resolve my problem.

Richard: Be truthful with her right now. Keep going. Tell her what you feel when she says stop.

Charles: I feel very irritated; I feel very . . .

Richard: (*whispering*) Go on—tell her!

Charles: I feel angry at you. And I hear myself softening my voice when I say that to you—

We have pointed out earlier that retroflection—carrying on an internal dialogue rather than being contactful with others—is another facet of Charles's script pattern. Richard continues to urge him to experiment with change: instead of observing himself, to be authentic with Rebecca.

Richard: Be authentic with her now.

Charles: Because I like you a lot.

Richard: Because you like her you can go ahead and be real with her, Charles. You're right on the edge, right now, of that little boy's decision. The social self, or the real self.

Charles: I'd feel very angry at you, Rebecca, if we were to stop now. Because I was hoping to, I was hoping to reach a point where I would experience a change in myself, as far as my anxiety's concerned.

Richard: What, in your mind, would that change—what would it be like?

Charles: Well, I was hoping that the resolution would, would lead to me having a drop of anxiety. Feeling freer to be myself.

Richard: Then it's almost a desire, then, that it be a dramatic drop? Like it was when you first got angry in group.

Charles: My desire would be—that's right. Even then, I think I've already mentioned it, in that I did not immediately experience it. As a dramatic drop. It was only a day later that I did. In the group that I was in, what I did experience was that I had done something I'd never done before.

Charles has condensed the memory of his previous group work, and out of that condensation comes an impossible criterion for feeling good about stopping: a "dramatic drop in anxiety" that may not be felt until the next day. If he can't feel the change now, he will be disappointed about his work. Rather than confront this self-sabotage (and invite Charles to feel even more disappointed and criticized, with no time left to deal with those feelings), Richard will return to the idea of extending the therapy out onto the volleyball court.

Richard: Um-hm.

Charles: And there was a sense of satisfaction that I had done it. But to me this was just a, in the group it was just an exercise. And I did not see a direct relationship between that exercise and me feeling less anxious. It was only when I got myself into a situation that previously produced anxiety for me, where I saw that I was no longer anxious.

Richard: Are you willing to do an experiment?

Charles: Yes.

Richard: How about letting your true self play volleyball tonight? Like the 10-year-old would have done, perhaps, with his buddies. Were you still free with them, or were you already adapted with them?

Charles: I was relatively free at 10.

Richard: What if you got out there and played with all the competition of a 10-year-old? With all the verbal freedom of a 10-year-old? With all the abandonment of a 10-year-old? With buddies that you knew really liked him and wouldn't humiliate him?

Charles: And wouldn't reject me.

Richard: Yeah. So that emotionally you go back before the haircut. And you take the risk, out there.

Charles: I feel like I'd be over half that court.

Ideally, this is the point at which Charles' work should have ended: He is experiencing, in fantasy, the excitement of being his "true self" on the volleyball court and has thus accepted the bridging between the formal work and other workshop activities. We end the transcript here to illustrate this ideal—but we would be less than honest if we implied that Charles allowed this to happen. In fact, he continued to request more time and to express his disappointment that he experienced no dramatic shift in his emotional state, finally forcing the therapists to end the work and thus reliving once more his old pattern of rejection and abandonment.

It would be easy to become discouraged here and to discount the gains actually made in the work with Charles. Indeed, this is what often happens in working with clients who exhibit these sorts of contact disruptions: The therapist gives up, labels the client as "untreatable" or "nonmotivated," and the therapy either ends prematurely or drags on and on with neither client nor therapist experiencing contact or excitement.

But disappointments are an important part of therapy with clients like Charles: Healing occurs when the disappointments can be dealt with in the context of a contactful relationship. In order to continue this process, the therapists here recommended that Charles find a therapist in his hometown, who would be available to him on an ongoing basis.

Although Charles was uncomfortable at the end of this work, he did carry some new behaviors into the activities of the workshop. He was more playful in the volleyball games, and began to initiate more conversations during meals and social times. The acceptance and understanding of the two therapists gave him a taste of what real contact can be like—and the experience of contact cannot be undone, however short-lived it may be. Charles will need much more of the same kind of slow, patient work in order to build a foundation of trust that will eventually allow him to let down his defensive barriers. Only when this level of trust is established will he begin to address directly the script beliefs and feelings that have so crippled his ability to relate spontaneously and joyfully with the world around him.

12

JON
Putting It All Together

We have come a long way and have met a lot of people in this book. We have introduced a variety of theoretical concepts, borrowed and adapted from the work of many of our predecessors in the gentle art of psychotherapy. We have described, discussed, and dissected many techniques and have shown how they can be used and what they can be expected to accomplish. And all of this has been a rather freewheeling consideration of ideas as they arise in the rich and varied context of ongoing psychotherapeutic encounters.

We have chosen Jon's work as the basis for this last chapter because it gives us an opportunity to wrap many of these ideas together: to show how one concept complements another, how one type of intervention grows out of a particular theoretical idea, and how a hypothesis about a client is often the product of (or refuted by) a particular series of interventions.

Jon's transcript, then, will illustrate many of the major theoretical underpinnings of integrative psychotherapy. We shall see examples of interruptions to internal and external contact, of Child ego state fixations, of the introjection of a segment of a significant other's personality, of the intrapsychic influence of a Parent ego state and the resulting defenses, and of childhood script decisions in which the entire script system maintains itself through a circular, self-reinforcing process. We shall also see many of the therapeutic techniques that have been discussed in previous chapters: the Parent Interview, the process of heightening awareness of defenses and enhancing contact, the attention to each of the major domains of therapeutic change.

In this piece of work, we can also follow with particular clarity the progression or flow of therapy. The work begins with a conversation between the therapist and Jon in which the goals of therapy are established and some background information is gathered. There is a rather rapid shift to Parent ego state therapy, with the final phase composed of a Gestalt therapy technique—"chair work"—which establishes in fantasy the contact that was missing between Jon's father (Parent ego state) and Jon himself. The fantasized contact concludes a major piece of unfinished business—a fixed gestalt that has blocked Jon from spontaneous and comfortable interaction with others. The "chair work," in turn, forms a bridge into a short (but intense) archaeopsychic regression and an invitation to Jon to make a redecision—a redecision that is now possible because of the decommissioning of the Parent ego state accomplished earlier in the work. And, finally, the piece terminates with a return to Adult ego state and a suggestion that Jon continue the redecision process on his own.

Jon is a heavyset, awkward young man, a psychiatric nurse who describes himself as ill at ease in social situations. He came to the workshop on the recommendation of his psychotherapy supervisor, a woman who trained with Richard and Rebecca and who suggested that working in the context of this intensively involved group might help him to resolve some of the countertransference that was affecting his practice of psychotherapy. Jon has been rather quiet for the first few days of the workshop, though intently interested in the other participants' work. Now he asks for time for himself:

Jon: I guess I'm wanting, I don't really know . . . I know I need to get some things taken care of, and I guess I don't really know how to do it.

Richard: Well, that's our job.

Jon: OK. I'll leave it up to you, then. Um . . . sitting back and listening to everyone else, I've gotten some major threads. And, uh, I guess I've felt basically, some of this I've hashed over before with my therapist, so some of this is going to be repetitive. (*sigh*) But basically I guess the feeling of being rejected has gone back ever since I can remember. I honestly believe I was the reason that my folks got married.

As often happens, Jon wants direction from the therapists. He doesn't know how to go about getting what he wants from his work, or even where to start. Once he is reassured that the therapists will, indeed, supply this direction, he is able to take the plunge himself, going directly to the issue that troubles him the most. "Direction," for Jon, is really a kind of respect for his own knowing, his ability to be aware of his process. We have spoken before of following the client's lead, of allowing the client to be in charge of the work. Richard and Rebecca waste no time in demonstrating that they will do just this: They will attend to whatever it is that Jon wants to talk about.

Rebecca: Were they pregnant with you before they were married?

Jon: Yeah. And I found that out back this summer.

Richard: Was that comfortable or uncomfortable? For you to know that?

Jon: Well, it's uncomfortable for me to know that, because it's . . . for 30 years, as I've been trying to piece things together, I can remember Dad making statements like, "Well, I promised your mother that I would stay with her until you were 21." And, uh, I can remember earlier years of Dad not really, not really wanting me. Or acting like he didn't want me. Uh, my dad is an alcoholic, or was an alcoholic, rather. And Mom invested a lot of her time in his illness. She really loved him.

Richard: Interesting that you call it an illness, rather than an alcoholic decision.

Jon: I guess I don't necessarily buy that theory. I view it as an illness.

Richard: It certainly *becomes* an illness. Because the liver malfunctions, and is unable to process food substances. Would it make a difference in how you saw your dad, though, if you thought of it as an alcoholic decision?

Jon: I would say I'd probably hate him more then. It's easier to accept the fact that he has an illness.

Richard: Have you considered that calling it an illness may be partly denial on your part?

Here is the first confrontation—light, respectful, clearly directed toward Jon's competent, problem-solving Adult ego state. Its purpose is more to discover how Jon will respond to this sort of challenge than to produce any therapeutic effect. Will he acquiesce, comply, go along in order to please the therapists? Will he resist the suggestion? Will he withdraw, or signal a need for support, or move against the therapists in some way? The answer to these questions will be useful in doing ongoing treatment planning as the work unfolds.

Jon: Oh, no, I know. I know how his drinking has affected my life.

Jon neither withdraws, attacks, nor collapses. Richard pushes a bit harder: Again, Jon's response will be diagnostically useful.

Richard: But do you suppose your calling it an illness has a cushioning effect? As opposed to calling it a decision, which puts much more responsibility, at least in the initial stages of his drinking, back on him.

Jon: Well, Dad didn't have a fair chance, really, from the very beginning. His dad was a moonshiner, and they had, talked about having five-gallon crocks in every room that the kids, anybody that wanted to could just come by and dip. Part of the trouble that I have in even entering therapy is reconciling the fact of the conflicting feelings about that relationship with him.

Now we have our answer. Jon doesn't back down, but is able to marshal facts that support his position. He also shows a bit of uneasiness—Richard is threatening to take over direction of the work, and Jon has not yet had a chance to tell his story. Richard quickly responds to this, putting Jon back in charge.

Richard: Go ahead, tell us more. I was probing to understand the importance for you in calling it an illness.

Jon: Uh, Mom worked basically three jobs. She was a full-time nurse, usually worked nights. And she worked, we had a jewelry store, she worked in there full time. And she tried to take care of the house until she quit. So I consider that three full-time jobs. Not a lot of time for me. Um . . .

Richard: What did you feel right at that moment, Jon? When you said "Not a lot of time for me," and tightened your jaw?

Nonverbal events—the physiological aspect of communication—are quite often more important than the actual verbal content. They are important not only as a major domain of therapeutic work (along with thoughts, feelings, and overt behaviors), but as indications that important processes are occurring in the other domains. This is the second time, early in the work, that Richard has structured his intervention in response to such a cue. We will see him do it often throughout the piece, just as we have in previous chapters.

Jon: Lot of hurt and anger. Mom said as a baby I never cried a lot. Only when I needed to be changed, and maybe a little bit when I was teething.

Richard: Does that mean you were contented?

Jon: I don't know. Didn't think of that.

Richard: I have one child, also, who never cried a lot, and I think it was primarily because she was contented.

Jon: I don't know if I'm contented.

Richard: Certainly not today. But do you think you were contented that first year of life? And therefore there was not much need to cry a lot? Except when you had to voice out some complaint . . . The way you said it, you implied that there was a problem that you didn't cry a lot. How do you understand that?

Jon: I understand that I was scared to cry. That I was scared.

Richard: Infants who are punished stop crying.

Jon: I don't know if I was punished. I don't have any clear memory of any physical abuse.

Richard: But you seemed to underscore that, as if that was a problem that you did not cry a lot as an infant. Is that accurate?

Still early in the work, the therapy is still exploratory. A number of things are being established in this segment. Richard is cementing the therapeutic alliance, the basic cooperative stance between therapist and client. Respectful even in his gentle confrontation, he conveys both his interest and his intent to look at all the possible meanings of each idea that Jon volunteers. He is gathering historical and process information that will help in diagnosis and (as we noted earlier) in ongoing treatment planning. And he is conveying information to Jon, both overtly—facts that will help Jon sort through his own memories and beliefs—and covertly—that things are not always what they seem, that there can be more than one way to understand or remember a particular fact.

Jon: Yeah. Mom and Dad thought it was a blessing.

Rebecca: Um-hm. Most parents do.

Jon: And, so anyway, as a kid I have never really been an achiever. I've always had a lot of difficulty in school. Basically a loner. I don't know how many diets the folks have had me on. And you see the result of it today; except maybe if I wouldn't have been on a diet I would have been twice the size I am. And, um . . .

Richard: Do you have a sense of what the excessive eating is about?

Jon: At times I do and at times I don't. I think in some ways now it's maybe the only way I can identify with my parents. Both of them are very, are big people.

Richard: Now why do you want to identify with them today, in the 1980s?

In common with many clients who have been in treatment for some time, Jon has some tendency toward psychological glibness: offering a pat theory as if it were in fact an explanation of himself. This sort of psychobabble may not only be misleading, but it can stand as a barrier to the search for valid, experience-based connections. Richard's response has challenged the finality, the patness, of the explanation Jon offers for his overeating. And Jon responds with a much more authentic, personal statement—a statement of a major script belief, which will recur again and again in his work.

Jon: That's what I'm trying to, that's what I'm trying to reason out. And, like I said the other day, life has been a struggle. Life is always a struggle. I've pretty much gotten over the fact of not wanting to exist. But that is still a prominent feeling. Anyhow, that's kind of the background.

Richard: You told us that your dad died—how long ago?

Jon: About seven weeks ago.

Richard: How did you feel about his dying?

Jon: I felt, uh . . . really mixed. Really, really mixed.

Richard: Can you describe the mix?

Jon: Yeah, I was really relieved. I was relieved that he was gone. Because I, I felt that an honest part of my hatred was buried with him.

Rebecca: What was the relief that he was gone? What are you now free of?

Jon: I'm free of him.

Rebecca: What does all that entail?

Jon: Dad and I had a very strange relationship, from about, intermixed, from about the age of zero to 10, and then I would say from about 8 to about 14 or 15 we were pretty happy together. Mom was the tyrant, Mom was the one who was the door-slammer, the kettle-banger. There was always a lot of tension between Mom and Dad, a lot of underlying tension.

Like a snapshot pulled from a Polaroid camera, the work is beginning to come into focus. The haze, the fuzziness, is beginning to clear; the major issue, Jon's relationship with his father, is moving into the foreground. It is not a matter of the therapists zeroing in on a theme, or even of Jon himself deciding what he wants to work on. Rather, it is like an intricate dance, with each participant contributing to weaving a pattern—a pattern that becomes more and more visible as the dance continues.

Richard: Precipitated by his drinking?

Jon: Yeah. Always a lot of financial stress, due to his—

Richard: (*interrupting*) Did it also *precipitate* the drinking?

Jon: (*sigh*) I think earlier that Dad drank more or less to get at Mom. At some point in time.

Richard: (*he has misunderstood Jon's statement*) What do you mean, drank to get a Mom?

Jon: Well, Dad was very—

Richard: (*interrupting*) To get at Mom, or to get a mom?

Jon: OK, both. Mom was a nurse, she was a very nurturing person. She was very, uh, take away the hurt of the world . . .

Richard: I just need to know something. Did I do a slip of the ear?

Jon: Well, no, both things that you said are true.

Richard: Yes, but what was your original statement?

Jon: To get at Mom.

Richard: OK. It's my slip of the ear, then. I thought I heard you say "drank to get a mom."

Richard's coined phrase, "slip of the ear," suggests that mishearings, like misstatements, are not mere random errors. Slips of the tongue, dreams, and humor can all be understood as reflections of our unconscious process—our out-of-awareness wisdom that puts together myriad tiny cues, memories, and feelings and presents the resulting product in a disguised way. So it is with a "slip of the ear." Experienced as an honest mistake in hearing, it may really reflect an important insight into the unconscious knowing or believing of the client, or may be a statement about the therapist. By staying with this fragment, Richard brings into awareness what was only dimly understood before: that Jon's father drank not only to punish Mom, but also in order to be nurtured by her. Jon's next question indicates that he does not yet understand the significance of this bit of information, and Richard does not pursue it. The work turns back to the original format: building contact, gathering information, planning the treatment strategy.

Jon: Uh, yeah. Well, he wanted a mother, that's why he married Mom. Mom was very mothering towards him. Is this going anyplace?

Richard: Oh, yeah.

Jon: Oh, OK.

Richard: It's going right between us—gives us a chance to understand you.

Rebecca: And we can speculate what he might have felt if he married your mother to have a mom, but had to compete with a newborn baby.

Jon: I don't really think Dad wanted to get married. And I don't think he really wanted me . . . And, uh, Dad was very dependent on her, and he was very angry about it.

Rebecca's "interpretation," as is so common in integrative psychotherapy, is framed as an invitation to "speculate," to consider or think about something. It gives the client plenty of room to deny the connection if he or she is not yet ready to deal with it, or if it is not accurate. Jon, although he still does not understand where this line of thought is going, is quite willing to stay with it. Indeed, his eagerness to discuss his father suggests that the father-son relationship will be an excellent place to focus the work. What is Jon's unfinished business with Dad? Does the "unfinished" relate to the grieving process (given that Dad's death was relatively recent) or to earlier script decisions?

Richard: Have you, in your personal therapy, had any conversations with Dad since his death?

Jon: Right after he died.

Richard: Think it's time to have another? (*long pause*) OK, your hesitancy is my answer. (*pause*) I'm going to assume, not yet.

Jon has been highly responsive to therapeutic suggestion up to this point. It seems clear that he wants to please the therapists (and the group), to "do it right" in therapy. His silence here, then, is eloquent—it says, more loudly than words, that the "conversation with Dad" is not what he wants from this piece of work. Gently, so as not to push him into adapting to the therapists rather than attending to his own needs, Richard and Rebecca explore this reluctance.

Jon: Not yet.

Rebecca: What are you feeling right now, Jon?

Jon: Relieved. I don't—

Richard: Tell us about that relief.

Jon: Well, I have been, I have been having some dreams about Dad. Lately. About the last, oh, well off and on, I've had three dreams about him since I came here. Two or three dreams. In which I'm just basically saying good-bye to him.

Richard: In the dream.

Jon: In the dream, yeah.

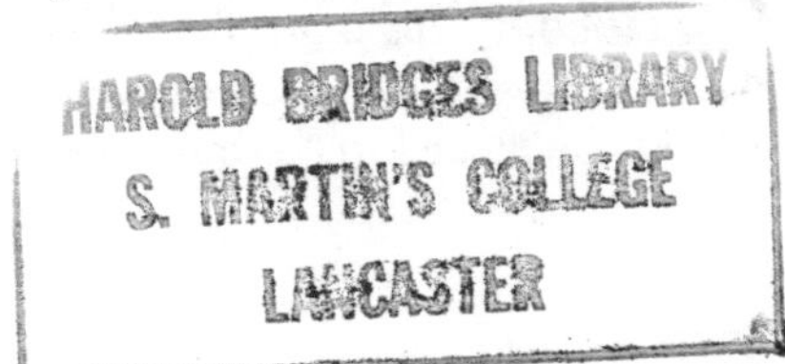

Dreams during a workshop of this sort are often highly significant, as we saw with Emily's work (Chapter 7). The therapists file this information away; they may choose to come back and work with one or more of Jon's dreams. First, though, they will need to finish with Jon's reaction to the suggestion about a therapeutic conversation with Dad.

Rebecca: Has it been helpful?

Jon: Yeah.

Richard: And yet here there's a hesitancy when I suggest the possibility that you have a conversation with him.

Jon: I don't think I need to talk to him about his death.

Richard: You need to talk to him about the way he lived. But not yet. Your reluctance is saying something important, and I want to respect that. Because if you're ready, it's going to be very spontaneous.

Jon: I'll know, in a couple of days, by how I feel? About that?

Richard: If it's an issue that needs to be worked with, it will get worked with.

Respecting and strengthening resistance, rather than breaking through it, is a basic tenet of integrative psychotherapy. The covert message to Jon is that he will be taken seriously, and that he himself knows what he needs.

There is another concern, however, at this point. Jon has been working for some time, and is beginning to show signs of impatience and discomfort at what he experiences as lack of direction. He needs some guidance, some help in accessing the problem that he wants help with, as he said in his opening statement. Knowing that Jon's emotional intensity has to do with Dad, and that Jon is resisting dealing directly with Dad himself, Richard hypothesizes that it is the introjected Dad—the Parent ego state—that must be decommissioned in order to free Jon to make changes in his overall script system. Once the internal influence of the Parent ego state is relaxed, Jon may be less resistant to expressing his feelings. Richard moves to set up a Parent Interview, but will be ready to back off if Jon signals a resistance to this plan. Alternatively, the therapists might help Jon to explore the dreams about Dad; this would be a second choice because Jon has indicated that he has been helped by the dreams and has begun to say good-bye to Dad (albeit prematurely). Richard speculates that it might be beneficial if Jon first says a real "hello" to Dad—makes full contact—before attempting to finish his "good-bye."

Richard: (*continuing*) How would your dad be sitting, if he were in this room right now? Would he be sitting on the mat like this, if he and I were going to talk to each other?

Jon: (*pause*) Dad would probably be sitting back on his, like this, and be going "Come and get me, sucker." (*Jon has assumed a suspicious, haughty expression*)

Richard: Is that his posture?

Jon: Well, more or less.

Richard: Just close your eyes a minute, see if you can move right into his muscular posture. See if you can re-create, in your body, what it would be like to be in his body.

Jon: Yeah. This is basically it.

Richard: Now, just close your eyes again. See if you can create the look he had on his face most of the time. Particularly if I were going to talk to him.

The induction procedure, which prepares Jon for the Parent Interview, invites him first to model the physical appearance of Dad as he remembers it, and then to take on his emotional and cognitive characteristics. As Jon moves into his father's physical posture and expression, his own kinesthetic cues will help him access the essence of "Dad" that he has introjected into his Parent ego state. As usual, the actual interview with Dad will begin slowly, gently, in a respectful yet concerned way. When an initial rapport has been established, the interview will develop into actual therapy with that Parent ego state.

Jon: This'd be it. (*his face settles into an artificial grimace*)

Richard: Plastic smile?

Jon: Yeah.

Rebecca: Also, you look angry.

Jon: Oh, yeah. Come and get me. Just you dare come and get me.

Rebecca: What's your name?

Jon: Herbert.

Richard: Will you close your eyes, though? See if you can get into that mood, of "Come and get me." (*pause*) And I want to talk to you, Herbert. But you as Jon keep your eyes closed. Cause I think that way you stay in the mood of Herbert better . . . Where you from, Herbert?

Jon (as Herbert): (*he now speaks with a decidedly different accent*) White Hill, Kansas.

Closing his eyes serves to block out the visual stimuli that would keep Jon anchored in the present time and place, and free him to move into the fantasy of being his father. The accent, so unlike his normal mode of speech, is evidence that he has accomplished the switch; he is not so much imitating his father as he is actually experiencing himself as Herbert.

Richard: Say that slower, that first word?

Jon (as Herbert): White Hill, Kansas.

Richard: White Hill. Why in the world do they call it White Hill? Is the ground white?

Jon (as Herbert): Yeah.

Richard: I've never seen that. Is it like a sand?

Jon (as Herbert): No. There's a lot of birds around.

Richard: Uh-huh. What grows there?

Jon (as Herbert): Oh, there's mainly trees and bushes. We, we have a farm.

Richard: In White Hill?

Jon (as Herbert): Yeah. Around White Hill.

Richard: Flat land there?

Jon (as Herbert): No, very hilly.

Richard: Hilly.

Jon (as Herbert): Yeah.

Richard: D'you like growing up near White Hill, Herbert?

Notice again the leisurely pace of these first questions and answers. It's chitchat, two people who have just met standing around the tractor or talking on the porch. It fleshes out the scene, paces the work, and gets Herbert/Jon more deeply in touch with his experience. Only with his last question does Richard depart from what might actually have been said by folks just introduced back in White Hill; and even this departure is very slight and nonthreatening. Herbert, though, as we shall see, is not going to be easy to reach.

Jon (as Herbert): Yeah, it was OK.

Richard: You ever live anywhere else, or did you spend your whole life around that area?

Jon (as Herbert): I lived there until I was about 21 years old, and then I went to the service.

Richard: So you finally got a chance to get out of Kansas, huh? How was that for you, going in the service?

Jon (as Herbert): I wish I would have stayed.

Richard: Chance to see the world. And what did you get to see?

Jon (as Herbert): Japan. And a lot of the southern USA.

Richard: That must have been quite a treat, for a boy who's grown up on a farm in Kansas . . . What kind of family did you come from, Herbert?

Jon (as Herbert): It was OK.

Herbert's answers have been terse, suspicious, truculent. This last one borders on rudeness; its whole tone does, indeed, convey the "come and get me" attitude that Jon described. It is an indication of how complete Jon's change to Parent ego state is. Richard decides to confront the resistance head on; earlier, he went with the resistance so as to communicate his respect for the struggle Jon was having with his father and to support Jon's own internal sense of what he needed. At this time, confrontation of the introjected Parent is appropriate: First, the significance of the relationship between Herbert and Richard will have to be established in order to set a constructive tone for what may follow; and, second, Herbert is denying his family situation. The defense must at least be brought to Herbert's awareness if any therapy is going to occur. Even in his confrontation, however, Richard maintains a respectful attitude:

Richard: Now, how come you're so reluctant to give me information, just give me a general feeling? When I asked the question, Herbert, I wanted to know, you know, the number of people in your family, and what you thought about it, rather than just a brush-off answer like "it's OK." Is there a reason you don't want to give me any details?

Jon (as Herbert): Why do you want to know?

Richard: So I can get to know you.

Jon (as Herbert): Why?

Richard: Because your son has come to me for some help with a very significant problem he's struggling with.

Herbert's suspicions need to be dealt with; he needs a convincing reason why he should talk to this inquisitive stranger. His very reluctance is another sign that Jon has indeed moved into "being" his father: Jon, so concerned with being approved of and getting things right, would never have answered Richard's questions this way. The reason that Richard gives is not only plausible, but true. It fits for both the Parent and the Adult ego states in Jon. And there is an extra, unanticipated bonus in Herbert's response:

Jon (as Herbert): And I suppose he's saying it's me, huh?

Richard: He hasn't said that. And that's what I'm trying to determine. In fact, when I probed to see if it might be you, he said several defensive things in your behalf.

Jon (as Herbert): (*laughs derisively*)

Richard: What did that laugh mean, Herbert?

Jon (as Herbert): That's a switch.

Rebecca: You expect him to be mad at you, huh?

This is the first clear example of the contact distortion between Jon and Herbert. Herbert does not accept the idea that Jon would defend him. We cannot know, yet, the exact form of the distortion—whether Herbert is retroflecting, deflecting, projecting his own anger, or using some other defense. But, whatever it may be, if it is a pervasive element in Herbert's way of dealing with the world, we can expect him to do the same thing as he relates to the therapists.

Richard: He actually said you had quite a disease.

Jon (as Herbert): Yeah, he always thought I had a disease.

Richard: What do you think, Herbert?

Jon (as Herbert): I drank a little.

Richard: Did it kill you?

Jon (as Herbert): I died of a heart attack.

Richard: Hm. So the drinking wasn't a problem for you, you think.

Jon (as Herbert): Not really.

Richard: What kind of family did you come from?

Jon (as Herbert): Why do you want to know?

Again the resistance—and again it surfaces most abruptly when Richard asks about Herbert's family. There is something here, something Herbert really doesn't want to talk or think about. Rather than confronting again, and quite possibly cementing the resistance even more strongly, Richard chooses to take Herbert's question at face value.

Richard: Same reason I told you three minutes ago. So I can get to know you.

Rebecca: Does that surprise you Herbert, that someone would want to get to know you?

Jon (as Herbert): I don't know why he would want to get to know me.

Richard: Cause I've never met anybody from White Hill Kansas before. And I suspect growing up there, in a moonshiner's family, has got to give you a unique perspective on this world. That growing up on the south side of Chicago, I never got. Now, I can tell you some things about growing up in the slums, that probably you'd really find intriguing.

With this response, Richard moves the focus from Jon's needs to Herbert's own appeal and interest. He also issues a subtle challenge: Was your boyhood as interesting and intriguing as mine?

Jon (as Herbert): Well, it was hard times, that I can tell you. I, I have my mother and my stepfather, that I found out was my stepfather after I was 10 years old. My parents divorced when I was about three months old. And I found out when I was 10. I have two brothers . . .

Richard: (*interrupting*) What do you feel about that? You sure swallowed hard there.

Even at the risk of getting into resistance again, this material must be explored. The nonverbal cue (swallowing hard), plus the repetition of information, indicate how important this business of the real father versus the stepfather is to Herbert. To ignore the cues, and allow him to continue his story, would not build trust; it would suggest that these therapists either don't care about his feelings or can't tell what is really important to him. And, even though the subject is painful, we can hear in Herbert's responses an ambivalence, a pull to talk about it even as he also resists.

Jon (as Herbert): Well, I always thought that old Ike was my dad.

Richard: Was that a good thought?

Jon (as Herbert): In some ways yes, in some ways no.

Richard: Were you disappointed when you found out the truth?

Jon (as Herbert): Yeah.

Richard: OK, now I understand why you swallowed hard there. Course, I don't imagine you're a man with a whole lot of feelings, are you?

Again, the tiniest hint of a challenge. Herbert responded well to the last challenge, so Richard offers him another chance to compete. And the intervention is successful:

Jon (as Herbert): Oh, I have a lot of feelings.

Richard: Hm. Somehow I got the impression from your son that that wasn't the case. That you had just learned to tough it out in life.

Jon (as Herbert): My son doesn't always know what goes on inside me.

Richard: I'd like to know, Herbert. That sure sounds like a painful statement. "My son doesn't always know what goes on inside me."

Jon (as Herbert): No one knows.

We can see here the depth of the contact disruption that Herbert experiences. Not only his son is out of touch with Herbert's real feelings; nobody in the world really knows how he feels. As was the case with Charles, in Chapter 11, the experience of contact with the therapist will be healing in and of itself for Herbert—for perhaps the first time in his memory, he will find himself being known, understood, cared about. And that experience will almost certainly serve to disconfirm and disprove the script belief, "nobody knows me," developed by a lonely boy on that Kansas farm.

Richard: Have you ever had a conversation like this with anybody who could understand your deep inner process, like I'm trying to do?

Jon (as Herbert): No.

Richard: Well, to answer your question of a few minutes ago, then maybe that's one of the reasons we should talk. That finally somebody's going to take time to understand your process. And what it's like.

Jon (as Herbert): I still don't know what it has to do with my son.

Richard: How about if I make a deal with you? Before we stop this interview, when the time is up, I'll detail how it affects your son. And then you can decide if you want to come back again for a second session. (*pause*) But, we really did get off the track. You were telling me something very important about you.

Richard offers a contract: Let me run things for now, trust me that I know what I'm doing, and I'll explain it later. When there is no dissent, Richard takes the silence as agreement. And the contract holds; Herbert does not again demand justification or explanation of the therapists' interest in him.

Jon (as Herbert): Well, I grew up in the '30's . . .

Richard: Yeah, you told me about old Ike. What is it like to discover that the man who you thought was your dad, really wasn't?

Jon (as Herbert): I found out about him after I had grown up, and I met him much later. He never had any contact with me.

Richard: What's that mean to you? The man who raised you is not your real dad, and your biological dad didn't put any energy into having contact with you?

Jon (as Herbert): It makes me wonder what was wrong with me.

This is a clear statement of a script belief: "Because my father was not there for me, there must be something wrong with me." We shall see several such beliefs in this work, but this one, the second to emerge, is central to Herbert's (and Jon's) way of experiencing himself in the world.

Richard: That's quite a wondering, isn't it?

Jon (as Herbert): Yeah.

Rebecca: Did you decide that your father had left you?

Jon (as Herbert): Yeah. I don't really know what happened. We didn't talk much about those kinds of things.

Richard: Yeah. That's one of the reasons it's good for you to talk to me now. Because I'll help you straighten out some of that confusion.

Richard makes explicit what has been growing implicitly: The interview, originally begun for Jon's benefit, has become therapy for Herbert. The session is following the same sort of pattern as

Ben's work (Chapter 4), although the contract with Ben's father, Max, was not made this explicitly. Herbert, in his response, accepts the therapeutic purpose even as he questions the strategy. Straightening out the confusion may be painful; he may not want to do it. The therapists shift quickly to attend to this concern, and at the same time (a few responses later) neatly connect Herbert's therapy to Jon's ongoing welfare.

Jon (as Herbert): What if I don't want to know?

Richard: Well, then I guess I'll have to stop.

Rebecca: Are you saying you don't want to know, Herbert?

Jon (as Herbert): It's in the past. What difference does it make now?

Rebecca: I think it still hurts.

Jon (as Herbert): And if it does?

Rebecca: It doesn't need to.

Jon (as Herbert): I don't know if there's anything that's ever going to take away the pain.

Richard: Well, you might be right, Herbert. But you know, at least you don't have to pass that pain on to the next generation. Do you want your son to carry your pain?

Jon (as Herbert): No.

Richard: That, we can help . . . I think I understand now, something important. Can I come back and check it out with you?

Jon (as Herbert): Sure.

What a difference from the hostile suspiciousness of Herbert's first interactions! With that "sure," Herbert takes a decisive step; he begins to trust these therapists. Herbert is in therapy now, and the work continues.

Richard: You said, "I don't know what's wrong with me, that my real father didn't make contact with me." Will you tell me more about what you feel with that?

Jon (as Herbert): (*pause*) Angry with him.

Richard: Um-hm.

Jon (as Herbert): He wanted to give me his name, but he wasn't there for me.

Richard: Did you use his name, or did you use old Ike's name?

Jon (as Herbert): I used Ike's name. That's the name that my mother chose; it was good enough for me. When I was born, he had me registered as William Walter Schmidt. And my name has always been Herbert Runkle.

Richard: Now what is the difference to you in having a Schmidt name or a Runkle name?

Jon (as Herbert): He lied to my mother. (*pause*) My mother did not know how to speak or write English; he did. And on the birth certificate he told her that it was going to be Herbert Schmidt. And now it was William Walter Schmidt. It was just another one of the tricks and lies he played on my mother. (*his voice is angry; his pain shows on his face*)

Jon/Herbert is no longer just talking about what happened; he is feeling it. The deception about the name, and the later abandonment, sent that young boy an implied message: "Who you are doesn't count with me; I don't care whether you exist or not." After acknowledging the feelings, Richard risks an interpretation:

Richard: You sound bitter about that, Herbert.

Jon (as Herbert): Yes.

Richard: Would you assume, then, that he really didn't want you to exist?

Jon (as Herbert): In later years, before he died, the only thing he wanted from me is money. And that's the only thing that my supposed stepbrothers, or half brothers, ever wanted from me also, is just money.

Richard: What about your existence, Herbert?

Jon (as Herbert): I don't know.

Richard: I think you do. I think you feel that pain, behind those tight jaws. Behind all that anger. What's it mean, that your father lies to your mother about the identity of your existence—what's it mean that you have no contact with him, not even the knowledge that he is your dad, until you're 10?

To not know what one feels and thinks requires denial; to deny requires holding in; emotional and cognitive holding in are always accompanied by some sort of muscular holding in—retroflection. And the reverse is true as well: Muscular holding in signals some sort of repression, something that must not be known or recognized. Richard calls this process to Herbert's attention and repeats the question. (It is called to Jon's attention as well, given that Jon occupies the same body as Herbert in this piece of work; earlier in the work, we also saw Jon tighten his jaws to avoid feeling hurt and anger.)

Jon (as Herbert): (*pause*) Don't know.

Richard: Um-hm. Boy, if I were in your place, Herbert, I think I'd really question whether I was even supposed to be alive in this world. Do you ever question that?

Jon (as Herbert): Oh, yeah.

Richard: Will you tell us about that questioning?

Jon (as Herbert): (*long pause*) You wonder, sometimes, what you're even around for.

The pause here is not one of resistance; it is a time to try to find a way to express what has not been said in words before. When it does emerge, it confirms Richard's hypothesis—but it does so tangentially, with you *taking the place of the* I *that would have firmly identified the question as his own. Herbert needs to experience an "I," not a "you," in order to feel fully the emotions associated with his wondering. The use of* you *instead of* I *is a defense, a deflection, a way to avoid the intensity of what he is saying.*

Richard: You mean you, as Herbert, wonder? Or are you speaking to me as Richard, I wonder?

Jon (as Herbert): I, as Herbert, wonder.

Richard: Yeah, tell me more about that, Herbert. That's what I want to know about. (*pause*) You say you wonder whether you should even be around.

Jon (as Herbert): People ask a lot of things of me, and I really do make an effort to try and accommodate them, but people just never do understand.

Another script belief. If "there's something wrong with me," and "I'm not supposed to be alive," then it certainly would follow that other people (who have nothing wrong with them, and are supposed to exist) would not understand him.

Richard: Understand how it is to be rejected as a little boy. Or to have a father who doesn't consider you important enough to put time and energy into a commitment to you.

Jon (as Herbert): Ike was my father.

Richard: Did you love him?

Jon (as Herbert): Ike was a good man.

Richard: Did you love him?

Jon (as Herbert): He said, "Herbert, you know the one thing I really like about you is you never tell me what to do."

Richard: Did you love him?

Jon (as Herbert): I cried when he died.

Richard: (*softly*) Did you love him?

Richard has now asked this same question four times. Each time, Herbert answers tangentially—that is, his "answer" is a non-answer. Repeating the question serves to confront the non-answering, but also underscores the therapist's interest and concern: The question, and its answer, are too important to slide past. With his last repetition, Richard's voice softens; with his voice quality, he is responding to Herbert's pain. It is as if he has said, "I understand how hard it is for you to answer this question, and I will support you as you wrestle with it." Herbert's response shows that he has heard this underlying message. He looks uncomfortable, his eyes grow moist, he swallows. Finally, he expresses his discomfort:

Jon (as Herbert): You know, I don't really know what you're trying to do with me. I really don't.

Richard: I'm trying to know if it was Ike you had the bonding with, or your biological father, Herbert.

With this matter-of-fact, respectful answer, Richard again establishes his trustworthiness. He will not put Herbert on the spot just to see him squirm; he will not encourage an emotional display simply for its own sake. He does have a rationale for his questions, one that he is willing to share, and one that will make sense both to Herbert and to the observing Jon.

Jon (as Herbert): Ike was my father. He is the man that raised me . . .

Richard: Then how come you hurt so much over the fact that your biological father wasn't there for you?

Jon (as Herbert): Because he lied to my mother.

Richard: And how come you hurt about a lie that occurred when you were too young to know even the language?

Understanding the flow of script from generation to generation is a fascinating aspect of integrative psychotherapy. In Herbert's system, as reenacted by Jon, we are now seeing hints of the thoughts, feelings, and behaviors that he introjected from both of his "fathers," the one who was present and the one who was absent. One might also explore Herbert's mother's beliefs about her husband's defection (and his deception), and the ways in which Herbert may have internalized—and reacted to—those beliefs. Grandparent Interviews are not uncommon in our work, and it may be that, as Herbert's system unfolds, his Parent ego state will need to be dealt with. For now, though, the therapists will stay with Herbert, providing a contactful relationship within which he (and Jon) can bring into awareness that which, flowing underground between father and son, has poisoned and distorted the life experiences of both Herbert and Jon.

Jon (as Herbert): Because Mom, she never, I never treated her right.

Richard: What do you mean, Herbert?

Jon (as Herbert): After I left the service, after I left the farm, I left her. And went for my own life. She wound up in a nursing home and I only saw her a couple of times a year.

Richard: You feeling bad about that, Herbert?

Jon (as Herbert): Oh, I feel very bad about that.

Richard: So you sort of treated her the way your dad had treated you at the beginning of your life, huh?

Jon (as Herbert): (*pause*) If you want to call it that, you can call it that.

Richard: Do you disagree with me?

Jon (as Herbert): Like I said, if you want to call it that, you can call it that.

Richard: And do you disagree with me?

Rebecca: Are you feeling angry right now, Herbert?

Jon (as Herbert): Damn right.

Here it is: The anger that we saw projected onto Jon, early in the Parent interview, now reemerges. Herbert, as predicted, does get angry at the therapists. And, also predictably, he will not acknowledge this openly; instead, he deflects his anger onto a vague, intangible "process."

Richard: You angry at me?

Jon (as Herbert): I'm angry at this whole process.

Richard: Want to stop?

Rebecca: What are you angry at, Herbert? That he's making you feel things?

Rebecca, concerned that Richard's challenge may have come too soon—before the therapeutic alliance with Herbert was firm enough to hold him in spite of his anger—chooses to intervene here. Softly and sympathetically, she pinpoints the source of his distress. Herbert doesn't answer her directly, but in his evasion provides an opening for Richard again to address the process that is occurring between them. Again, stressing the contact is a way to invite Herbert into a new (for him) kind of healing experience.

Jon (as Herbert): It's all in the past. I got a wife that doesn't understand me. She doesn't . . .

Richard: Herbert, I'm willing to understand you.

Jon (as Herbert): I've got a son who doesn't come around to see me.

Richard: I'm willing to be here and listen to you.

Jon (as Herbert): I don't know if I'm willing to be here.

Is this a response to Richard's challenge of a few moments ago, a warning that Herbert will, in fact, quit if he is pushed too hard? The threat that "I will walk out if I don't like this" makes it difficult to do good therapy; the client needs to stay and deal with whatever emerges in the work. Richard, sensing the need for some sort of boundary here, offers a minicontract.

Richard: How about another 30 minutes?

Jon (as Herbert): I don't know if you're going to be here with me when I'm . . . how long you're going to be here with me ever again.

Richard: I'm only going to be here about another 30 minutes. But I'm going to be fully here, with every attempt to fully understand you, for that whole time.

No phony promises here, no guarantee that Richard will stay as long as Herbert wants or that Herbert can come back again. Such a promise or suggestion would be disrespectful, and Herbert would experience it as a put-down. Instead, Richard is again open and believable about what he intends, and what he is willing to offer. After a pause, during which Herbert might have argued but (significantly) did not, Richard continues, using the silence as a tacit acceptance of the contract.

Richard: (*continuing*) When you started getting angry is when I started asking you about that sense of rejection from your dad. That sense that in some way he implied that your existence was unimportant.

Jon (as Herbert): Well, he sure as hell said it, didn't he?

Richard: Yes, he did. And what's it like growing up, in essence being told by your father, "Don't exist"?

Jon (as Herbert): It's hell! It's the plain shits!

Richard: Tell me about that shit.

Jon (as Herbert): You think you've got a sense of belonging and then someone comes and pulls the carpet right out from underneath you. Then when you're 62 years old you find out that your given name was not your real name at all. It's given to you by a man that's not even there, to be around for you. Who doesn't even have any contact with you for 20 or 30 years.

In our discussion of the script system, in Chapter 1, we detailed the three major components: script beliefs, script display, and reinforcing experiences. Herbert, here, describes two memories. First, someone "pulls the carpet right out," referring to the abandonment by his biological father as a young child; later—much later—he learns that he has been deceived about his name. The experience of each of these events, mulled over in pain and anger hundreds of times, serves to reinforce his beliefs. We will hear these beliefs emerge again in a few minutes: "Life is the shits" and the implied "People can't be trusted."

Richard: And what does that mean about living?

Jon (as Herbert): That means living is the plain shits.

Richard: So how come you didn't kill yourself?

Jon (as Herbert): I don't got the guts.

Richard: You mean it takes guts to kill yourself?

Jon (as Herbert): Yes.

Richard: Why?

Jon (as Herbert): Because.

Richard: Would you like to have done it?

Jon had said earlier in the workshop that he was very suicidal at one time; at the beginning of this piece of work, he also referred to his suicidal feelings. With this as background, it becomes especially important to explore the suicide issue with Herbert. Did Herbert pass on to Jon, along with his other script beliefs, a belief that life is not worth living? Did he, in any way, withhold from Jon the same permission that was withheld from him—the permission, from father to son, to exist in this world? Understanding how Herbert has dealt with the question of suicide will help the therapists to understand and assess how much Jon may be at risk.

Jon (as Herbert): Yes.

Richard: Tell me about that.

Jon (as Herbert): It's a pain that goes right through the middle of me.

Richard: Where at?

Jon (as Herbert): Right here (*indicating his chest*).

Richard: Um-hm. Like right around your heart?

Jon (as Herbert): Yes.

Richard: That was my thought.

Jon (as Herbert): To feel so down and so out and then know that no one cares, or gives a damn whether you're here today or gone tomorrow. The only thing they want is their goddamn watches fixed or their radios repaired.

Richard: God, you're pissed!

Jon (as Herbert): I'm not.

Richard: You're not?

Jon (as Herbert): That's just the way things are. That's the way life is.

Richard: How come you're not more pissed?

Jon (as Herbert): What in the hell good would it do?

Richard: Hm. So what you're saying is "There's no use."

Herbert obviously feels anger, it exudes from his very pores. And he has reason to be angry! Expressing his anger openly, directing it at an appropriate target, would be healthy for him; it would combat his depression and provide a way for him to resolve his suicidal impulses. Instead, true to his pattern, he denies the anger, turning it inward so that it contributes to rather than counters the depression. His "that's just the way things are" is a good example of the way cognitive defenses are used to repress the emotions that were present at the time of script decisions and threaten to emerge later in life. "Why be angry; what in the hell good would it do" is also just another way of saying "What's the use," as Richard notes—and "What's the use," as a core script belief, is nearly always associated with strong suicidal tendencies.

Jon (as Herbert): You're damn right. People, they're all out to use you. That's all they ever want from you. Is to see what they can get from you.

Richard: Um-hm. It was a pretty good thing for you to get away from Kansas, huh?

Jon (as Herbert): (*pause*) I went back.

Richard: Yeah, why?

Jon (as Herbert): Because it's a sense of home. I left the state seven times, and each time I've always come back to it.

Richard: D'you have that same sense when you traveled in the South?

Jon (as Herbert): People are the same no matter where you go.

Richard: So you really believe that people are out to use you.

Jon (as Herbert): You're damn right.

Richard: And what's the use.

Jon (as Herbert): And what is the use.

Richard: What else do you believe?

Jon (as Herbert): About what?

Richard: About life.

Jon (as Herbert): (*pause*) That no matter where you go, you're never going to escape it.

Richard: What's the "it"?

Jon (as Herbert): Life. You're never going to escape life.

Richard: Um-hm. What's that mean?

Jon (as Herbert): That means that it follows you wherever you go. The misery, the hard work, the being misunderstood. That hurts.

Herbert's script belief structure is clear and explicit: Life is hard and painful, it can't be escaped, so what's the use of trying. His is a particularly tenacious system. Herbert truly believes that all people are out to use him—it isn't just a feeling, a response, but is for him a fact, supported by hard data. It's true now, always has been, always will be. There is nothing to argue about. And yet, even as he expresses this fatalistic position, something new emerges: It hurts. The feeling part of him is responding to the therapists' uncritical interest, to the sense of contact and relatedness that he has been experiencing. Those last two words are the expression of Herbert's long-buried, but not quite smothered, need to be touched and known at a deeper level, to share a tenderer, more vulnerable part of himself. It is the most hopeful sign he has shown thus far in his work.

Richard: Yeah.

Jon (as Herbert): It makes a man wonder what's, what is the purpose of being around. You're just going to die.

Richard: And what's your conclusion on that?

Jon (as Herbert): Well, then I'm going to live it to the fullest. I'm going to do what I damn well want to do. I'm going to do what makes me happy.

Richard: Which is what, Herbert?

Jon (as Herbert): I'm going to eat and drink. I'm going to buy whatever I want.

The child (or adult) who believes he cannot get what he wants will make a second choice—because I can't have what I really want, what will I try for instead? Often, this second choice is made outside of awareness; the need or want itself is blocked from consciousness, and the person experiences only the secondary process. The derived "need" is satisfied by the second choice behavior, but the original need remains unmet; thus the satisfaction is only illusory. This is the essence of the "fixed gestalt" pattern: Meeting the secondary need appears to close the gestalt, "fixes" it in a cycle of apparent satisfaction followed by a reemerging sense of deprivation, which is met by more secondary need-satisfying behavior. Herbert's description fits this pattern exactly. Wanting to make full contact with good, caring people, and to experience life as worth living—he has decided that these are impossible. His second choice is a kind of hedonistic bravado, which provides short-term relief but leaves the underlying loneliness and despair untouched.

Richard: What about your wife and kid?

Jon (as Herbert): You had to bring them up, didn't you?

Richard: All right. Want me to leave them out?

Jon (as Herbert): I know there are probably some things that I haven't done that they needed me to do.

Herbert's voice sounds truculent again. He is back in his old projective defense, experiencing his self-criticism as if it came from outside—in this case, from Richard.

Richard: Herbert, stop. I'm not making an accusation.

Jon (as Herbert): Well, you're the first one that hasn't. (*laughs sarcastically*)

Richard: All I asked is, what about your wife and kid?

Jon (as Herbert): What do you want to know about them?

Richard: Well, let me back up with that question for a minute. You assumed I was making an accusation. (*Herbert laughs again*)

Herbert's laughter is so harsh, and so inappropriate to the content of his speech, that it must have some important symbolic meaning to him. The risk in asking him about it is, of course, that he again may project criticism into the question. Yet to ignore it would mean overlooking a significant part of what he is, at some level, trying to communicate. Richard decides to solve this dilemma by using Herbert's own defense: He projects a criticism of himself onto Herbert. This provides a subtle frame for joining Herbert (we are both people who are accused); it also allows Herbert freedom to talk about the laughter or not, as he chooses. And if he chooses not (which, in fact, he does), Richard can always come back later as the "accused one" and pick up this thread.

Jon (as Herbert): You're the only one who hasn't made an accusation.

Richard: I don't know enough yet.

Jon (as Herbert): Oh. You will, then. I was right. (*laughs*)

Richard: I might.

Jon (as Herbert): OK.

Richard: But tell me, what do you think the accusation was that I was making?

Jon (as Herbert): That I don't do enough for them.

Richard: Hm. Do you think that's true?

Jon (as Herbert): I give them a house over their head.

Richard: Do you think it's true, that you don't do enough for them?

Jon (as Herbert): I don't do all that I'd like for them.

Richard: Do you do enough?

The pattern recurs: Herbert does not answer Richard's question, and Richard patiently repeats it. It is confrontational without directly confronting the evasion. And this time Herbert does, finally, answer directly.

Jon (as Herbert): I think I do, yeah. According to them I don't.

Richard: I bet you give them more than you ever got.

Jon (as Herbert): When the only thing you get for Christmas for the whole family is a pound of butter, and that was one Christmas . . . When you talk about eating, scraping the lard out of the frying pan to put on your bread—yeah, I give them more.

Richard: I bet you in some ways thought you were real generous, even with your emotions, compared to what you got as a kid.

Jon (as Herbert): I never heard the word "love."

Richard: Would you like to hear it?

Jon (as Herbert): (*long pause, then very softly*) Ya.

Here, at last, is real contact with his innermost desire. Herbert has allowed himself to feel, and to share his experience. Even though he answers with a single word, all of his nonverbal behaviors signal that this is an emotional moment for him, and that Richard is very much a part of his emotional field. Richard is quick to capitalize on this, inviting Herbert even deeper into experiencing his previously blocked feelings and need to be loved.

Richard: Who most would you like to have heard say the words, "I love you, Herbert"? If you could have only heard it from one person, one time in your whole life, whose voice would you like to have heard those words come from?

Jon (as Herbert): (*long pause*) Phil. My father.

Richard: Your biological father . . . Oh, Herbert, that would have made all the difference in some ways . . . What would have been the difference, Herbert, if Phil could have said to you, "I love you, my boy"?

Jon (as Herbert): Then it would have made, made me want, then it could have helped me under— . . . then I wouldn't have felt like such an outcast.

With the reexperiencing of the forbidden feeling comes a new facet of Herbert's script beliefs: "I am an outcast." It fits, underlies, and helps to explain his other beliefs—"Life is hard," "What's the use?" and "People are out to use me." Naturally, these things would be true for an outcast, someone who doesn't belong anywhere.

Richard: That's one of the things you believe, isn't it? "I'm an outcast." In some ways you really were, from him, weren't you? And then you perpetuated it the rest of your life. Were you even an outcast when you were in the service?

Jon (as Herbert): No, I was somebody in the service. I wish I would have stayed there.

Richard: But you came back. Seven times you left the state, and seven times you came back.

Jon (as Herbert): I've always wanted to belong somewhere, to have a sense of belonging.

Richard: Particularly to have that father say, "I love you, my son."

Jon (as Herbert): To have anyone say that, I guess.

Richard: How about your wife?

Jon (as Herbert): Huh? . . . Oh, she's a pretty good woman.

Richard: Did she ever say, "I love you, my husband"?

Jon (as Herbert): Oh, yeah, that's her, that's what she's supposed to say. I don't really know, I don't really think, though, that she wants, I don't really think that she loves me. I think that she loves having a husband.

Evidence that might challenge or disprove a script belief is either filtered out of awareness or redefined to be consistent with the beliefs. "I'm an outcast" or "No one loves me" is experienced as reality, like sunrise in the east or cold weather in winter. Herbert's script beliefs serve as a cognitive defense against the awareness of both the need to be loved and the emotions related to that need not being met.

Richard: You mean any man would do?

Jon (as Herbert): Ya.

Richard: So you're really an outcast in your own family.

Jon (as Herbert): Ya.

Richard: What about your son? Did he ever say, "Dad, I love you"?

Having uncovered a core script belief, "No one loves me," Richard now begins the slow and careful process of tying all this back to Jon, to how things were and might have been between Jon and his father, and to what is now needed to heal that damaged relationship so that Jon can get on with his life.

Jon (as Herbert): Oh, when he was about 21 or 22.

Richard: How'd you feel with that?

Jon (as Herbert): It really felt good.

Richard: D'you ever want to hear it when he was a little boy?

Jon (as Herbert): Ya.

Richard: And what actually occurred, when he was a little boy?

Jon (as Herbert): (*pause*) I had so many hopes and dreams for him . . . But he wasn't, he wasn't exactly what I had planned at the time.

Herbert's pauses and nonanswers are becoming almost as revealing as what he actually says. Again, he signals that the question has hit home, and that the feelings it stirs up are painful. This nonanswer, though, is different from many of the others in that Herbert is now talking freely about his feelings: his broken dreams, his lonely longing. It is as if he now feels so close to the therapists that he doesn't need to evade or to answer directly. The answer, given inside his head, is taken for granted, and his verbal response simply picks up and elaborates on the thought. Richard's response supports that sense of shared understanding, and asks Herbert to go farther yet.

Richard: What do you mean by that, Herbert?

Jon (as Herbert): He was a commitment. He was a commitment out of honor. I married his mother.

Richard: Well, that's to be respected.

Jon (as Herbert): Yes. To give the child a name. That's the most important thing there is, isn't it?

Richard: Certainly important when you were born, wasn't it?

Jon (as Herbert): Ya.

Richard: The name . . . So you did what your father abandoned.

Outcasts neither have nor need names; they don't belong, and nobody cares what their name may be. Herbert, by marrying Jon's mother and giving Jon a name, rescued him from that outcast status. He broke the script curse, the belief about self that passes from generation to generation. As he becomes aware, and proud, of this choice, he may be open to other beliefs and feelings that he would now choose not to hand on to his son.

Jon (as Herbert): Ya.

Richard: How did that feel, to know that you were not going to repeat the mistake that your dad had made?

Jon (as Herbert): I thought that I was doing the best for him that I could.

Richard: Well, I think that in some ways you ought to be honored for that. Cause that took a lot of guts. (*Herbert laughs*) Just plain guts, Herbert . . . So you stuck it out. And you gave him something you never had.

Jon (as Herbert): Oh, those early years, they were hell.

Richard: What do you mean?

Jon (as Herbert): Well, I wasn't really sure whether or not I was ready to settle down yet. And my wife, she must have felt that, because she was always checking up on me. She knew the miles out to work that I would go, and every night she knew how long it would take me to get from work to home. And she used to check. And oh, the hell Sue used to raise, when I wasn't home within that certain amount of time.

It's hard to imagine what it must be like for Herbert—so accustomed to criticism, so ready to agree with it himself, so certain that he is an outcast doomed to a lonely and painful life—to experience the understanding and respect that he is getting here. From a shiftless drunk, he has been transformed into a man who had the courage to give his son that which he himself most wanted and never got. This is so alien to his whole self-concept (and yet rings so true in a deeper part of himself) that he becomes acutely uncomfortable. Predictably, to deal with the discomfort, he retreats into script: He begins to tell a story that will again show him in a bad light and will invite criticism. Note how Richard avoids delivering the criticism, without in any way denying the truth of Herbert's recounting.

Richard: What would you do, stop off for a beer?

Jon (as Herbert): Ya. I'd stop and talk with the boys. And every now and then I'd give a girlfriend a call.

Richard: Just a call?

Jon (as Herbert): Ya, just a call.

Richard: You were looking for something, weren't you?

Jon (as Herbert): I wasn't ready to settle down. I never went any further than that, but my wife, she didn't believe it.

Richard: That must make that commitment to your son's name mighty important to you then, if you weren't ready to settle down. If you wanted to be in the service and see the world. Makes it even more of a sacrifice. (*pause*) Also adds to your belief that life is a struggle. And that you can't get what you want. Right? That's what I hear coming through this all the time, "I can't get what I want."

Going back again to those core beliefs, Richard is preparing the ground to decommission the introjected Parent system and to free Jon from Herbert's crippling view of the world.

Jon (as Herbert): (*long pause*) I've done good for myself, though.

Richard: Did you just expect me to criticize you, Herbert?

Jon (as Herbert): I don't know.

Richard: I was sure feeling empathetic with what sadness permeates your life. Underneath that well-polished anger. Real sense of sadness.

Jon (as Herbert): Well . . . if you haven't criticized me yet, ya, well I'm waiting for it.

He is not only waiting for it, but will manufacture it if it isn't there. With this admission, we can see the central importance of the therapists' refusal to criticize. To say anything that sounds like disapproval of Herbert would only serve to reinforce his beliefs about himself, would provide one more memory to shore up his role as an outcast who will never get what he most wants in life.

Richard: Herbert, how am I going to criticize that deep sadness that permeates your life? The sadness that goes with that belief, "I'm an outcast." The sadness underlying the belief, "I'm misunderstood." That sadness underlying the belief, "People are out to use me." The real depression that goes along with "What's the use?" That "life is a struggle."

Jon (as Herbert): Life is life. What are you going to do about it but carry on?

Richard: Well, I think what you did is, you drank, not to feel that hurt.

Jon (as Herbert): I like to drink.

Richard: And what happens when you get the booze in you? What happens to that hurt?

Jon (as Herbert): I start feeling like I'm somebody. Like I'm somebody important.

Again, we can see here the repeating pattern of the script system. The person who is not given permission to exist, to meet his innate need to be recognized and attended to, finds an artificial solution. The unclosed gestalt is closed, temporarily, by drinking. For a short time, the emptiness is filled. But, as with any fixed gestalt, Herbert's solution becomes itself a new problem. Although he feels like "somebody important" when he drinks, his drunken behavior invites others to treat him like an unimportant nobody. He needs a new way to solve the problem, a way to meet the original need directly.

Richard: Well, Herbert, you've been somebody for me. And you haven't been drinking while we've been talking (*Herbert laughs*) What's your laugh mean?

Jon (as Herbert): You've got a way with words, don't you? (*laughs again*)

Richard: Well, more than that, I've got an understanding with people. I can understand you.

"I can understand you" is not only another move to underscore and intensify the sense of contact between therapist and client, but also speaks directly to Herbert's need to be somebody. "You are a person who is worth understanding—you are important to me." Herbert is being introduced to the experience of meeting his primary need in a primary, rather than a secondary, way.

Jon (as Herbert): If you do, you're the first one.

Richard: I'm sorry that's true. And yes, I guess it's got to start sometime . . . I think your son struggled to understand you. And you know what he did?

Jon (as Herbert): It's hard telling what *he's* done.

Richard: I can tell you. It's not hard.

Jon (as Herbert): I'm listening.

Richard: In order to get the same thing that you've always wanted from your dad, real support and encouragement for existing; in order to hear "I love you"—but more than to hear it, Herbert, in order really to feel that he belongs, rather than being an outcast in his own relationship with you—he's carried your sadness. He's carried your belief that "I can't get what I want out of life." That "Life's the shits," and "What's the use." But mostly he's carried your pain. In the hopes that if he carried your pain, and stayed depressed for you, you'd be relieved enough that you could be there for him. Your son is very loyal.

In this interpretation, Richard speaks both to the activated Parent ego state (Herbert) and to Jon's observing Adult and Child ego states. Jon, as well as Herbert, will experience being understood, being important enough to be worth understanding. Moreover, there is a relabeling of Jon's symptomatic behavior, as his depression is defined as loyalty. Will Herbert go along with his son's being depressed in order loyally to support Dad? Or will he now give Jon permission to change, to have a better life? And will Jon, with this new frame of reference, decide that there are better ways to express and experience his relationship to his father?

Jon (as Herbert): It's . . . it's hard to believe. He, uh . . . I tried to talk to him many times.

Richard: Oh, he's also pissed off at you.

Jon (as Herbert): And it seems like, ya, I used to be able to talk to him, but in recent years I've not been able to. It's as though he's pushing me away, and I don't like that.

Richard: He is, externally. But you know, during those formative years, he took on your pain. And he bears it for you. Except, he's forgotten it's yours. Because it's almost identical to his own . . . Herbert, you hurt. You've hurt all your life. You even hurt about your relationship with Jon. You hurt about life, and your existence.

Jon (as Herbert): That's life, isn't it?

Richard: No, it's not. But it is your life. Will you do something? Just imagine Jon in front of you right now. And tell him about your pain, and the burden he's carried for you . . . Just talk to Jon right now. This is your chance to be understood by him.

With this abrupt shift to a fantasy dialogue between Parent and Child ego states, Richard invites Jon/Herbert to neutralize the poisonous effect of that withdrawn, withholding Parent ego state. Although it is too late for Herbert to change his own life, he can still give Jon permission not to live in the same way. Speaking directly to Jon will deepen the emotional intensity of this permission, so that it will feel to Jon like a real event, rather than a wished-for dream.

Jon (as Herbert): (*pause*) What am I going to tell him?

Richard: Start with the hurt. Particularly how you've denied it. Don't hide it, Herbert. Just begin by using his name. And the words will flow. And if you don't say it right, you can always say it again.

Jon (as Herbert): It is hard.

Richard: Yeah, say that again, to Jon.

The statement to the therapist, about the difficulty of Jon's Parent ego state (Herbert) attempting to talk to Jon, might have sidetracked the work into a blur of discussion about whether or not he can carry out the task. But the statement may also refer to Herbert's script position: "Life is hard." Richard responds to this deeper meaning, and simply redirects the comment from himself to the fantasy Jon, to whom Herbert must talk.

Jon (as Herbert): Jonny, it's hard to tell you these things.

Richard: Just let yourself feel it, Herbert. Just repeat that sentence over, and elaborate.

Jon (as Herbert): It's hard to tell you these things . . .

Richard: Keep going.

Jon (as Herbert): Since I want to tell you these things, my body is just shaking, all inside.

A good sign: The physiological reaction indicates that he is, indeed, experiencing this interaction as real. He is responding as if he (in both ego states, Herbert and Jon) were really there, talking to each other in a way that both desperately wanted yet could never achieve. The shaking feeling results from the opening of long-closed emotional energy channels in the body, channels that can now be used for healthy emotional expression and release. The retroflections are relaxing.

Richard: Yeah. That's the part of you that's been raised that it's not manly to talk about deep feelings. You know, I really believe it is manly, Herbert. Your son needs to know your deep feelings so that he can be a man that doesn't get stuck between being a boy and a man, in that midzone . . . Tell him about how it is for you to feel so deeply, Herbert.

Jon (as Herbert): It's hard to tell you how I feel, because the feelings are so deep. And they're so hard to express. (*he reaches out in a curious half-gesture, and then pulls back*)

Richard: Yeah, but your arms and shoulders and hands are expressing them. Do that little gesture again, Herbert.

Herbert, a man of few words, says with his body what he cannot yet say with his voice. Although his verbal shutting down is not as intense as that of Glenda (Chapter 10), the therapist's attention to and use of Herbert's gestural communications is often similar to the work with her. Asking Herbert to repeat and intensify his gesture will heighten his awareness of what he is trying to express.

Jon (as Herbert): Sometimes I just wonder what is even the use of telling you.

As the system opens up, script clues come often. Herbert, in talking to Jon about his feelings, is about to break the rules by which he has lived his life. And the old core belief, "What's the use," emerges again as a barrier to change, an illusory safeguard that protects him from the risk of exploring new and unknown territory. The protest is a weak one, though; the process of change is gathering momentum and needs only gentle encouragement to continue.

Richard: There is a use, so keep going.

Jon (as Herbert): I've tried reaching out to you in so many ways, but my ways are limited. I have tried talking to you, and you have always been a good listener, and I like, I love, I . . . I love you, Jonny.

Richard: Louder, Herbert.

Jon (as Herbert): (*crying*) I love you, Jonny.

Richard: Do it again, Herbert. Do what you never heard.

Once or twice is not enough. Herbert needs to repeat himself, to feel it all. Repetition, along with raising his voice, helps him to break the cognitive restraints, to feel intensely what has been held in for so many years. To the extent that this process is fully involving, both Herbert and Jon (Parent and Child ego states) will be cleansed and freed to experience themselves in a different way.

Jon: (*sobbing*) I love you, Jonny!

Richard: And tell him what it's like to have never heard it. (*Jon/Herbert is sobbing so hard that he cannot speak*) Tell him what it's like to finally say to your son what your father never said.

Jon (as Herbert): (*speaking through his sobs*) Those words seem so strange to me. To say them to you. I never heard them as a kid.

Richard: (*supporting Jon's diaphragm*) Now let that come right out of here, Herbert.

Richard's touch, just below the heart, serves a number of purposes here. It calls Jon's attention to how he is still physically holding back, and invites him to break through in this area. Richard's touch is gentle, yet firm; as he pushes against Jon's diaphragm, he encourages the deep release that Jon needs. Also, his touch provides contact and emotional support; it is an unmistakable reminder that he is with Jon, and that Jon/Herbert does not have to do this alone, that he—they—are important enough to be helped and encouraged and cared for.

Jon (as Herbert): I never heard that as a kid.

Richard: Say that word "that." Say what it means. The whole sentence.

Jon (as Herbert): I never heard them say that. That they loved me. And I don't believe it. I never believed it could be possible.

Richard: Tell him what you believe about Jonny.

Jon (as Herbert): (*sobbing again*) I do believe you love me.

Richard: Yeah, let that come, Herbert. He's been very loyal and loving to you, by carrying your burden about life, to make life easier for you. The only problem is that it didn't work. Even though he carried your pain, you still had your own pain.

Jon (as Herbert): I don't want to make your life miserable.

Richard: Tell him more, Herbert.

Jon (as Herbert): (*reaching out with his hands*) I just want someone to be there for me.

Richard: Yeah, do that again with those hands. "I *want* someone there for me."

Jon (as Herbert): I *want* somebody there for me!

Richard: Louder, Herbert.

Demanding, with his voice and his gestures, what he wants, rather than giving up because "what's the use," is a behavioral change. In order to do this, with genuine feeling, Herbert must *give up his belief that everything is hopeless: The feeling can only emerge from a sense of hope, of possibility, of opening to contact with others. And, having opened here in therapy, Jon/Herbert can carry that potential for openness out into the real world.*

Jon (as Herbert): I want somebody there for *me*. (*sobs*) It's so lonely, knowing that no one's there; knowing that no one cares!

Richard: Tell him what it was like when Jonny was Mama's little boy.

Jon (as Herbert): (*still sobbing*) She had to spend time with you, and she couldn't be there for me . . . I hated you. But I loved you. You were mine.

Richard: Tell him both parts again.

Jon (as Herbert): I hated you, but I loved you!

Richard: Tell him, elaborate on each one.

Herbert is clarifying the split in himself, a split that confused and damaged his relationship with his son. Herbert's Child ego state was jealous of the attention given to Jon, and hated Jon for taking what Herbert wanted; Herbert's Adult ego state was proud of his son and wanted good things for him. Feeling the split, talking about it, intensifying it, clears the way for integration, bringing the two parts back together into a new and healthy whole.

Jon (as Herbert): (*still sobbing*) I loved you because . . . you were the only thing I ever really made, and you were good. And I had so many dreams for you. I wanted you to have the things I never had . . .

Richard: Tell him . . . about hating him.

Jon (as Herbert): And I hated you, because you took from me what I did have.

Richard: Tell him more about that.

Jon (as Herbert): I wanted someone to take care of me . . . (*each phrase is punctuated by sobs*) And who'd be there for me . . . and only for me . . . But that changed when you came . . .

Richard: Let it come right out of your heart, so it doesn't have to fail you.

Jon (as Herbert): I wanted you to be close to me. And I was so scared of being close to you.

Richard: Yeah, say that confession again.

Jon (as Herbert): I wanted to be close to you, but I was so afraid of getting close to you.

Richard: Cause you tell him what you believed would happen if you got real close.

Jon (as Herbert): You'd leave me if I got too close . . . (*still crying*) I needed to keep you weak. And I needed to keep you down . . . So that you would depend on me. So that you would stick around me. I was always so threatened whenever you would bring people home with you . . . or be friendly with someone, because that took you away from me.

Again, another split. Herbert needed a parent to be there for him when he was young. He fantasized Jon as potentially meeting these early childhood needs. Alternately, he anticipated rejection from Jon. Jon thus becomes the fantasized and then projected "good" and "bad" parent.

Remember that one of Jon's initial concerns was his social awkwardness and isolation. Another signal that the work is on course is the way in which it is beginning to circle around and pick up bits and pieces introduced earlier. Herbert is not only making redecisions for himself—as this happens, Jon's old, caustic Parent ego state is being decommissioned and the destructive intrapsychic influence is subsiding.

Richard: So what I did to you was . . .

Jon (as Herbert): I put you down.

Richard: In order . . .

Jon (as Herbert): To keep you weak.

Richard: In order . . .

Jon (as Herbert): To keep you, for me. (*sobs*) I had so many hopes and dreams for you, and I wanted you to be a repairman like me. And I was so disappointed when you had bad eyes. I wanted you to take over the business. And it hurt to see you stray from that.

Richard: Cause if you and I were in business together, Jonny . . .

Herbert shows some signs of wandering from the immediacy of his encounter with Jon, into a more detached storytelling mode. Richard brings him back, by focusing on the relationship meaning of his story, and further fuels the emotional intensity by using Herbert's pet name for his son.

Jon (as Herbert): Then I could have had you for me. (*sobs*)

Richard: Let it come, Herbert. Just like with you and your dad, isn't it?

Jon (as Herbert): I was so threatened whenever you would get something for you, because it would take you from me . . . (*still sobbing*) If only you could understand the struggle for you, that I had! The pain that I felt whenever you left me. And the pain that I felt not being able to tell you.

Richard: Just like the pain when your daddy left you. The fact that your dad never told you anything about you and him. Yeah, let that come now . . . Just let yourself shake . . . Yeah, let it come even louder . . . Cry it out, right out of your broken heart.

Throughout this speech, Herbert/Jon's crying has become more and more childlike; by now he is doubled up on the mat, crying and shaking with grief. Herbert has regressed to an archaeopsychic ego state, the Child ego stage within the Parent: It is Herbert, not Jon, who is reexperiencing his childhood deprivation. Yet Jon will benefit, because it is his introjection of Herbert who is doing this therapeutic work.

Richard: (*continuing to support Jon's diaphragm*) Just let that sobbing come, from way down there . . . And say the words that go with that deep crying.

Jon (as Herbert): I don't have any . . .

Richard: Try these: "Love me, Jonny."

Jon (as Herbert): Love me, Jonny. (*sobs*)

Richard: Shout it at him.

Jon (as Herbert): Love me, Jonny! (*the words are gulped out, through the tears*)

Richard: Now try, "Love me, Daddy."

Jon (as Herbert): Love me, Daddy (*sobbing even harder*)

Richard: Say it again; right out of your guts.

Jon (as Herbert): Love me, Daddy!

Richard: If you don't love me, Daddy . . .

Jon (as Herbert): Then I can't be any good. (*sobbing, but more quietly*)

Here it is at last, a decision upon which many of Herbert's other beliefs rest. Without Daddy's love, I am no good. So life is hard, what's the use, and all the rest. Just saying it out loud seems to give some measure of relief, as if the hiding and the defending, at least, can be relaxed. Herbert, the flesh and blood father, cannot change his life, for he is dead. But therapy with the Parent ego state can free Jon to do it differently; Jon need no longer carry this belief as part of himself.

Richard: Listen to that decision, Herbert . . . Listen to that little boy's decision. "If you don't love me, Daddy, I can't be any good." Is that how you want to live your life, Herbert?

Jon (as Herbert): (*through his sobs*) It's true, isn't it?

Richard: No. It isn't true, Herbert. I think you made a decision, around 10 years of age, that "my daddy doesn't love me, therefore I'm no good. If my daddy doesn't love me, something's wrong with me." And you know something, Herbert? By living out that decision, you actually are programming your son to do the same. Because he's been carrying your legacy for you. You know the word "legacy"? Means like he's wearing your old hat. You know how little kids will put on dad's old hat? He's living your life-style. Is that the decision you want Jonny to carry? That he's no good, and something's wrong with him? You want him carrying that life burden?

Jon (as Herbert): I want him to have the things I never had.

Richard: Tell him that.

Jon (as Herbert): Jonny, I want you to have the things that I never had. I want you to have a name that you can be proud of. And I want you to be happy. I want you . . . to be . . .

Richard: Just put the period there. "I want you."

Jon (as Herbert): I want you. (*he cries softly*)

The shift in the quality of Herbert's affect indicates that something has indeed changed. He is no longer gasping out his sobs, but weeps softly, almost with relief. It is as if something tight and strangling has been released, allowing him to breathe and relax. Herbert can now express his wants for Jon in a caring and contactful way—which he does.

Richard: Now go on. I want you . . .

Jon (as Herbert): I want you to be happy . . . and I want you to have the things that I never had . . . I want you to be successful in life . . . I want you to be trusting.

Richard: He's heading there, Dad. Most of all, he's been carrying your beliefs. That something's wrong with him, and that life is not worth living . . . And you want him to go through life carrying your old decisions?

Jon (as Herbert): No.

Richard: Then tell him about that.

Jon (as Herbert): Jonny, I want you, I want you to find out for yourself that life is worth living. And I want you to find out for you that you're OK.

Something doesn't ring quite true in these last sentences. Herbert sounds stilted, forced. Is Jon/Herbert adapting, saying the "right" things in order to please the therapist?

Richard: Do you believe that, Herbert?

Jon (as Herbert): Not really.

Richard: Do you believe it's possible for your son, who has a father who will say "I love you"? Who has a father that will make a commitment to be there, *even* if you don't know how to do it well?

Jon (as Herbert): Perhaps.

Herbert/Jon has run head on into the Parent ego state's inability to go back and make changes in the real parent's life. Whether because of this dawning realization, or fatigue from the length of the piece of work, or something else, Jon's cathexis of Herbert is beginning to slip, as is that Parent ego state's contact with the therapists. Herbert is beginning to sound more defensive, as he did at the beginning of the work, and, in so doing, his whole presence is taking on an "acting" quality, rather than the genuineness of the last several minutes. It is time to close off this Parent session, before it begins to unravel and lose its impactfulness.

Richard: (*pause*) Well, Herbert, anything else you want to say to me, before we stop?

Jon (as Herbert): You sure know how to get a guy talking, that's for sure.

Richard: Thank you. That's quite a compliment. You know, it's sort of like having a broken mainspring. You gotta find out where the break is, put it in and wind it up.

Jon (as Herbert): I usually just throw them away.

Richard: Well, unfortunately now, your mainspring is finally broken, irreplaceably. But you know, Jon's got a lot of time to tick away yet. The one thing that concerns me, though, is that he may love you so much that he'll follow in your same footsteps. And he may have a heart attack. So I'm concerned about his health. But I think that's another chapter, when we focus on his eating appropriately, so that he can live much longer than you, and have a full, complete, happy life. Would you like that for him?

Jon (as Herbert): Yes, I would.

Richard: So that curse of your life is over now. Your son doesn't have to carry it. If that's OK with you.

Jon (as Herbert): Can Jonny still love me?

Richard: Ask him.

Herbert/Jon has provided the opening for a way to move out of the Parent ego state therapy, back to Jon's own response to his father. Asking for information about Jon's feelings is a signal that he is ready to cathect either Adult or Child ego state, to speak for himself rather than for his father. Richard will underline the therapeutic relevance of both sides of this question and answer: Herbert's need to ask the question that he could not ask before, and Jon's need to answer the question that had not been asked.

Jon (as Herbert): (*long pause*) Ya, I think he can.

Richard: Ask him. So that you hear the question that you never got to ask your own daddy.

Jon (as Herbert): Jonny, will you still love me even if you don't have to bear my pain?

Coaching Herbert to ask the question directly of Jon allows Richard to direct a switch out of Parent ego state. It is important to end the Parent ego state therapy by moving the client back to Child and finally Adult ego state, in order to facilitate the full integration of the work. In Jon's case, the ensuing conversation also allows for symbolic contact, contact that Jon never experienced in reality. Richard directs the shift, emphasizing it by asking Jon physically to move to a different spot on the mat, and talk toward the place where he, as Herbert, had been sitting.

Richard: Now switch. Put your dad there, and talk to him.

Jon: (*moving across the mat*) Yes, Dad. I'll still love you.

Richard: Tell him what you love about him.

Jon: In so many ways. You're such a kind and compassionate person. And you've got a neat sense of humor.

Richard: Just let yourself see his face now, Jon. Just as though he's right here. Tell him about that humor. That kindness.

Jon: (*beginning to cry*) In the midst of all your crossness, and harshness, you could still have time for a funny story, or a joke. And we could laugh a lot together. (*sobs loudly*)

Jon is experiencing the loss of the father he knew as a child, the dad who joked and laughed when he wasn't abusing his body with alcohol. The reality of a dad often drunk, dour, and withdrawn has been pushed back—the laughing dad did exist some of the time, and this is the dad to whom that young child was bonded and for whom the child grieves. Just as Herbert had no chance to express his feelings to a father who was gone, so Jon couldn't express his feelings to a withdrawn and drunken dad. Expressing them now can break the spell, the script legacy that goes from father to son.

Richard: Tell him what you appreciate about laughing with him.

Jon: (*sobbing*) We'd laugh a lot. You had a smile that was so neat . . . When you laughed, all of you laughed.

Richard: Tell him what it did inside of you.

Jon: Made me feel good inside. I wasn't scared when you laughed. (*sobs*) You could appreciate the beauty of a flower, or a nice poem. For an eighth-grade education, you were a very smart man. It was fun talking to you about neat things, . . . and I miss you! (*he breaks into loud sobs*) I've missed you for so long! . . . Instead of always being mad at you, I always wanted to love you! (*still sobbing*)

Richard: (*pause*) Tell him what else you appreciate.

Jon: (*pause, then quietly*) You are my dad.

Richard: Yeah, say that louder.

Jon: You are my dad.

Richard: Now shout it, Jon.

Jon: You are my dad!

Richard: All the way to Kansas!

Jon: YOU ARE MY DAD!

Richard: Tell him what that means.

Jon: I love you . . . I have your name.

Richard: And tell him what you also resent about him.

Jon has experienced and expressed his deep caring for his father, and he is ready to deal with the resentments. Those deep feelings have established the bond, the commitment; he can now talk about the negatives without fear of destroying the relationship. And the negative things need to come out, lest they fester and poison the new decision that Jon is making about himself.

Jon: (*crying again*) That you never, that you gave me very little chance to get close to you in a fun way.

Richard: Yeah, and tell him what else you resent.

Jon: And I always had to be your caretaker, and I always had to listen to you, and you wouldn't listen, you took very little time to listen to me. You never had time for me. Only it was always, I had to meet you on your terms. You were very critical of me, Dad.

Richard: Say it again, and tell him how much you resent that.

Jon: You were very critical of me.

Richard: Tell him what goes on inside . . .

Again and again, when a client begins to move the focus outside, to attend too much to the other person in the relationship and not enough to him- or herself, one of the therapists will gently bring the client back home, to his or her own inner process. This intervention, "Tell him what goes on inside you," is typical of that redirection process. It doesn't criticize, but rather guides the client back to what needs to be looked at and expressed.

Jon: I tried so hard to be a good little boy, and I was never good enough for you. (*crying*) *I'm still a good little boy*!

In this case, the redirection succeeds in helping Jon to a new awareness: that, in continuing to try to please his father, he is keeping himself small. While Richard suggested this earlier, in the work with Herbert, Jon's comment at this point has a quality of fresh discovery. In looking "inside," he has found the pattern in himself, in his own thoughts and feelings and behaviors.

Richard: Unfortunately . . . Tell him how long you're going to stay a little boy, just to get him to attend to you.

Jon: I wanted to stay a good little boy until you came to me. But that's not, there's not a chance (*sobs*) . . . I resent the way you've always treated Mom . . .

Richard: Tell him how long you're going to stay a good little boy. How many more years.

Rather than go back to the resentments, Richard chooses to stay with Jon's script decision to stay little for Dad. By asking Jon how long he intends to stay young, Richard invites him to look into the future, and to begin to experience his own ability to choose either to continue or to take another route—to redecide.

Jon: I don't know.

Richard: Sounds like you're not ready to give that up.

Jon: That's *me*. (*crying*) That's me. I'm a good little boy.

Richard: That's choice.

Jon: What's wrong with being a good little boy?

Rebecca: Nothing wrong with being a good person. You hold yourself back if you stay a good little boy.

Richard: You have to go incompetent.

Jon: I never felt competent with you, Dad.

> *Richard's earlier statement is accurate; Jon is not yet ready to give up this decision. He first expresses his sense that the decision has become a part of himself (and, implicitly, his fear of what will happen—who will he be?—if he gives it up); then he defends against the further confrontation from both Richard and Rebecca by moving to blame his father. Further pushing at this point would be more preaching than therapy, and would either drive him further into his defensive position or invite an adaptive, please-the-therapist pseudoredecision. As he did with Chris (Chapter 3), who also was not yet ready to make a firm redecision, Richard chooses to end the work by giving Jon some summary information, inviting him to cathect his Adult ego state in order to think about his decision, and then assigning "homework" that will carry the therapeutic process on outside the one-on-one work setting.*

Richard: Listen to the decision, and you'll know why. "I'll always be your good little boy, Dad." Is that the decision you want to reaffirm? Or is that a decision you want to change? I'm going to stop here, and let you think about it a while. I know you were going to say something just now, and my concern is that you not say the result that you think we're looking for. But that you deal, inside of you, with what your choice means, for the next 50 years. What it's going to like 5 years, 10 years, 25 years from now. As you get older, while being a good little boy. Or what life would be like, if you make some alternative decision . . . You willing to stop at this point? Think about it. And imagine what the ramifications are, of whatever choice you might make? Whether it's a reaffirmation of the old decision—it's a promise, to Dad: "I'll always be your good little boy." Or, now that he's dead, are you released from that promise, and can choose something else. You come back and tell us about your thoughts later?

Jon: OK.
Rebecca: I'd like to hear them.
Richard: I'd like to know what you think.

Jon's work is particularly useful for a "wrap-up" chapter because it illustrates so clearly the two major aspects of integrative psychotherapy: an understanding of client dynamics, and the way in which those dynamics shape and structure the therapeutic intervention. Let us consider each of these aspects in turn.

The primary "maps" of client dynamics used in integrative psychotherapy are the notions of ego states and life script. The major defenses, including decisions and introjects, form the basis for the fixation or archaeopsychic and exteropsychic ego stages. The presence of archaic defenses and nonintegrated ego states is confirmed by the script beliefs. While there are a number of ways in which life script can be conceptualized, we have found the notion of the script system generally most useful. Regardless of where the script beliefs come from, introject or decision, they are the warp and woof of the client's experiences in the world: They color interactions with others, problem-solving strategies, understandings of him- or herself. As a result of these script beliefs, and repressed needs and feelings, the client behaves in certain ways—the behavior is based on what the client believes has happened, is happening, will happen, and how he or she feels about those happenings. In turn, those behaviors lead to responses from others, responses that invariably are selectively remembered in such a way as to reinforce—to "prove"—the script beliefs and maintain the repressions. It is a closed, self-sustaining system, and will continue to operate as such indefinitely, unless a major shift can be induced by some external event. Integrative psychotherapy is intended to create such a shift.

In Jon's case, the script beliefs became clear early in the work. Jon introjected from Herbert a set of beliefs, including "People are out to use me," "I'm an outcast," "What's the use," and "Life is hard." Herbert's behaviors—his alcoholism, his withdrawal from contact, and his denial—make sense in the context of those beliefs. And he certainly collected many memories, memories of Father not being there for him, of people using him, of deprivation and loneliness, to support his beliefs. His script is a repetition of his early life, and a repression of awareness of his unmet needs and resulting emotions. His treatment of Jon, his son, not only provided the conflict between father and son, which Jon introjected, but also set the stage for Jon to make the same decisions for himself. For a son with an alcoholic father, a father who refused contact, who refused to respond to his son's need for attention and affection, life *was* hard, and it would be easy for the son to conclude that it was his own defects that caused Dad to reject him. The little boy's solution was to try even harder to please Daddy, to be a very, very good little boy. Out of this decision, and the related constellation of beliefs and repressed needs/feelings, emerge *Jon's* script behaviors and fantasies, his social awkwardness and inappropriateness, his overeating, his isolation and despair. And Jon, in turn, behaving consistently with these beliefs, invites others to treat him in ways that make his expectations come true.

Within the context of the script system, intervention may be made so as to change the script beliefs themselves, to change the script behaviors, or to change the reinforcing memories. Often, in the course of a piece of work, all three components of the system may be challenged. Additionally, defenses are relaxed and repressed needs are brought to awareness through the expression of the previously unexpressed emotions.

Challenging the script beliefs may occur through work with the introjections; this is the strategy of Parent ego state therapy, which constituted the greater part of Jon's work. Here the beliefs of the parent himself are challenged; when the client cathects—becomes, psychologically—that Parent part of himself, he opens the Parent ego state to the possibility of change. As the Parent ego state shifts its position, the introjected material loses its potency and no longer intrapsychically influences the Child ego state. Herbert (the Herbert in Jon's head) found his own script beliefs confronted. As we have seen, he was also confronted at the level of behaviors and memories. The other major challenge addressed Jon's Child ego state solution to the problem, his decision to be a good little boy. Because his script beliefs *are* that decision, changing the decision will again shift the beliefs and feelings.

Work in the area of script beliefs and repressed feelings, then, requires that the client cathect either Parent ego state (in order to deal with introjected beliefs) or Child ego state (in order to deal with early decisions). Working with the script behaviors, in contrast,

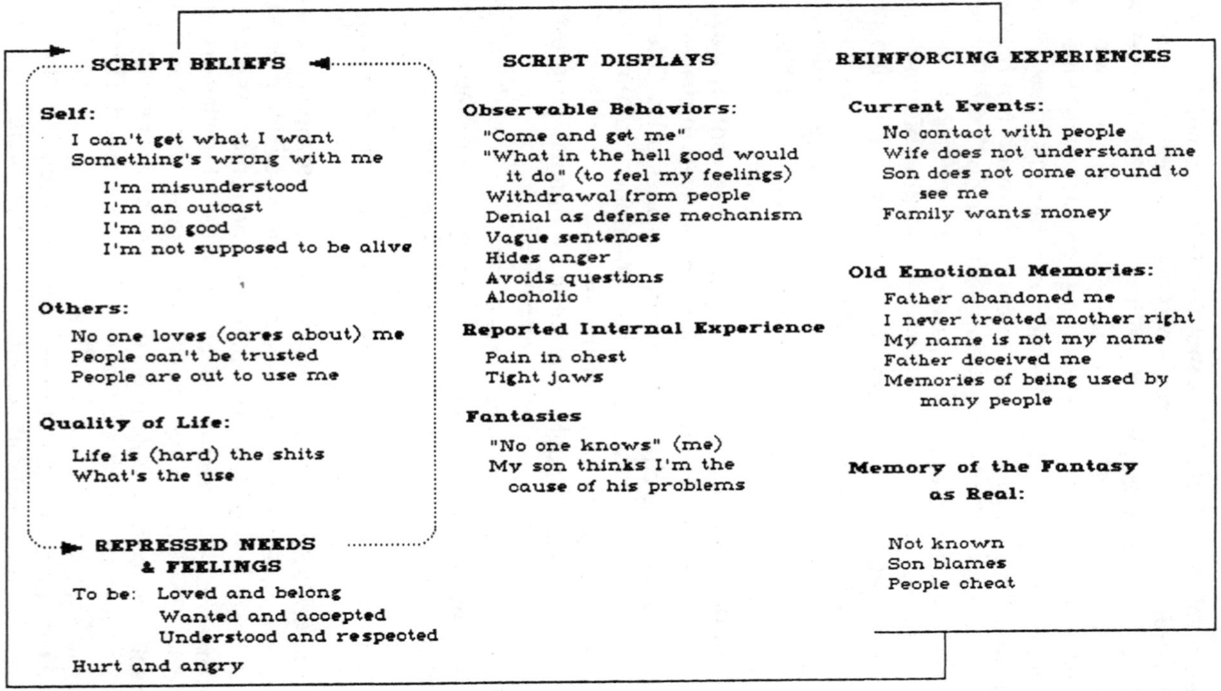

SCRIPT BELIEFS

Self:

I can't get what I want
Something's wrong with me
I'm misunderstood
I'm an outcast
I'm no good
I'm not supposed to be alive

Others:

No one loves (cares about) me
People can't be trusted
People are out to use me

Quality of Life:

Life is (hard) the shits
What's the use

REPRESSED NEEDS & FEELINGS

To be: Loved and belong
Wanted and accepted
Understood and respected

Hurt and angry

SCRIPT DISPLAYS

Observable Behaviors:

"Come and get me"
"What in the hell good would it do" (to feel my feelings)
Withdrawal from people
Denial as defense mechanism
Vague sentences
Hides anger
Avoids questions
Alcoholic

Reported Internal Experience

Pain in chest
Tight jaws

Fantasies

"No one knows" (me)
My son thinks I'm the cause of his problems

REINFORCING EXPERIENCES

Current Events:

No contact with people
Wife does not understand me
Son does not come around to see me
Family wants money

Old Emotional Memories:

Father abandoned me
I never treated mother right
My name is not my name
Father deceived me
Memories of being used by many people

Memory of the Fantasy as Real:

Not known
Son blames
People cheat

Figure 12.1 Jon/Herbert's Script System

is most usefully done when the client is operating out of a clear Adult ego state. This is best illustrated at the very end of Jon's work. Here Richard challenges Jon to *do* something different. The subtle and unstated implication, of course, is that Jon is, in fact, able to choose to behave differently, and that these different behaviors will lead to very different life experiences from those he has known up to now.

Challenges to the reinforcing experiences of both Herbert and Jon occur throughout the work. "Did your not crying mean that you were contented?" "Were you an outcast when you were in the service?" "Your son defended you." "You've been somebody for me, and you haven't been drinking." "Tell your Dad what you love about him." More important, though, the whole process of the work, experiencing the contactfulness, the respect, the attention of the therapists, questions Jon's (and Herbert's) collection of memories in that it runs exactly counter to what has been harbored up to now. It is a new interaction that doesn't fit the old expectations; if the script beliefs are true, this process simply cannot be happening. Through full contact, Jon gained the support that makes change possible.

Going back to the notion of domains of work, which we introduced in the first chapter of this book, we can again see each of the domains illustrated in Jon's work. The cognitive domain was involved in (a) the initial contact, setting up a goal for the work; (b) the challenge to Herbert and Jon's reinforcing experiences and beliefs; and (c) the ending, when Jon was challenged to think about his choices. Affective work was intense during the latter part of the Parent ego state therapy, and in the short conversation that Jon had with Herbert. Work at the behavioral level typically is prescribed or assigned to be done outside of the actual session, as was the case with Jon. And, finally, there were numerous instances of the therapists picking up on physiological cues and using body responses to enhance the impact of the work.

Throughout the work presented in this and the preceding chapters, there has been a consistent commitment to two principles of integrative psychotherapy: first, the affirmation of the integrity of the client through the therapist's expression of respect, kindness, and contactfulness; and, second, the expressions of the possibility of positive life change—no matter what has occurred in life, we each can learn and grow from the experience.

There is much more that could be said here: There are many loose ends, many questions that could be asked, or could be answered more fully. There isn't any good stopping place—perhaps that's why therapy, and writing about therapy, are like real life. In therapy, as in life, we continue to learn, to grow, to change. So it is that this description of integrative psychotherapy cannot be complete. Our understandings change, grow, shift; in the very process of writing about our approach, we continue to refine it. Each answer suggests new questions, just as each question demands many answers.

So, our solution to the dilemma of how to end is—to stop. Stop, with our thanks to you, the reader, for your interest in our work, and our hope that this book has been as useful to you in the reading as it has been to us in the writing. May we all—clients and therapists alike—continue to question and answer, to learn and grow, and to enjoy our journeying together.

Index

About the Authors

Richard G. Erskine received his Ph.D. in Emotional and Cognitive Development from Purdue University and is a licensed psychologist specializing in psychotherapy. He is the author of numerous articles on psychotherapy theory and clinical practice with individuals and families. He is a former professor at the University of Illinois, where he taught child and family therapy. He has also taught at Purdue University and Chicago City College and has served as consultant and staff trainer to mental health agencies throughout the United States and in several other countries. He began his professional life on the southside of Chicago as an elementary school special education teacher, working with emotionally disturbed and socially maladjusted children. From his experience and training in education, child development, and clinical psychology, and 20 years of practice as a psychotherapist, he has synthesized diverse concepts of theory and clinical practice to present an integrative perspective. He currently serves as the training director of the Institute for Integrative Psychotherapy in New York City where he conducts a postgraduate psychotherapy training program and continuing education courses for professionals in the mental health field. His current theoretical interest and research are with ego function in narcissism and multiple personalities. He is certified to practice clinically and teach Transactional Analysis by the International Transactional Analysis Association, which in 1982 conferred upon him and Marilyn Zalcman the Eric Berne Scientific Award for advances in the theory of transactional analysis. He is a faculty member of the New York Institute for Gestalt Therapy and an institute instructor and full member of the American Group

Psychotherapy Association. He is the father of three children and an avid gardener.

Janet P. Moursund is an Associate Professor at the University of Oregon, where she currently serves as Director of the DeBusk Counseling Center. She also is a licensed clinical psychologist and maintains a part-time private practice at the Eugene, Oregon, Center for Integrative Therapy. She has been teaching at the University of Oregon for some 20 years, first in the School of Community Service and Public Affairs and more recently in the Division of Counseling and Educational Psychology. She also founded and served for five years as Director of Aslan House, a low-cost community counseling center. She was born and raised in rural Illinois, and graduated from Knox College with a B.A. in psychology in 1958. She entered graduate school at the University of Wisconsin and became affiliated with Dr. Carl Rogers's research program on psychotherapy with schizophrenics, where she was responsible for the psychometric evaluation of all clients involved in that project. Working with Rogers, Charles Truax, and Eugene Gendlin provided confirmation that psychotherapy was indeed the profession for her. It was to be several years, however, before that intention became a reality: after receiving her doctorate from the University of Wisconsin came a move to East Lansing, Michigan, and a position at the Human Learning Research Institute of Michigan State University. Only after joining the faculty of the University of Oregon, in 1967, was she able to return to counseling and psychotherapy as a primary career orientation. As a mother of four, she has divided her time between homemaking and her professional activities. She has authored five previous books: *Us People* (Brooks/Cole, 1971); *Evaluation* (Brooks/Cole, 1973); *Learning and the Learner* (Brooks/Cole, 1977); *Approaches to Personality* (with James Geiwitz) (Brooks/Cole, 1979); and *The Process of Counseling and Therapy* (Prentice-Hall, 1985). In addition, she is an active member of the Episcopal Church, a builder of doll houses and miniature furniture, and (she announces proudly) is learning to ski.

* * *

Rebecca L. Trautmann, cotherapist in much of the psychotherapy presented in this book, is a psychiatric nurse who also received a

Master of Social Work degree from Washington University in St. Louis. She divides her time between a clinical practice and teaching in the postgraduate training program at the Institute for Integrative Psychotherapy in New York City. With her background of living in India for 18 years, she is interested in the integration of Oriental and Occidental approaches to "wholeness" and their combined effectiveness in psychotherapy. She is certified to practice clinically and teach Transactional Analysis by the International Transactional Analysis Association, is a practicing Gestalt therapist, and a full member of the American Group Psychotherapy Association. She travels extensively conducting continuing education seminars for practitioners in the mental health professions.

NOTES